The Contractor worked in domestic and foreign intelligence organisations before returning to his first trade as a builder. He now divides his time between building houses and taking private intelligence contracts.

Mark Abernethy is a journalist and professional writer. Born in New Zealand, he has lived in Australia for most of his adult life. He is the author of six spy-thriller novels and is the ghost writer of many commercial titles.

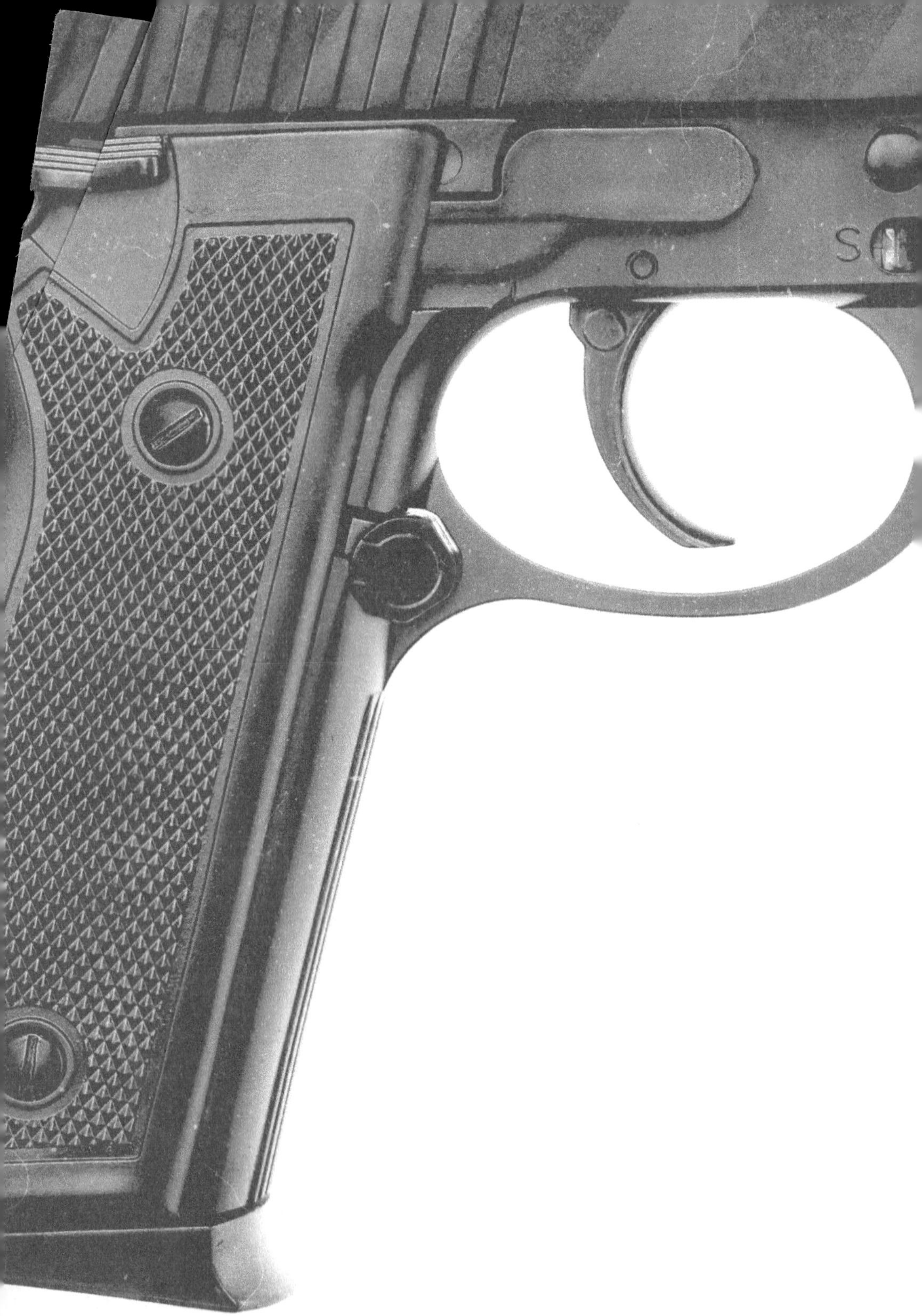
S

THE CONTRACTOR

6 TRUE TALES OF COUNTER TERRORISM

AS TOLD TO
MARK ABERNETHY

A BIG UNIT TRUE STORY

MACMILLAN
Pan Macmillan Australia

Some of the people in this book have had their names changed to protect their identities.

First published 2017 in Macmillan by Pan Macmillan Australia Pty Ltd
1 Market Street, Sydney, New South Wales, Australia, 2000

Copyright © Mark Abernethy 2017

The moral right of the author to be identified as the author of this work has been asserted.

All rights reserved. No part of this book may be reproduced or transmitted by any person or entity (including Google, Amazon or similar organisations), in any form or by any means, electronic or mechanical, including photocopying, recording, scanning or by any information storage and retrieval system, without prior permission in writing from the publisher.

Cataloguing-in-Publication entry is available
from the National Library of Australia
http://catalogue.nla.gov.au

Typeset in 11.5/16 pt Janson Text by Post Pre-press Group
Printed by McPherson's Printing Group
Gun image: Shutterstock

The author and the publisher have made every effort to contact copyright holders for material used in this book. Any person or organisation that may have been overlooked should contact the publisher.

Aboriginal and Torres Strait Islander people should be aware that this book may contain images or names of people now deceased.

For the men and women of the intelligence community, who make our world a safer place and accept that they will never be acknowledged for their service.

CONTENTS

1	From Pakistan, with Love	1
2	Paris au Go-Go	81
3	Man Alive	131
4	Talking to Animals	185
5	Palace Coup	237
6	Code Rouge	295

Author's Note

The following is a collection of true stories. They describe episodes in the life of an Australian 'contractor' who works for foreign and domestic security agencies. 'Mike' is an alias but The Contractor is 100 per cent real. I have used 'novelisation' techniques to protect identities of individuals and organisations but what you will read is Mike's voice. Remember: sometimes fact is stranger than fiction . . . and a tradie is not just a tradie.

Mark Abernethy

FROM PAKISTAN. WITH LOVE

1

The heat came early to Melbourne that year, pushing the building site temperature to thirty-five degrees in October. I worked through it, trying to duck my baseball cap into the afternoon sun while I nailed wall frames into the joists, but sweat ran down my face like rain.

Hoodie, one of my offsiders, read from his smartphone, updating me on the temperature in the hope that when it hit forty I'd send everyone home. I just punched nails with my rattly old Paslode, giving it a bang and a shake between nails, hoping it would hold out for another ten minutes. I wanted the place tarped down by 3 pm with all the frames up. This had been a big catch-up week after days of rain and my schedule for this house meant finishing the frames and the roofing trusses well before Christmas. But Hoodie and my labourer, McKenzie, were overheating, it was a Friday and they just wanted their cash and a cold beer so they could go feral for the weekend.

'Thirty-six, boss,' Hoodie told me, holding a brace in one hand and his phone in the other.

I ignored him and checked the loose nail-feeder in the Paslode, my hands slipping on the metal slides as the sweat poured down my forearms. I'd recently seen a new Makita nail gun kit on sale in the Gasweld catalogue; the special offer was a big green site radio along with the gun, but I'd decided to save the 500 bucks, so here I was relying on a nailer that no one could operate except me. I hated being wrong about tools – I hated stopping because they failed. But with a few of my patented whacks and slaps, I got the old girl working again, slammed ten final nails into the frame and stood up.

'Thirty-six's a working temp,' I said, breaking my rule that if it's over thirty, and you're over thirty, you put down the tools. 'Now brace that frame and let's get this tarped. Could be a beer in it for you.'

I left the boys to it and drove across town to the bank. I could have used the Westpac in the Glen shopping centre, but I don't like covered shopping centre parking. You see convenience – I see one large choke point. I see a perfect place for a snatch or a hit. Parking buildings are a fact of life in the city, but if there's an alternative, I'll take it. Westpac had another branch in a nearby high street, so I parked the ute with open skies above me, withdrew $2000 in cash and tucked it into my bumbag. That was $1000 for Hoodie and $800 for McKenzie. He had a first name but Hoodie never used it so neither did I. It hardly mattered since I paid these guys in cash and I never begrudged it. I don't have a problem with paying someone to start at 7 am and keep up with me all day – if you can do that, you've earned your dough.

I walked into the cold room of the Bottlemart and the sweat under my orange hi-vis turned cold. I could have pulled up a poolside recliner and taken a little holiday in that cold room, I don't mind telling you. Fucking bliss.

Grabbing a carton of VB I made for the checkout. A couple of concreters were in the queue ahead of me so I propped the carton on a wine stand and checked my messages. I use a Nokia 6110, which in phone terms is prehistoric, but it suits me and my lifestyle. No internet, no metadata, no nosy bastards getting into my business.

There was an envelope icon on the top of the screen – which, for those youngsters who've never used a Nokia, means there's a message. I clicked on my messages and saw a number that started with a '+'. Always promising, and when I recognised the first few numbers as a London code, that was even better. Even as the centre of the world has moved away from the UK, London is still one of the capitals of the insurance industry, in particular the underwriters who write the life policies for executives in foreign territories – policies that cover things like kidnap, ransom and emergency evacuations.

I don't take my interesting calls in a public place so I stowed the phone and bought the beers. When I got back to the site, the tarps were on and the tools sat in a neat stack. We drank in the shade and talked about footy and women and money. I heard about Hoodie and McKenzie's nightmarish girlfriends and thanked God that I'd chosen well on that front. And then I paid them for the week and let them take most of the stubbies with them.

Me? I headed for home, glad for the progress on the house but thinking about London, and my other contracting job.

2

I don't make a big thing of what I do. I wear a hi-vis shirt and drive a tradie's Ford Falcon ute. I'm a chippie by trade, from back in my teens, before all this international drama began. I left school early, I drink beer, support the Manly Sea Eagles and I take shit from the missus like any working man. There're only a couple of things that set me apart. One of them is obvious: I stand around six-foot-three and weigh 125 kilos. I'm a former rugby league front-rower, and when I first came to Sydney from the bush I worked on the doors of some pretty heavy venues in Kings Cross, and was bodyguard for some people you'd recognise if I named them. So I can take care of myself.

That's the part you see. The part you don't see is that I fix things for people. I can build you a house or remodel your bathroom, but I can also make bad situations – and bad people – go away. Some people make money from shares, some from hard work and some from technology. I make a living from threat: I identify it, neutralise it and manage it. I see it where you don't even know to look, and I move on it quickly, matching the threat with my own equal and opposite reaction. And if I get it right, the threat never makes another pass. Ever.

This needn't be sinister or spooky. Sure, when I worked for

governments as an intelligence operator it could be those things, but I went 'private' a number of years ago, and as the Contractor I no longer have to scan the radar every hour of the day, watching for the bad guys. When you're working for governments, you're in what we call The World, and that kind of life burns you out, wears down your circuitry. It isolates you, pushes you further into a spiral of work-related friendships and away from real life. That's why we refer to it as The World – when you live inside it that's all you live and not much else.

Now? I can live a life, have a wife, and be called off the bench for specific assignments, and that suits me fine.

I had a shower and heated up a chicken curry that Liz had left in the fridge. Liz works in A&E in the hospital system and she was doing a weekend of night shifts, so I had a stack of ready-made meals to choose from. I microwaved some rice and sat down with a cold beer to watch the telly. Sky News powered up and I got two fork-loads of curry into my mouth before my phone rang. Looking down at the handset beside me, I saw that London number again – I picked up.

'Yep,' I said.

'Is that Mike Daly?' said an English voice.

'Who's this?' I said, not even thinking.

'My name is Darcy Milne from Allardyce Insurance,' said the voice. 'I have something you might be interested in.'

*

First things first. Any muppet can find my number and call me. So I said to him, 'Darcy, hang up now, I'll call you back.'

I went into my office, fired up the laptop and did a quick search on Allardyce Insurance, a search on Darcy Milne, a search on Darcy Milne in Google Images, and then went to the London White Pages and got the main corporate number for Allardyce. I dialled it on one of the 'burner' phones I keep in the drawer – these are the pre-paid disposable mobile phones you buy at the convenience store, usually with some minutes and some data. They're also untraceable, especially when you buy them in South East Asia, as I do. Someone answered and I asked for HR. When the woman answered I said, 'I'm doing the paperwork for the Darcy Milne car lease – does his Darcy have an "e" in it?' and she said, 'Let me check,' and came back and said no. I said Darcy had been listed as the head of security services, but did that have a technical-preferred term like VP or director? And she said, 'Give me a second,' and she verified the title was Director of Corporate Security Services – Allardyce Insurance.

I wanted to place him, so I said, 'I need to get something to him this morning, is he handy – is he on the same floor?'

And she said, 'No, he's on the eighth,' and I thanked her very much. For making my job easier.

I called Darcy at his office and he sounded like a man under pressure. 'I have a problem and Charles thought of you for it,' he said, referring to a security executive I knew at another insurance company. 'He says you're highly effective but not too clumsy – that's what I'm looking for.'

'Talk to me,' I said, and listened.

The gig was a doozy. Allardyce underwrote a major oil and gas services company which built pipelines, refineries and LNG terminals. And they had this bigwig in a place called Islamabad. That's right up there in the north of Pakistan, the eastern end of the Peshawar Valley that leads into the joys of Afghanistan. But while Islamabad is in the middle of some pretty wild country – like the Tribal Areas and the Kashmir border – it's also the capital of Pakistan. Purpose-built to replace Karachi, it is sort of a Canberra of the subcontinent. I'd been there once before and I distinctly remembered a 'twin city' arrangement: the new part is all laid out with big houses and wide boulevards, and numbered streets, as in Street 23 or Street 46. I'm serious – look it up. But adjacent to this new, antiseptic, planned city is the original city to the south, Rawalpindi, which is ancient. There's a demarcation line called Inter Junction Principal Road – or IJP Road – and once you cross that you're leaving the bright new and entering the dirty old. In Islamabad you get lawyers and diplomats; in 'Pindi' it's bookmakers and currency scammers.

I picked up my pad and pen and I let Darcy tempt me: it seemed the oil executive – the Person of Interest, or PI – was an Australian living in a security compound with his wife and two kids – also Australian – within an expat compound, which itself was in an expat zone of Islamabad.

'He should be okay, then,' I said. 'He's got security?'

'Well, yes,' said Darcy. 'But that might be the problem.'

Darcy told me he was a former 'government employee', which means in our world that he had an intel background. He'd been let in on a disturbing tip-off. An MI6 team that had been tracking Guardal Alpha – a notorious Indian organised crime boss – had intercepted emails and texts from some of Alpha's operatives in Islamabad. A communication pointed to a couple of Pakistanis who wanted to kidnap an oil executive and his family from a compound and sell them back to the oil company. The Pakistanis who were proposing the deal wanted to do the dirty work, and they wanted Alpha's people to arrange the payment and secure the cash. They wanted to split the proceeds fifty–fifty.

'Sounds like the same scam going on all over Asia, a hundred times a day,' I said. 'Who are these kidnappers?'

'Well, that's the thing,' said Darcy. 'It's our client's bodyguard and his personal assistant.'

'Fuck me,' I said, before I could stop myself.

Darcy snorted. 'That's what I said.'

'How much time do we have?' I asked.

'The emails suggest end of the month,' said Darcy. 'But that's what they're proposing to Alpha's people – they're also negotiating.

They're saying, "We're here, in place – you let us know when you're ready. End of the month is good for us."'

I looked at my watch. We had about twenty days before the end of the month.

'We're initiating a claim on a kidnap and kill policy,' said Darcy, putting on a formal voice. 'We have a thirty-day expiry date.'

That means, by the way, that the attempts to extract you, protect you and get you on a plane out of your shithole, have a thirty-day limit on them. That's how long the gig lasts before they no longer pay me. Remember that the next time a corporation wants you to go manage something in Andean Peru or Northern Burma. Yes, the insurance policies are consular-grade, but everything has its limits.

We talked it through a bit. I was obviously interested, and this was my bag. But I immediately pulled back on the details of what I'd do, and with whom. It is very unusual to fully brief the client on the operational details because inevitably people in hierarchies have to report to other people and once the Chinese whispers start, you lose control of your op-sec – your operational security. And when you lose control of that, you're not in business: you're in freefall, and real pros won't work with you.

Darcy respected that. He was talking to me because he was worried that a gung-ho mission would get his clients hurt, or that a British, French or American outfit would be too obvious; would maybe tip off the crims. There're plenty of cowboys out there who would take his money, believe me. He was also concerned about Guardal Alpha's reach into the security scene in London; he wanted any action to be dark. I got that. When you go in-country you are stripped of so many advantages and resources enjoyed by the local bad guys that if you can put some basic rules of operational security around the gig, you can at least slip into their midst without them knowing it. So, Rule Number One is op-sec: every bastard shuts his mouth. Rule Number Two is op-sec: if they don't know it, they can't spill it.

So, no offence to the good people at insurance companies, but from the moment I take the gig, I go dark. You get a time and a date and an airport, and I'll be there with your clients, and you can be there with my cheque.

For all my interest in this job, I was very nervous about the Guardal Alpha connection. I knew the basics about him and I did some searches and reached out to some of my colleagues around the world. Alpha's early criminal career saw him controlling bookmakers across India, Pakistan and Bangladesh – and therefore controlling all the sports-betting scams and plunges. But in the post–9/11 age he'd evolved into an arms dealer and financier for a whole bunch of al-Qaeda splinters, of which ISIS was the best known. Jihadist splinter groups are lucrative for arms dealers because as soon as they break from the main Jihadi group, they need their own armaments, vehicles, fuel supplies, explosives, detonators and all the other materiel of terrorism.

These days Guardal apparently lived on a ship that moved around South East Asia and into the Indian Ocean, and he seemed to control a number of banks without having his name officially associated with them. One of his scams involved gold bullion swapped for ISIS crude oil. I didn't know how it worked, exactly, but Alpha had reach, and he had power, and whatever I agreed to do, it would have to entail Alpha never discovering the identity of me or my crew. It would have to be like that.

'You need someone on the ground, quick smart,' I said. 'You got anyone in Islamabad?'

'No, I got the tip-off fifteen minutes before I called you, Mike – you're the only person I've brought in.'

'Keep it that way,' I said. 'I'll take the job, but it won't be cheap.'

3

How does it work? What does Darcy actually do? It's insurance by any other name but this mob doesn't do comprehensive on your car, or replacement value on your house. They underwrite risk to people, who – because of where they live and what they're worth – are in much greater danger than your average Aussie suburbanite. Let's say your next level of promotion at an American oil and gas multinational sees you doing a five-year stretch in a shithole like Bangladesh. I don't have anything against my friends in what used to be called East Pakistan, but believe me, there's a criminal community in that country who sees this executive and his family purely as a means to make money: kidnap, ransom, extortion, fraud, standover, theft and good old-fashioned stacking of the household staff with one's own family, whether they can do the job or not.

In order to ensure their executives agree to live in Bangladesh or Gabon or Myanmar, the oil company underwrites them with a consular-grade insurance policy that covers just about every eventuality, as if they're in a nation's diplomatic corps. You can't buy these policies over the phone. There're too many strange contingencies, including the costs of greasing palms, private-hire helicopters, medical teams and the cost of people like me. And sitting behind these policies is a person like Darcy. When the crap starts, Darcy has to get the facts, assess the situation and assign someone to fix it. He has to be straight enough to deal with very wealthy clients for a large insurer, and bent enough to be trusted by people like me. I mean, the money's good, but I value my life more, and people like me don't work for any old muppet who can find my phone number. In my world, people we don't know are people we don't trust. We can be clubby that way.

So this is how it goes. I make someone at an insurer look good on one job, and when a juicy gig comes along, and another insurer needs a job done, my name is recommended. That person shoves every contractor, security company and mercenary to the back of the queue, and tells his buddy – in this case, Darcy – to call Melbourne. And it isn't like London isn't filled with security firms who do this work for their bread and butter. I'm in favour, so I get the tap.

With the gig in the bag, I waited for the deposit on my quote in my British Virgin Islands bank account. With internet banking, I can see very quickly if a deposit has been paid – with Darcy, it came up in under ten minutes. You might be wondering how a London insurer can clear funds into a BVI bank account in the space of minutes? My understanding is that the London insurers have their own bank accounts in the BVI, Caymans, Dutch Antilles and Singapore, so they can make payments to people like me as fast as a local payment. And why do I bank through the British Virgin Islands? When I was first setting up as a private contractor, I paid for some time with an accountant who has many clients like me. His advice was to bank in a place where your banking records are unlikely to be seized by a government. So I opened an account in the BVI.

With the start-money in the bank, I got moving. I needed a tourist visa for Pakistan, which I applied for the following morning using the passport photographs that I kept in a stash of around thirty in my desk. I explained that I was a bit pushed for time because my plans for visiting the country had been brought forward by a month, out of my control. The fellow was understanding, and having checked my return tickets printed from my online booking – and sighted my bank statements – he pushed it through fast. I also had a building job to keep on top of, so I asked my building mate, Si, to oversee it for me. He'd done this before and Hoodie and McKenzie knew to toe the line with Si or get a shellacking from me when I returned. I drove over to the site he was on in Hawthorn and handed over my bumbag: it contained four envelopes of cash, representing two weeks of pay for my labourers, the keys to my ute and my tools lock-box, and a To-Do list that laid out what he needed to get done. Two years earlier, Si had broken his foot and I'd stepped in to manage his two projects, so I had some favours in the bank.

For this job I needed a team of six, myself included. I've been on jobs where they short-hand you, and while it's true that fewer people creates less of a profile in-country, it's also a disaster on many other fronts. One of the important aspects of black operations in a foreign country is gaining full ground intelligence. This doesn't just mean that you have the PI under surveillance, as well as the people who are a threat. But you should also conduct surveillance-detection: that's when you set up observation posts to observe who might be observing you. This takes people – professional people. Also, when you're getting a family out of a threat situation, your extraction plan inevitably comes down to one of your teams travelling with the family, and another team behind them in the security car. So six, for my gigs, is a good number and I line them up before I leave, and 'stagger' them into the area in which I need them. You don't want a gang of former soldiers and spooks rolling down the airport concourse – the immigration and security people would be too interested in that.

I always get my game face on before I leave the house. This is where I do my farewells with Liz – usually with a few wines and an early night. She doesn't want to talk about what might happen and neither do I. So we play some music, have a laugh and I find myself holding her hand quite a bit. Because of her profession, Liz knows just how bad life can be, so she doesn't do hand-wringing and sobbing. She stays strong and asks me to be careful. It's the best way to go into a gig and much more supportive than the crap many blokes have to put up with.

Ninety-nine per cent of the time, I go into a job clean, which means I leave my laptop and smartphone in the desk, and I carry a passport, a credit card and some cash in an otherwise filleted wallet. This time, everything I was taking in-country was in the Rip Curl backpack sitting between my ankles in the departures lounge of Melbourne International, which is where I was sitting the morning I set out. This was my acclimatisation time: I always make sure I get to the airport early, make my way through the immigration gates and security screening, and have a wander around; look at who's looking at me. I like to stand at t-shirt racks, browse through the shops or get a bite to eat while I survey the area, looking for watchers, identifying the 'types' who are trained to blend in and not be noticed. They're not really reading that magazine; they're not reading a text on their phone – they're holding it up so they can look over the top at you. I don't get too worried about it. Australia's international airports have a fair smattering of undercover Federal Police as a matter of course. It isn't personal, but if someone like me is on the international move, they might want to know about it. Sometimes they know me and just sit down and have a chat. Or they eyeball me and then ignore me.

Today I grabbed a coffee and found a table where my back faced the wall, my body faced the room and I could legitimately face the TV screen yet also scan the area. My dress code was strictly tourist: jeans, polo shirt and dark sneakers. Actually, they're really tactical boots that look like trainers. Footwear is my one non-civilian indulgence, but an important one. You try handing out a decent kick or putting a hold on a big bastard if your shoes are slipping all over the place.

It's in this environment that I usually start compressing, like a commercial diver who's going to be working in a pressured state for two weeks. I get into my very focused but very relaxed state – a state of body and mind where I look like someone on holiday but inside I'm coiled and scanning everything like a cyborg. I get into character, doing some small talk with other travellers, just loosening up so that by the time I walk into the arrivals concourse of my destination, I *am* the tourist.

For this trip, I had the Lonely Planet guide to Pakistan in my bag, a malaria kit from my doctor and a booking at the Marriott for the date of my arrival – I may not use the hotel, but having the booking completes the tourist image. So if someone at Pakistan customs wanted to brace me, by the time they pushed the issue I would just be Mike the builder, on holiday in sunny, beautiful Islamabad. It pays to have done some research on your destination and have a feasible tourism story. Mine was that I was interested in the Mughal-era architecture of northern Pakistan, hence my camera bag. I was also interested in taking a drive across the Himalayan foothills and into the highlands of India. So I knew the names of the highways, roads and passes which would explain my interest in 4x4 vehicles, if pressed on the matter.

Sometimes I carry a burner phone – which I dump before my ultimate destination – and other times not. That morning: not. I'd already received a text from one of my operators, MG. I got the message before leaving the house, giving me his mobile phone number and affirming that he was in place. As soon as I'd got the go-ahead from Darcy, and got my 50 per cent of the quote up-front, I had sketched a plan. It required a point guy to go into Islamabad as a tourist, hole up in a non-chain motel, and secure several things for the arrival of the main team: two 4x4 vehicles; a garage or warehouse to park the cars inside; and six small arms, preferably handguns but assault rifles if that was all he could get. Rounds to go in the firearms, and a special package that MG would have ready for me.

MG was my chosen guy for the role. He's a lean Texan special forces operator, formerly US Marines Force Recon, and now taking contracts from his base in Dubai. Not only did he have significant combat experience in Iraq, Afghanistan and the southern Philippines, but his career was filled with the sort of soft infiltration work I required for this job: blending in, finding the life pattern of a place and becoming perfectly camouflaged without really hiding. I'm good at this, but MG is excellent, so he was my point guy. His job was to assess the ground in both the big ways and in minute detail, before the rest of us arrived in three distinct waves. By the time he picked us up from the airport, he'd have a log in his mind of how the city works, who's who, the main driving routes we'd use, and the choke points. He'd be able to tell us what we had to do to blend in.

MG's what we call 'heavy', in that if you point a firearm at him he's immediately working out how to take it off you and kill you. But MG also has a brain, and that Force Recon training, and I totally trusted him to be first on the ground. He's also about five-foot-ten with dark hair and dark eyes. You put MG in a man-dress and he could move around places like Islamabad without advertising the fact that he's an American soldier.

The other four people I'd assembled were Rich – also from Dubai – Intel from Canberra, Frank from London and Doug, who usually worked out of Singapore or Melbourne but for this gig was flying in from Moscow. I'd given all of them small amounts of pictorial information on the family we'd be looking after and the two bad guys – well, the two bad guys that we knew of. With the involvement of the Alpha network, we couldn't be sure about that. The files my team had seen before coming in to the gig were in an electronic lock-box that Darcy had set up. These lock-boxes were used by big law firms and they were set up so that – for instance – you were authorised to open them once, and you couldn't download or print from them. My own lock-box had the bodyguard's emails in it and of course my letter of engagement acknowledging the secrecy of the gig, and spelling out my quote, which was US$690,000. I'd explained to Darcy that I'd need a team for this job – which included me – because we'd have to establish ourselves in Islamabad long enough to be satisfied that we were not ourselves under surveillance. The Alpha connection had me on edge and I wasn't going to put my own people, and the PI and his family, in danger by just charging in there and affecting a rescue.

The departures board at Melbourne International clicked over and it said my flight was now boarding. I stood up, and went to work.

4

I flew into Benazir Bhutto International Airport from Jakarta in a Garuda A330, and wandered with the rest of the throng through the 1960s-style building. The customs and immigration officers were not interested in me and by now I was deep in my tourist cover, even believing it a bit myself.

I had no checked luggage, so having got the stamp on my visa from the immigration people I moved down the concourse with the other travellers, dodging the big mobs of Pakistani families who always seem to move in groups of fifteen or twenty people. There was a newsagent-type convenience shop and I ducked in, playing the wide-eyed Aussie tourist, and bought a Mobilink prepaid phone – an LG flip model, the cheapest I could find. Standing near the front doors to the terminal, I set up the phone as I casually took in the scenario. Nine times out of ten, the security police – if they're on to you – will track you before you land. And if they let you through immigration, it means they're going to tail you and see what you're up to. And of course the pick-up point for the tail would be the dispersal area at the terminal entrance. So I took my time with the phone, fired it up and watched the light show begin on the screen, but still positioned so that if I had a tail inside the building they'd have to be twiddling their thumbs and doing silly things with a tourist map while they waited for me to move. I couldn't see anyone like that – and my radar's pretty good for these people. So I scanned the terminal's front apron, looking for late-model sedans or vans with no personal accessories on them. You see twin overhead foxtails on the aerial of a 1976 Charger, then you're probably looking at a private car. You see a new Toyota Tarago in Asia, with heavily tinted windows down the sides, and there're two nondescript dudes in the front seat? If they're looking at you – you're made. Same goes for late-model Nissan Maximas: they're comfortable enough to sit in all day, and when things get out of shape, they go like a rocket. Plus they're built like a truck, so people like me use them because they can still be driven after a collision.

The entire drop-off area of Benazir Bhutto International was covered in cross-shaped anti-tank bollards and anti-bomber fencing. Cars couldn't get close to the apron and people were having to walk across a pedestrian mall–like zone, and into the car parks and bus stop lanes. There'd been bombings and assassinations in Islamabad and the place looked on edge. I saw a soldier in a steel pillbox, with a machine gun, but no government men poised in their Tarago. I input the number I'd memorised for MG's in-country burner phone, and sent a text: *here now*.

Only then did I move out of the building, into the light and the strong smell of Pakistani cooking. It was late October so it was dry and temperate, about twenty-four degrees, which I was happy about. Extreme heat and humidity makes everything that bit harder. There was a sun umbrella across the pedestrian area with a bloke scooping a brown goo into naan bread. I walked past him and kept with the flow into one of the car parks, my cap pulled low. The place was clear of tails – or to be more precise, I didn't feel followed and I couldn't see the telltale signs. The phone buzzed against my leg and I flipped it open. There was a text saying, *here 2*.

While there were no vehicles near the actual apron at the airport entrance, there was a narrow drive-by lane with bays to pull in to, and I left the car park and walked along this lane, keeping a smile on my face. In front of me was a mess of cars, cabs and buses, and big groups of Pakistanis poured out of vehicles, even though I suspected only one of every group was travelling. It seemed like a great way to clog the transport infrastructure, but what did I know? As I looked around, a dark blue Mitsubishi Pajero pulled up and its headlights flashed once. I got in the front passenger door, beside MG.

'Lovely place you got here,' I said as MG dropped the clutch of the fifteen-year-old Pajero and surged into the traffic.

'Well, we like it,' said the Texan, blending a little too well into the local driving style for my liking.

The airport was actually in Rawalpindi, and as we made our way across town, through the throng of Honda 70s and Suzuki 50s, I was hoping we were going north, into clean Islamabad. I listened to MG as he briefed me on the layout of our new home. He'd been keeping a low profile, playing a backpacker wanting to drive a 4x4 across the Himalayan passes. He'd grown his hair way beyond the old Marines style and the locals had accepted the tourist story and found a couple of Pajeros for him.

'This is the good one,' he told me, keeping a straight face.

'You're having a lend,' I said, and was rewarded with a small smile. Another thing I like about MG? He's Texan, which means a dry, Aussie-like sense of humour.

Rather than driving north into the gleaming jewel of Islamabad, we drove west, into the bowels of Rawalpindi. After twenty minutes we pulled up in front of a crappy garage, located in a side street in a part of town where the roads were neglected and the gutters were filled with rubbish. As I got out of the car the smell of human sewage hit me like a slap and I moved quickly from the Pajero, under a roller door that MG was lifting, and into a dirt-floor garage where another Pajero was parked.

MG had set up cans of soft drink and packaged snack food on a box in the garage. It was in line with my rules in these gigs: no local food or water. And I include bottled water in that. Our job was to get in, secure the subject, and safely lift the subject to where the client wanted him or her. My job was not to play nursemaid to a bloke who's going hard from both ends, simply because he wanted to eat at a street stall. For me that's part of op-sec: stay healthy, stay strong, don't shit the bed. Some blokes get toey about this rule, especially when they're holed up for two or three weeks eating potato crisps and drinking Pepsi. But they understand the rule when I put it this way: *You want to go local? Okay, buddy, but you're on bedpans and sheet-scrubbing.*

That stops most food mutinies. As well as the food and beverage, MG had sourced piles of blankets. But no beds.

'Where am I sleeping?' I asked, looking around.

MG shrugged, his boxer's shoulders straining momentarily through his shirt. 'Back of the cars?'

We cracked a Red Bull each and took a seat on some old fruit boxes. MG took a sip and then filled me in on the roads, the routes, the location of the executive and his family, and he confirmed he hadn't been made. Then, looking at his watch, he was off again, to meet Intel at the airport.

Over the next day, MG collected the crew and dropped them one by one in the garage. This was where I'd organise the gig and each night MG would have to go back to his motel, to a real bed and a shower – purely to keep up his cover, you understand.

We made our beds in the back of the cars – with the back seats folded down – and Doug slept on the 'top bunk', the roof of one of the 4x4s. It was hot and muggy in that building; plus it was dark and it smelled like shit. Not surprising when you consider that running along one of the side walls was an open sewer drain, about one foot deep, which carried the effluent from the houses that ran up to the top of the hill. The advantage to us was having a toilet right beside our abode.

Everyone present had an area of expertise, which started with MG as my main recon man. He'd help me get my mapping right, aid with situational awareness and design the surveillance-detection.

From the minute he arrived, Frank – an Englishman with an almost bookish presence – started tinkering with the cars, ensuring they'd work when we wanted them to work and not break down halfway to the airport. Frank was in his early forties and came from a British Army background, and while he could work on high-tech engines with computer diagnostics, he was also handy with a basic kit. He had a Geordie accent and was the opposite of the stereotypical whingeing Pom: if you asked him to do something, he'd just do it.

Doug was an Aussie IT and electronics guy. He came from an intel background, and had also spent a lot of time in the IT consulting world, devising security systems for data and voice comms. He was a tall, young-looking thirty-five year old who had that computer nerd image but with a wicked sense of humour. He was also useful on firearms and basic infiltrations, and if the need arose, he'd be good for a fight. I needed Doug to assess the security systems around the PI's compound and come up with a plan to disable them, or trick them, or whatever we decided to do. The only problem with Doug was his way with women. They really liked his looks and personality and when I'd hooked him into the gig I'd stipulated, 'Keep your hands to yourself, okay, mate?' and he'd laughed himself silly.

And then there was the muscle. Intel (former Aussie 2nd Commando Regiment) and Rich (former British SAS) were my door-kickers, the blokes who go from zero to 100 in a split second to bring up the speed and intensity of the gig right when it's required. You need every type, which includes smart IT and comms people and deep experience like MG's. But when you deal with the kind of adversaries who come at you in this job, brains and guile aren't always enough. Sometimes you need to overcome violence with greater violence, and Commando and SAS operators bring that. You need genuinely *heavy* people, and I'm not talking about poseurs with lots of tatts who hang out in the gym. I'm talking about soldiers with combat experience who stay calm around gunfire and seize on a bad guy like a Rottweiler.

So I had my team assembled, but before we went too far into the op, we had to have a confab. On the first evening that we were all together, MG presented us with a gift: a white plastic shopping bag filled with clothes.

'What's that?' I asked, squinting under the one dim light bulb in that stinking cesspit.

MG reached into the bag and handed out a selection of garments. When we held them up, they looked like dresses.

'You're fucking kidding,' said Rich, a Liverpudlian tough guy. 'It's a fucking dress!'

'Shit, mate,' I said to my Texan friend, who by now was having a chuckle. 'I'm gonna pull some gorgeous blokes with this, I tell ya.'

'Always the bridesmaid, eh, Big Unit?' said Intel, addressing me.

There was a bit of grumbling and pushback and I said, 'Come on, boys, let's get the man-dresses on.'

I stood, took off my polo shirt and whipped on the man-dress. Mine was an off-white cotton number, collarless at the neck and reaching to below my knees.

'See?' I said, pretending I was on a catwalk. 'If it's good enough for Boy George, then it's good enough for me.'

Taking my lead, MG got to his feet and followed suit, and pretty soon the whole crew was in a selection of man-dresses. It's actually classic Force Recon behaviour, to hide in plain sight by using what's around you. Add to that a story about wanting to go driving across the Kush and the locals eventually look straight over you. Especially if you have the Pajero parked in front of the garage all day, with the hood up, and someone working on it. Which was the plan.

We were all sitting around in our man-dresses, and MG threw another shopping bag in the middle. This one contained a selection of woollen hats he'd bought at the market. They were similar to a French beret, except bigger – wider. Most of the men in northern Pakistan wore them. I picked up one that was a pale-beige colour, trying to show leadership, and put the thing on my head. There was a pause, and then the whole crew started laughing, and I don't mean a few polite chuckles. They fell about the place.

'Okay,' I said, throwing the hat at the bag. 'Man-dress, compulsory – silly hat, optional.'

5

We slept in the cars, in an environment that smelled like one of those old blocked-up toilet blocks at a beachside car park. At least we all had to put up with it, so there was plenty of humour about the living conditions. The next morning at 6 am, MG tapped on the roller door, I opened it and we went for a drive. I pulled the tourist map of Islamabad from my backpack and got my bearings. Tourist maps are both useful and sometimes quite detailed, and they also serve as a prop to the cover of 'tourist'. We drove north, over IJP Road and into the Westernised city of Islamabad and towards the expat compounds. As we cruised along the relatively safe roads, I had a chance to ask MG about the tools.

'Got a guy who knows a guy,' said the Texan.

I was only interested in one thing. 'Discreet?'

'Showed him 100 US dollars,' said MG, lighting a smoke and cracking the window. 'He'd take a vow of silence for another fifty.'

I noticed MG had changed back into his cargo shorts and travel shirt; one of those Columbia stop-rip ones that Bear Grylls wears. Lots of pockets and an internally zipped one somewhere as well. He was staying with other travellers at the motel and so he was in character as the adventurer with the driving plan.

When we got off the main boulevards, the streets were still modern and wide but they became more reminiscent of the type you get in Asia: lots of different vehicle types and speeds sharing the roads, making it anarchic. Along with my rule on eating, we also work dry – no booze unless it's part of the locals' social scene – and certainly no dumb shit on the roads. The number of intelligence ops that go south every week because of poor driving or overconfidence? Enough to make you wonder, believe me. A lot of Westerners think they're great drivers and they carry their superiority into places where it gets them nowhere. I don't care how smooth you think you are; Saigon, Tehran and Mumbai's roads can humble any outsider.

'Just up here, over the hill,' said MG, and we slowed among the local traffic, came over a rise and the road was noticeably less crowded as it sloped downhill for about a kilometre towards a series of security walls, mostly brick or painted cinder block.

'This is the expat section of town,' said MG, steering with a flat palm the way many Americans do.

From our vantage point I could see a precinct that looked to be about two square kilometres. It was obvious because of the walled nature of every property. The walls surrounded flat-roofed, two-storey houses that also resembled bunkers, with their satellite dishes and aerials sticking out the top. Since it was Islamabad, I knew there was a diplomatic compound in there and a corporate expat compound, one of which belonged to Allardyce Insurance's client, currently lived in by the Johnson family.

The downhill stretch was almost deserted by the time we hit the T-junction with a road that went along the perimeter walls of the precinct. There were not many kids or street hawkers along this street, probably because of the American SUV with the word 'Security' along the side which was cruising down the street.

We watched the security guards drive past and turned left into the wide street, so now we were driving west, with twenty-foot security walls and bolted steel doors on our right, and dusty old shops with a few Pakistani loiterers to our left. MG drove for about 120 metres, then took the first right into an interior street, which was now cleaner and less populated by street people than anything I'd yet seen in this part of the world. There was no litter, dirt didn't cover everything, and the few vehicles passing us were Mercedes sedans and Range Rovers.

'It's like *The Lion, the Witch and the Wardrobe*,' I said, opening my morning can of Red Bull. 'Step through one door into a whole new world.'

'There're suburbs like this in Dallas,' said MG, flicking his smoke out the window. ''Cept there's a golf course in the middle.'

We drove for less than a minute before he said, 'On the right, black locks on a terracotta door.'

I kept my body pointing forwards and saw a terracotta-painted cinder block wall, about twelve feet tall, with a terracotta-painted steel door set in a steel frame, with a black locking mechanism on it. It looked secure and so did the steel vehicle access door alongside it – a slider, by the looks of it.

We kept driving, and MG took us out of the precinct. 'What do you think?' he asked when we knew we were clear.

'Looks pro,' I said. 'Camera on the gate. Any others?'

'Could be a pinhole camera in the vertical frame of the vehicle door,' said MG, getting back into the normal swim of Islamabad traffic. 'It's either a bolt head, or a camera. If that was my set-up, it'd be a camera; check cars as they try to enter.'

I thought about that as we circled around and headed for higher ground again. MG did a couple of driving tricks to see if we had a tail and then we parked beside a 1960s building which had a government sign on it. MG led the way through the front entrance and we rode an elevator to the fifth floor. When we emerged it was into a large room filled with locals queuing for something. I followed MG around the back of the room and through a door onto a verandah that looked out on the city, and over the expat compounds.

'This is where I took my surveillance shots,' he said, pointing. Through a line between other buildings we could see over five or six of the expat compounds and into the PI's house. Behind that wall was a garden, a driveway that led to the front door and a fountain in the middle of the lawn. On the driveway was a black Mercedes sedan and a small red 4x4, a BMW by the looks of it. MG had his tourist photography bag with him, and had the Canon D series out, complete with the zoom lens. He touched a couple of shots and then handed it to me. We could have been a couple of tourists, having a perv at Islamabad. The 70–300 millimetre zoom lens was excellent and it took me right into the front yard of the Johnsons' house, with pretty good detail. It was a two-storey rendered cinder block mini-mansion with steel frames in the windows, but the glass probably wasn't bulletproof. The house design was symmetrical, so on either side of the front door portico were two sets of windows, with three sets across the top storey and the middle set directly above the front door.

I couldn't see any people, but for now I was most interested in the front door and the approaches around it. Most of us in this business would love to be able to enter premises with a clever *Ocean's Eleven* work-around, but when you can't make that happen, you have to go to Plan B: the door-kickers. And if that's the mode of entry, you have to know about that particular door and what's around it: cameras, a security guard inside, guards in the window over the front door, etc.

I zoomed all the way in and took a few shots. There were two outbuildings: a garden shed, which I didn't expect to contain people, and the garage – at the end of the driveway, down the side of the house – which had what looked like small living quarters above it.

I took my shots, gave the camera back to MG and we went downstairs to the Pajero. We spoke quietly about the house and the gig. If you think about Americans on a spectrum, from loud and bragging to quiet and highly effective, MG was on the quieter side, but all about results. He wanted to know more about the security measures around the wall, the gate and the entry to the house, and he wanted more information on that front door: you don't want to be all revved up only to find that no one can kick in the door. You lose the element of surprise and you give a big warning to whoever you're after. And, of course, you look like an idiot.

'And, seriously,' I said as we crossed back into Rawalpindi, 'are we being watched?'

MG shook his head, popping a stick of gum into his wide face. 'I'm saying no to that, Big Unit, but you know what these places are like: they ignore you but you're always being watched.'

I laughed. I'd worked security contracts in Kabul – about three hours' drive away – and he described the scene perfectly. They didn't stare at you but they didn't miss anything.

I asked MG to drop me five blocks from the garage and to go back to the garage and go over the pics of the house with Doug. The IT–electronics people always see the things I don't and I wanted Doug to start giving us an advantage.

I walked the streets, dressed in my man-dress, looking at my map and establishing some surveillance-detection points. Surveillance-detection is not the same as counter-surveillance, in which you pick up the watchers and evade them or deceive them. With surveillance-detection we find an OP (observation post) from which the watchers would be conducting surveillance on us, and we set up our own OP at another tier behind them. Now we are watching the watchers – it's also known as 'third tier surveillance', or 'overwatch'. If you do this properly, you learn more about your enemy than you otherwise could. You might also save your own life, especially if you're a bunch of Westerners in Pakistan and the Alpha crime network takes an interest in you.

From the garage door I'd seen a perfect OP that I would

expect any professional to use. It was on the top-storey balcony of a 100-year-old hotel, two blocks away. A watcher who used this balcony would be in shade, would look down on the garage door, and when we looked at this balcony in the afternoon, the sun would be in our eyes, blinding us to the watchers. If I was the one doing surveillance, that would be my OP. So I wanted to find another OP – further back, and on an angle where I could look at this balcony. According to my tourist map there was a large mosque with public visiting hours, and I wanted to have a look at its minaret, because its balcony looked down on the hotel balcony (from behind), and I figured that this was where I could do some surveillance-detection.

There was a nearby market, and I strolled through it, blending in. I didn't want any of the vegies or rice but I bought a can of Coke and had a look around. This was the 'old' city, Rawalpindi. It was a one-time Hindu city with the same seething anarchy as all the large cities in the subcontinent. It was cramped, loud, dirty and smelly. Its contrast to adjacent Islamabad was extreme.

The mosque opened at 11 am and I joined a group; we took off our shoes and were led around a large, airy space with natural light coming in, and me looking very respectful in my man-dress. The whole experience was very nice, actually. The tour moved upstairs into the minaret and I lollygagged at the back of the bunch, noticing some small lock-up structures on that roof, perhaps for the maintenance people. They'd be handy for someone to hide behind. I looked out to the east, where as I moved along the parapet, the balcony of the hotel came into sight. I couldn't quite line it up with the garage door – which would have been perfect – but I had a fairly clear view of that hotel balcony. The group moved on and I brought out my burner phone, took a quick snap from my OP and put away the phone.

There was no one on that balcony, but that didn't mean there wouldn't be.

6

I was laid out on a stack of blankets on the floor of the garage while Frank worked on a Pajero in front of the building, out in the early morning sunlight. I was having a big think about the gig and wanted more information. This is not unusual, by the way. I always want more information – everyone does. But when you do this work you have to identify the potential problems and come up with a way to neutralise them, or to avoid them altogether, or accept them and change something major in your plan, such as the exfil – the getting out of Dodge – or the timing of the whole thing. One of the potential problems in this case was that we were a group of outsiders who had to disrupt an Alpha kidnapping and then try to make it to the airport and get out of Pakistan without the Alpha operatives getting to us. The Alpha people wouldn't necessarily come in their black hats and behave like bad guys; they were probably connected in the Punjab Police and the Federal Investigations Agency, and given my experience in such matters, the Guardal Alpha organisation was surely on good terms with the ISI, Pakistan's version of the CIA. The ISI are fabled among military and intelligence people from the West because so many of their executives, senior operators and managers are under contradictory mandates. At the top level, they're very educated and smart, and at the operator levels, they do what they're told. And the middle ranks? As an American intel person once said to me, *They're dumb and dangerous.*

Here was I, with a crew, on Alpha's home ground, and I didn't want to be known as the white boys who diverted a million bucks from Guardal Alpha. I wanted to know more before I struck. My crew was going to take turns in the mosque tour. My guys could secrete themselves behind the structures on the mosque roof and take their time with the surveillance-detection detail. While they were doing that, I wanted MG to take a different person with him every day, and case the movements of our subject – Mr Johnson – and his bodyguard. That's where MG and Intel were right now. MG had already made some initial passes at the Johnson compound and could confirm that the bodyguard was also the driver, and he and Mr Johnson left the compound around 8 am every weekday for the oil company offices downtown. I wanted at least four tails on four consecutive days so that we could nail down their routine. If the personal assistant was staying in the house every day, were the wife and kids already under threat? Or were they oblivious to the plot?

So while MG was doing the go-to-work tail, I wanted a second team observing the compound to see if there were any other comings and goings. It was a Monday morning, and the Johnson kids were seven and ten – they'd be going to school. Or they should be.

I wanted Rich to drive and take Doug on the surveillance job. Doug could form a view about the security and video systems in the house, and hang around long enough to see if the kids were being taken to school and whether Mrs Johnson went out anywhere. When that morning job was over, I wanted them to make a visit to the government office balcony, and for Doug to assess the house wiring.

The second team left at around 9 am and that left me and Frank in the garage. By now we were into the third day of the gig and we were smelling pretty bad. We were keeping to ourselves and staying out of places where they'd ask for ID or where we'd be caught on CCTV. The open sewer beside the garage was losing its charm and our man-dresses were starting to look raggedy. The only person getting a shower and a real bed was MG, and his backpacker cover was also giving him the freedom to move around. One Western man in Rawalpindi is slightly unusual; six of us would be a honey pot for the security forces. My rules were resented but the guys also understood why I wanted to be below the radar in this stinking, ancient city. Because, regardless of what they thought of the garage and the man-dresses, they'd hate a Rawalpindi prison cell a lot more.

Frank took a seat on another blanket bed and read an old Indian news magazine that the boys had found in one of the Pajeros. And I pulled out my burner phone and took a quick look at my G-Shock watch: a little after 9 am, making it a little after 11 pm in Washington. Late, but what the hell: I dialled a number I kept in my head.

It rang five or six times and I figured no one was there, then as I was about to hang up a deep voice said, 'Yep?'

'Stan, it's Mike,' I said. 'Did I wake you?'

'Only from a deep sleep with a beautiful woman,' said my buddy. 'That's all. You're welcome, really.'

'Yeah, yeah,' I said.

Stan was one of those Americans who pull your leg harder than even an Australian can. Stan and I went back to the old days, back to a certain government agency in Australia, when we pulled some hairy gigs in South East Asia and some scary-crazy stuff in Baghdad and Kabul. Stan and I had dealt with the highs and lows of international scumbaggery, from Sydney's western suburbs to the most lawless neighbourhoods of Baghdad. A big guy, ex-US military, he'd gone into military intelligence, risen high in government and ended up an adviser while I'd gone private. Stan is the best of the Good Americans: a handshake is a contract and friends are never forgotten. (Yes, they still exist, and they're in positions that count.)

'Just sleeping on the sofa, it's all good, Big Unit,' Stan said.

'Sofa?!' I said.

'I'm in my office, Mike,' he said. 'Do you mind?'

'Okay, brother,' I said. 'Need a favour.'

'Like every bastard. Shoot.'

'Our Friends' intel on Guardal Alpha's operation,' I said, trying to keep it broad and using the American term for British SIS. 'You hearing anything?'

'Last I heard on that asshole Alpha, he was trafficking RPGs and SAWs to Islamic State – he still on that fucking ship?'

'Thought you could tell me?' I said. 'Hear anything on Alpha and Pakistan?'

'They're kissing cousins,' said Stan.

'ISI?'

'The only game in town,' said Stan. 'You in trouble, brother?'

'Not yet.'

'Want me to look?'

I said yes, and I could hear him tapping on a keyboard. Stan was a stalwart of our world, and on the occasion he'd taken me through the Pentagon building, I'd marvelled at it: there was a whole secret operations office inside the Department of Defense building that did nothing except make constant alterations and renovations, not only to the décor but to the actual layout, right down to changing the numbering protocols of whole wings of the building. The idea was that even if you could get inside the Pentagon building without authorisation – which you can't – you'd be lost very quickly, even if you could find a porter with a golf cart to give you a lift.

'Pakistan?' said Stan.

'Yep, try northern.'

Stan tut-tutted. 'You be careful, Tonto.'

'Careful doesn't come close. I'm looking at kidnapping, extortion scams.'

'Well, the only product from our Friends says a drug cartel that answers to Alpha is now active in Western expat kidnaps.'

'Where?' I asked.

'Says northern Pakistan, which I suppose means Islamabad, Abbottabad – all that . . . Christ, Mike, you're not up there – tell me you're not in that shit.'

I tried to duck the question. 'What's the cartel, Stan?'

'Called the Mardan Group,' said Stan. 'You be careful, you hear?'

'Any dates, imminent actions?'

'No, brother. I'll call if that changes. Christ, Mike!'

'Yeah, yeah, I know,' I said, and I hung up.

Frank was peering at me over the top of his Indian magazine. 'You okay, Mike?'

My voice must have squeaked out some stress while I was talking to Stan. 'Yeah, mate,' I said, standing and stretching. 'Dude wants to borrow some money – fucking Yanks!'

He seemed to buy it, or at least see the humour. I told him I was lying down, and I cycled my breathing as I thought through the op and Stan's warning. There was a time in my career when a Middle Eastern government's operatives grabbed me from a hotel in the middle of the night, and when I came to after passing out from the beating and the hood they pulled over my head, I was in a concrete-walled basement that you'd expect to see in a really bad Steven Seagal movie. Only in that basement, the tractor battery was real, the pliers were of tradie quality, and the soldering iron was actually plugged in. The only thing not from a B-grade movie were the interrogators, who don't – as I found out – dress like demons or talk like villains. They're the bureaucrats of the building, just going about their business. I lost a couple of toenails in the ensuing discussion in that basement, and the tractor battery was freshly charged, believe me. The soldering iron? Then I'd really have to kill you.

I learned an indelible lesson from my Arab hosts: don't wander into something without knowing the exit. Me? I check into a hotel and I check the fire escapes, do a walk-through of the kitchen into the loading dock and have a good old look around the service elevator and the stairwells. Ask my wife: I like to know the way out. So as I dozed off to sleep in that garage, this is what gnawed at me: if the kidnappers took the Johnson family while we were in the vicinity, should we take them back? And if we did rescue those people, what were the chances of getting out of Pakistan before the Alpha group or their surrogates pounced?

Even worse – if we did get out of Pakistan, what were the odds of the Alpha people leaving us alone?

I had to get the timing right, and it had to start with a surprise snatch of the Johnson family.

*

I woke up when MG got back with Intel. We debriefed and went through the basic morning routine for Mr Johnson: the bodyguard drove, Mr Johnson in the back, straight to the office block in downtown Islamabad and into the underground security car park, which had a guard and a boom gate.

MG took me through it, showing me the streets on his tourist map, and doing small sketches where he didn't have photos. A couple of blokes drawing is not exactly macho, right? But that's one of the big overlaps between my tradie life and the intel world: blokes have to be able to draw what they need another bloke to understand. The route Mr Johnson used to get to the oil company building was along the main boulevards. It was a twenty-two-minute drive, according to MG.

'Any tails, any nosy bastards?' I asked.

MG made a face. 'None that I could see.'

If these inside guys were doing the job, then the set-up was probably going to be that they deliver the family to the Alpha people.

MG had to go, and said he'd be back in half an hour. I grilled Intel on the drive and he repeated MG's take on it: nothing unusual, standard route. It wasn't as if the driver-bodyguard was sneaking in a secret route so it would be easier to snatch the family. Or, he wasn't using it yet. If these guys were smart they'd take Johnson on his way to work and take the wife and kids when they were elsewhere. If it was me doing it, I wouldn't try to take the whole family in one hit.

I sucked on another Red Bull, probably a mistake, but these are the sacrifices we make. MG got back in under half an hour and delivered a large cardboard box from the front seat of the Pajero.

'What's this?' I asked.

He tore open the box flaps and what I saw in there was, honest to God, like a collection of rusty junk. I picked out one of the pieces – it had a rusty spring attached. It had once been a Makarov semi-automatic pistol, a staple of officers in the Red Army. But I wondered how long it had been living underwater. I was incredulous, and when I delved further into that box of tricks I found a pile of other weapons in varying states of disrepair, wrapped in sheets of old newspaper. I pieced together a Russian assault rifle that looked like it had been buried. The magazines had dings in them.

'AKM?' I asked MG.

He nodded. 'Two of them, boss.'

'Fuck,' I groaned, looking at my hands, which were now covered in orange rust powder. I feared being faced with a lot more firepower than we'd get from a corrupt bodyguard and a personal assistant. And we might have to use firearms to get out of the city, or even out of the country, against a foe that could be a coalition of organised crime and security forces. It was a worst-case contingency, but it wasn't far-fetched. Not in northern Pakistan. And to defend us was a bunch of junk that belonged in the garbage.

'That's all I could get,' shrugged MG. It was dim in that garage but I could see he was embarrassed.

'Jesus, mate,' I said.

MG lit a smoke. 'Two rifles, four handguns. You wanted me to shop local, stay off the grid, and this is what I could get.'

I'd told him to avoid the big arms dealers because in northern Pakistan they could easily be linked to Alpha's gang, or the ISI – or both – and I didn't want that attention.

'Okay, you're right,' I said. 'Let's get cleaning and see how we go.'

I wasn't happy, but whining or finding a scapegoat is a pointless exercise when you're holed up in a garage in Pindi, crapping in an open drain and trying to stop a kidnapping without being killed. So I did what I've done either in the field, or on a site, many times: concentrate on what you can do. Focus on putting one foot in front of the other, and making progress.

Frank, our mechanic, had an armourer specialisation from the British Army, so we let him lead the effort. Of the four handguns, he reckoned only two were salvageable – maybe three – based on the state of the firing pins and slides. He was bullish about the AKMs because these weapons were designed to be buried and resurrected. We'd have to start with those four weapons and if we got lucky with the last two, then so be it.

We had a look around and the best we could come up with was Listermint mouthwash, toothpaste, some petrol and an old peaches tin lying in the corner. I could have pulled rank, but it was my fault we had such shit weapons so I volunteered my toothbrush for the scrubbing brush. We poured Listermint in the peach can, wet a rag with petrol, and all afternoon we took turns dismantling the guns and scrubbing and wiping the parts to the point where we could actually use those things without having our fingers blown off or losing an eye. My fingers were aching by the time I'd worked on one of the AKMs with a petrol rag, but we were getting those weapons back to a workable condition.

When Doug got back with Rich, I took him aside and we debriefed on the technology around the house. He said he'd seen a housemaid coming in through the gate, and she had to stand and wait, having pushed the buzzer. She looked up while she did so, suggesting a camera. He said Johnson's wife didn't venture outside the house except to say goodbye to the children at around 8.40. They were driven to the International School inside the ex-pat precinct, by the personal assistant, in the BMW 4x4. The assistant returned to the house without diverting.

Doug turned the debrief to the access points: he knew the mechanism on the sliding vehicle gate. Doug said it wasn't on an IT network, it wasn't hack-able, and it had bolt locks that slid sideways into the wall. Very secure and probably not the way we'd go in unless we followed Johnson's car inside. I didn't like that scenario because it would trigger a gunfight and then the personal assistant would be inside with the wife and kids, and we'd be outside going at it with the bodyguard. The only scenario that made sense to me was taking down the two bad guys in the same area, at the same time. They were kidnappers, so guess what one of them would do if the plan went to shit and the other one was caught? He'd probably take a hostage, and I was being paid to stop that.

'Where is the vehicle entrance gate opened from?' I asked.

'There's a remote in the Mercedes, and one – probably wall-mounted – inside the front door, in the vestibule area. Probably where the alarm box is.'

'I see,' I said, not happy.

'We might get lucky,' he said. 'There's a 50 per cent chance of a manual override on the other side of the gate. Most of them have one in case the remotes don't work.'

I thanked him and let the information sink in. There was a very straightforward way to do this that I was starting to favour. It wouldn't be high-tech, but it would be highly effective.

7

Just planning an operation properly doesn't mean it will work that way. You can plan and scheme and out-think the bad guys and it's almost scientific. Then someone pulls out one small pin, the whole thing falls over and you're back where you started: one bunch of guys having to out-muscle another.

So I wasn't feeling overconfident about the gig and I had a big dose of paranoia about what could happen once we poked the hornet's nest. But some of the pieces were in place: there was no surveillance that I could detect; the morning routine was simple and began at 8 am; the alarm and door-opening systems were not able to be overridden, but we could deal with that. It didn't look too bad, actually, and I reckoned we'd given ourselves enough time to get in front of any problems. Once those firearms were in better shape – at least four of them – we'd be close to 'Green'.

I was lying on my back in the Pajero, it was just after 10 pm, and I was scrolling through a newsfeed you can pick up on text and going through things in my head. Intel was sitting on the roof of the garage, having a look for undesirables. It was quiet, people were dozing, so I almost jumped out of my blanket when the phone rang, all buzzing and lighting up.

It was a No Caller ID call, and I took it. 'Yep,' I said.

'Mike, it's Stan.'

I relaxed a bit, trying to calm my heart, which was racing from all those Red Bulls. We small-talked briefly and then he said, 'The matter of our Friends?'

'Yep?'

'I'm looking at an intercepted phone transcript, taken earlier today, between an Alpha operative in Peshawar – named Faisal,' and Stan spelled out the name.

'Yep,' I said, sitting up.

'This Faisal is apparently the genius who turns opium into AKMs and RPGs,' said Stan. 'Makes the Taliban real happy with that trick.'

'Who's he talking to?'

'Other caller named Mohammed, logged 16.48 Pakistan time. Not much else on it – the Friends aren't interested in Faisal or Alpha, per se. Seems they're looking for a British asset who is probably working with Alpha, when he's supposed to be working with the Friends, if you see?'

Stan was saying that this transcript wasn't important to British SIS because they were trying to catch out a potential double agent. In other words, this transcript was a piece of garbage that was about to disappear into a hard drive archive, but Stan had caught it because he'd made a request of the system – probably around 'Guardal Alpha', 'Kidnap' and 'Pakistan' – and he'd been alerted.

Stan kept reading. 'Mohammed says, *I'm bringing you those things, remember, that we spoke about?* And Faisal replies, *I'm in Jalalabad, and then Kabul on Thursday.* So Mohammed says to him, *When are you back in Pakistan?* And Faisal says, *I'm gone for a month.*'

I was now fully up and moving around the garage, listening intently, my breathing growing shallow. 'Yep, and then?'

Stan continued. 'So – let me read this – okay, so Mohammed is saying, *Jama says you're interested. These people are Australian, work for the big oil company and they have insurance*, and Faisal says, *Can we do this on Wednesday – I'm busy tomorrow*, and Mohammed says, *Yes, we can do Wednesday, we're here with them all the time, but what do you want to do with the hand-off – you want us to take them to Peshawar?* And Faisal says, *No, my people will let you know. You do the kidnapping and we'll take them from you in Rawalpindi.*'

My heart was thumping and the sweat on my forehead was clammy. 'Shit, Stan – you sure he says Wednesday? Like, two days' time Wednesday – is that it?'

'That's what he says.'

My ears were ringing. 'Thanks, mate,' I said. 'This was from this afternoon? Sure?'

Stan read out the date and time stamp on the page he was reading from.

We signed off and I woke the crew. It was Monday night, and this was our window. We had the night to plan this, run through it and then execute it. We had a narrow slot to stop this family being kidnapped and escape ourselves.

I texted MG, asking him to come down from the motel, and I cracked another Red Bull. By now my eyes were bugging out of my face and I felt a bit of blood pressure in my temples. When MG arrived ten minutes later, I put the guys in a circle around me and used a stick on the dirt floor, beneath where the only light bulb was hanging.

'We're on for tomorrow morning,' I said. 'I have live intel that the bodyguard and assistant are ready to kidnap the Johnson family. Their target date is Wednesday.'

The blokes nodded and looked at me. There's a lot of ego and machismo on these gigs but when things start to go down everyone stands back and lets each person do their job.

Using my stick I sketched the way we were going to enter

the compound – over the wall – then how we'd open the vehicle gate, pick up Johnson and his family, and I outlined the route we were going to take to the airport. We'd gone over the ground and looked at the property and the bad guys so many times that we were comfortable with how it was going to go. It's one of the benefits of spending some time in-country and investing in situational awareness. We'd driven and walked the routes and we were happy with the choke points and traffic flows, and we'd detected no surveillance of us or the Johnsons.

Our drivers were MG and Frank, the muscle was Rich and Intel, and Doug would cover the ground between the vans and the bad guys – he'd be a cover person with a handgun at the ready, in case some nosy bastard walked out of a garden shed or the garage and wanted to make something of it.

'Johnson leaves the house each day just before 8 am, so we'll be at the house at 7.30.'

They nodded.

'Any questions?' I asked.

'Where are we headed?'

This was the last piece of the puzzle and one I usually left until we were almost there. 'Benazir Bhutto International,' I said. 'Final instructions on approach.'

This didn't mean I distrusted any of them specifically. It's just that when I promise op-sec to the guys, I mean it. If you're being bugged or tailed or someone can monitor your conversations, they can eavesdrop on everything you say. Just ask me about that time in Malaysia: I made a last-minute confession to my crew that we'd take three taxis to Penang and catch a ferry to Sumatra, but the room I was talking in was bugged by Malaysian intelligence. So guess who was waiting at the ferry building? That snafu was fortuitous because we'd helped an English mining executive stay clear of a blackmail scam. So the security folks just wanted more on who we had thwarted. But you see how I became like this?

In the end, if I don't disclose the exit strategy, there's nothing for the listeners to hear. Your escape hatch has to be clean and unimpeded, and I guard it.

Instead I filled in the boys on our Plan B. If the race to the airport went to shit, the intention was to hit the softest road border, and find the nearest friendly embassy. The strategy is always to walk into an Aussie, American or British diplomatic post and say, 'I'm lost and confused.'

To my mind the best option for Plan B would be crossing into Afghanistan, but that wouldn't be easy. I would find a lot of sympathetic people in Kabul, given my networks and the contracting work I'd done in that death-trap city. But the border? I wasn't sure about it. It was always changeable, and I was standing in front of the experts on borders in that part of the world – I wanted them to set me straight if there was a better idea.

'Any alternatives to Kabul?' I asked.

'Crossing into India, at Wagah,' said MG. 'Usually pretty smooth and you're on a highway east out of Lahore. Easy driving.'

I nodded, but not really in agreement. 'That's a lot of time on Pakistani roads, especially if the Alpha people have a bead on us.'

'Okay,' said MG. 'You comfortable with the national highway?'

He was talking about the highway that goes westward straight out of Islamabad-Rawalpindi, over the border and into Kabul.

'You don't like the crossing?' I asked, and MG shrugged.

'If Alpha has border guards working for him, they're probably on that road. That's the big contraband route; it's the big money earner for the guards.'

I accepted that. I had no way of knowing what that crossing would be like if we were blown. 'What about the crossing on the Khost road?'

Rich gave me a look. 'That can be hairy.'

'That can be bribed,' I said. The Khost road was a terrible mountain pass, entering Afghanistan south of Kabul.

'With two car loads of rich white civilians?' said MG. 'That won't be cheap.'

'I throw ten grand at them, what are the chances?'

MG nodded. 'That would do it.'

I looked at them. 'Everyone okay with the Khost road as our Plan B?'

Some nods were slower than others, but they all went for it.

I asked MG to bring over the last two bags of items he'd been collecting before we arrived. One held a bunch of Kevlar-insert ballistic vests, stab vests and cargo pants. This is what we'd be wearing under our man-dresses on game day. In the other sports bag were two body bags, some zip-ties and a roll of duct tape. We were going to take the bad guys out of play while we exited this country – there was no other way to do it safely. They had to be bagged, placed somewhere non-public, not able to use their mobile phones, not kicking up a drama.

'Up at 6.30; we got full tanks in the cars?' I asked Frank. I never assume we have enough fuel.

'Roger that,' he said, and I suggested we turn in.

*

It was a nice night, clear air and stars visible, so I reached under the front passenger seat of MG's Pajero and pulled out the special package in a jute bag that I'd asked him to hide. It was MG's BGAN satellite phone, which he usually travels with. I took a walk around the block as the guys assembled guns and checked their passports and what have you. On the night before a gig, people don't talk much – they go through rituals, usually of the triple-checking variety.

I walked the streets, where women threw dishwater into the gutters, dogs looked for scraps after the dinner hour and parents raised their voices at kids. There were still a number of lights on but I found a shadowy shopfront and put in a call to AAA Freight

Corp plc., a Dubai-based provider of aviation services to organisations which would prefer not to operate in public.

'We're Green for location A, tomorrow zero-900,' I said.

They responded that they'd see me there, at nine in the morning. When I go in-country for these things I like to stay flexible in terms of dates and times, so I pay an extra bond on the private jet charter and have them not exactly on stand-by but at short notice and wide window. This was very short notice but they said they'd be there, which in my experience meant they'd be there.

I breathed out and took a quick snort of air through my nose. We were Green.

Back inside, the adrenaline was palpable even though these people were pros and didn't let their nerves show. We were all a little strung-out, to tell the truth, having gone a couple of weeks with no showers and crap food, living in the dirt-floor garage, and knowing that there was an Alpha crime gang connection. I hadn't told the boys my latest intel, because I didn't want it colouring my final mission brief. But as I walked in and saw four handguns now assembled and loaded up with 9mm rounds, I decided they should know.

'Something I want to share with everyone,' I said, weighing one of the Makarovs. It had come up nicely and I would not have recognised it as the pistol I'd seen in that cardboard box a day earlier. 'I got reliable intel today – these guys working with Johnson are certainly involving the Alpha gang in this kidnapping.'

MG whistled low. 'Shit, Mike. We made?'

'No,' I said. 'The transcript I heard contained no mention of us or anyone coming in to wreck their party. They think their snatch is going to be easy.'

'They in Rawalpindi?' asked Intel. 'The Alpha people?'

I shook my head. 'They're in Peshawar – they're arms dealers for the Taliban. They're pretty heavy, but we're going to get in first, do it fast and clean, okay, boys?'

They nodded, no emotions. If they were worried about getting caught in this part of the world by one of the world's biggest crime networks, they weren't letting on. I just hoped they couldn't see how worried I was.

8

I didn't get much sleep. I lay awake most of the night, thinking about what had brought me to this place. I thought about choices and life paths. How did a footy-playing apprentice builder end up in a Rawalpindi garage, about to save a family from kidnappers? The simple answer is, *Because this is what I do – this is what I've been trained for.* When I moved down from the bush in my late teens, I started working doors in Kings Cross and then became a bodyguard to a couple of well-known identities. When it became apparent that I had a knack for counter-intelligence and staying one step ahead of people, I came to the attention of a government agency. They trained me in the security arts: personal protection, intelligence, counter-intelligence, counter-terrorism and all the infiltration and information extraction skills that most people would associate with a secret agent. I did training secondments with other governments in specialties such as firearms, cyber-security and counter-measures, and paramilitary tactics that I would later deploy as a security contractor in Kabul.

Over the years I've been taught so many things by some of the world's experts in their fields. But operationally, it always seems to add up to the same thing: my strength is finding the threat and moving on it before it hurts the good guys. I see threats very clearly and very early, and I don't scare easily. And who was to know there was a living in it for a boy from the bush?

The alarm on my phone buzzed me awake at 6 am. I shook off the fatigue and the bad taste in my mouth and saw that MG was up and moving, sipping on a can of Coke and eating potato crisps.

'Happy with the route?' I said, seeing that he was poring over his own tourist map.

'Just doing last-minute rat runs,' he told me through a big mouthful of chips. Rat runs are the secondary and tertiary routes you might have to take on the basis of a split-second decision, and when you make that decision you have to know exactly where you're going. Experienced people like MG don't just memorise the main route, but all the other ones they might have to take.

'We're clear on surveillance?' I said.

'Check.'

'Cars working?'

MG gulped his drink. 'Check.'

'One man over the wall, using two men to lift.'

'Check.'

We went through it, breaking the whole gig into pieces. I wanted the vehicle gate opened quickly so we weren't parked in the street and I wanted to take custody of the Johnson family while both of the bad guys were around. I wanted all the players under one roof when we struck. As we did our thing, Frank sauntered over and grabbed a drink. Now I had my two drivers with me.

'Now that you're both here, location A is the Punjab Air Services Depot, Benazir Bhutto International.'

They both nodded, looking down at the map. I pointed to a freight zone on the western side of the airport, which also doubled as the private jet terminal.

'Can't drive onto the tarmac, sorry, mate,' I said to the Texan. 'This one's by the book – well, sort of.'

MG laughed. 'What's the play?'

'Punjab Air Services Depot is a bonded freight hub with an accredited customs and immigration official,' I said. 'We park on the street, clear immigration through the depot, and the charter will be parked on the other side.'

MG and Frank mumbled together, agreeing on the route to the building, and I asked them to keep it to themselves.

'Sure, boss,' said Frank, testing the ejector slides on the pistols and letting them catapult home. He and the boys had done a fantastic job with the weapons and I told him so.

Within two minutes I had the whole team on deck: me, MG, Frank, Intel, Rich and Doug. I asked them to eat and drink because the way this business goes, you can get caught up in shit and suddenly you don't eat for twelve hours and it's no good for anyone. So we munched down the snack food we'd grown sick of, then pulled on our man-dresses. We stood in a circle, knowing we wouldn't see this place again, and I went through the phases of the gig, numbering them on my fingers. I got eye contact and nods from each of the guys, and then we opened the garage door and walked into the gloom of pre-dawn.

We made fast time across town, out of the stinking, brown-tinged oldness of Rawalpindi and into the gleaming newness of Islamabad. There were few people around and the early morning cool wafted into the car as we drove down the incline towards the expat compounds, the Pajero driven by Frank right behind us. I turned slightly as we approached the compounds and saw Frank tailgating us in the security vehicle. When you have more than one vehicle on a gig, you close up the gap and move as one. One of the worst things you can do is have the lead vehicle separated from the security, and that doesn't always happen because bad guys are after you; if you're too far behind the lead car, you can be caught out at a traffic light or interrupted by slower traffic from a side street. This can easily happen in Asia because scooters will simply emerge right in front of you from side streets and alleyways and then your convoy is separated. So I ask my guys to tighten up – I'd rather have a few bumper taps from the security vehicle than lose them and have to wait.

The most knowledgeable person on this gig was MG and he was driving the lead car, so there was not much to say. He chewed on gum and drove, while Intel checked his AKM and I checked my handgun, we went through the plan in our minds. Approaching the business end of a gig can set off your nerves, but the people who do this professionally operate under a basic code: *Don't tell me your fears and I won't tell you mine.* As you count down to a full Green, you can't have people who want to think aloud or ponder the worst case scenario. The worst case scenario was fairly evident: this was northern Pakistan and we were about to deny a crime gang their million-dollar payday. What you do instead is focus on your job and see it all in your head, so when the pressure comes on you walk through it. It makes for a quiet car, but chatty types don't gravitate to this sort of work.

MG took a right turn and then another right corner and then we were slowing and moving the Pajero up against a wall neighbouring the Johnsons' compound. On the off-chance that there was a surveillance camera in the top of the vehicle door frame, I wanted to make us as hard to see as possible.

MG and Frank stayed in the cars and left them running, while Intel, Doug, me and Rich spilled out and stealthed along the footpath until we were against the compound wall. Intel pushed back against the terracotta-painted cinder blocks and linked his fingers and Rich stepped into his hands and levered himself up to the top of the wall. I stepped in behind him to help push Rich's foot skywards, but I felt him stall.

'Oh, fuck,' he said under his breath, and Rich was suddenly back on the pavement. 'Glass. Fucking broken glass along the top.'

Six men had looked over this compound and none of us had seen the glass. I didn't have time for this. We were committed and we were in the open, trying to climb over an expat compound wall in a neighbourhood where you get shot for that. We couldn't stand in the open so I whipped off my man-dress and put my hand out for Rich's too. I folded them together and over one another, and handed the mat I'd created to Rich. Intel got back in position, linked his fingers and Rich stepped in. On the count of three, Intel lifted and I came in behind to hold Rich while he arranged the mat over the broken glass. Then the ex-SAS man planted his forearms on the top of the wall and took his own weight. I watched, waiting for a seep of claret through the white fabric. But it didn't come. Rich pulled his right knee up onto the wall beside him and paused, his head low and scanning the compound. It was getting light quickly but the sun hadn't yet fully hit the front lawn or gardens. It still felt like we had some cover.

'Clear,' he said and heaved himself onto the wall, straddling his knees and thighs sideways across the broken glass to stay clear of the jagged edges. Then he swept himself over and disappeared from our sight as he dropped to the lawn below. I jumped slightly and grabbed the mat of man-dresses from the wall, tearing the cotton as I pulled the evidence off the glass tips.

'We made?' I asked. 'Anyone see anything?'

'Negative,' said Intel.

'Doug, you ready with that piece?' I asked.

'Roger that,' he said.

Doug was going to slip a piece of duct tape over the camera above the vehicle gate, and work the gate while we lifted the Johnson family. He'd be the person making that initial call if we were interrupted by people who might want to stop us, such as cops and security guards. His split-second judgement would have a big impact on the whole group's safety and I wanted him focused.

'As soon as we're safely to that door, you shut the gate, okay?'

'Roger that,' he said.

If we took too long in or around the house, I didn't want the drama being visible from the street. So the gate had to be shut, but then it had to be opened again as we exited.

'And no one comes at us from behind, okay, Doug? Someone comes at you, just drop 'em – I'll do the paperwork later, got it?'

'Check,' said Doug, looking calmer than I felt.

'Ready, boys?' I asked Intel. Intel nodded.

The gate buzzed and rattled and started moving sideways and I motioned for Frank and MG to drive the cars in behind us. As soon as the gate was cracked wide enough for one man, I pushed through and found Rich. 'We clear?'

'Clear, boss,' he said, taking the AKM handed to him by Intel. Now both of them were armed with assault rifles. I led them across the front lawn in a crouching run, the sun just about to hit the house. I felt the nerves hit my stomach and I burped slightly, feeling Red Bull fumes rise and fill my mouth.

Three, two, one . . . and we were at the door, the security camera lens seemingly huge, staring down at me from over the doorway. The car engines roared in my ears as they edged up the driveway, and then I heard the gate being sent back to its closed position.

We stood at the front door and I could feel Intel's breath on my neck – he was ready for action, I could smell it on him. I turned and saw Doug at the vehicle gate, giving me the thumbs-up as the gate rolled back and the gap to the street reduced to nothing.

Turning to the front door I peeked through the windows down the side of the frame but the glass was so heavily frosted that I couldn't see anything – another detail we hadn't been able to ascertain from long range. I looked at my G-Shock; it was 7.41 am.

Two choices in these situations: you kick in the door and storm the place, or you ring the bell and in doing so at least bring one or more of the occupants to the door. I was sure that either the bodyguard-driver or the personal assistant would answer the doorbell, so I wanted to start with that approach. It gives you more control – you then know precisely where at least one of your adversaries is standing.

So I took a breath and rang the bell.

I could feel Intel tensing behind me as we stood to the sides of the portico. Down the hall a dark shape moved to the door. The shape came straight towards us and I thought it was going to just answer the door – which would have suited my purposes – but at the last second, when the shape was less than a metre from me, it paused. I stayed still, because if all I could make out through that glass was movement, then the person on the other side had the same problem. We'd also gone over the security camera set-up and Doug had modelled the vision that would be transmitted. We were fairly certain that we were not being picked up by the door camera, and the Pajeros were now parked alongside the house, also out of range.

The shape stayed in one place on the other side of the door; we could see the shadows of his feet under the door. We held our breath while the dude inside the house held his. No sound, no movement, no breathing. Four men stayed in that holding pattern for at least a minute, by which time my heart was banging in my temples and a cold sweat had erupted on my forehead. In this kind of stand-off you can't see your adversary's face to get a hint of what he's going to do and you don't know if he's armed, and if he is, with what?

Intel and Rich had their AKMs stowed flat across their chests, but with their hands gripped around the trigger guards, ready to start shooting. I looked back to the big Aussie Commando. If this went on too much longer, I wanted him to kick in the door and we'd storm the place. I held up my spread hand – meaning five seconds – and he nodded and looked at Rich, who also nodded.

I counted down the seconds on my hand and as I did, Intel lifted his AKM with two hands over his left shoulder, and readied himself. As he got ready, and the stress became unbearable, the shape through the frosted glass moved, and a few clicks sounded from the deadlock on the door. In the circumstances, those tiny clicks sounded like an alarm going off. I held my hand up in a blade to put a pause on Intel, and as the final click came from the lock, the door opened a fraction. Whoever was on the other side of that door was touchy, and they knew all was not right.

The door cracked by half a centimetre and stopped, and I locked on a dark eye looking straight at me through the small gap. I changed my blade hand into a finger pointing at the door and Intel launched into the biggest stamp-kick I'd seen for many years, at a point just below the doorknob and lock. Intel is a former Aussie Rules footballer who saw seven combat missions in Afghanistan with the 2nd Commando Regiment. He's around six-foot-two, built like a tank, and his boot went through the door like it wasn't there. As the door flew back it hit our silent adversary so hard that the force tore the top hinge out of the frame and drove the leading edge of the door into the marble floor. Intel and Rich poured into the entrance of the house, weapons shouldered. Lying in front of us was the person I knew from my briefing notes as Mr Johnson's personal assistant. He was dressed in black pants and shirt and his face was quite damaged by the blow he'd just taken. He writhed and groaned on the floor, his phone in pieces along the marble.

Intel was the first through, and as the assistant opened his mouth to scream, Intel hit him in the face with the stock of his AKM, sending blood everywhere. I slid to my knees and put a carotid choke on the man to hold him in an upright position where he couldn't make a sound. But as I got my left arm around his neck, he overcame his shock and yelled, and tried to crawl and scrabble away from me.

Down the end of the hall, where the marble hallway opened into a living area, a large man appeared, his hand going to his hip to draw his handgun. This was the bodyguard – also dressed in black and a much bigger man than the assistant. As I got another hold on the assistant and punched him in the side of the neck, stunning him, Intel and Rich descended on the bodyguard. Intel grabbed the bloke's gun hand and dropped his shoulder into the guy, who fell against the wall, his gun clattering across the floor. They wrestled a bit, Rich looking for an opening to whack the kidnapper in the head with his rifle stock but not finding an opportunity.

A woman appeared – Mrs Johnson – and started screaming. And then an Anglo man who I recognised as Mr Johnson came in behind her and started yelling, about *what the fuck* and *who are you people?*

Rich finally got his hands on the bodyguard and put the muzzle of his AKM in the bloke's mouth, putting his finger to his lips. Now the bodyguard stopped struggling and panted, wide-eyed. The PA was semiconscious on the floor, and I checked behind me, out on the lawn where Doug stood guard. He gave a thumbs-up. So the Pajeros were in place and we had no unwanted attention.

Mrs Johnson continued to scream and her husband tried to protect her, so I walked up and told them I was from the insurance company. Mr Johnson looked confused, but at least he put his hand over his wife's mouth so he could hear what I was saying.

'Your assistant and bodyguard were about to kidnap you and your family and sell you back to the oil company,' I said. 'We've been assigned by the insurance company.'

Mr Johnson shook his head. Too much information – too much shock.

'Anwar?' he said, looking at the bodyguard.

I gestured for Intel to let Anwar speak. The rifle muzzle came out of the bloke's mouth and the begging hands and pleading eyes gave the game away instantly.

'Please, Mr Johnson, sir,' he started, but Johnson didn't let him go on.

'Fuck, really?!' he shrieked. 'I trusted you with my kids, you piece of shit.'

I put my hand out to stop him moving towards Anwar. 'I'm the good guy,' I said. 'My job is to remove you from this country, right now.'

Johnson let go of his wife's mouth, and both of them looked at their employees and the blood all over their marble hallway. Disbelief would about cover it.

The bodyguard tried to plead a misunderstanding and made a small movement towards Mr Johnson, and Intel dropped him with a very fast blow to the head with the rifle stock. Mrs Johnson leapt back into her husband's arms and I stood between her and the bodyguard so she couldn't see the mess.

'We need to keep quiet,' I said as calmly as I could. 'They have accomplices and we need to get you out of here with as little fuss as possible, okay?'

Mr Johnson nodded and asked his wife to calm down.

'Where are the kids?' I asked, and as I spoke, the bodyguard – who could have played second row in a rugby league team – broke loose from Intel and came at me. I stepped back slightly and hit him with a left hook, which flattened him. Intel leapt on the guy and choked him out, right there on the marble, while I asked for the husband and wife to move back into the living area. Intel and Rich were going to deal with the bad guys and I'd get to play management. I could see Doug standing in the doorway. 'Get the wet gear,' I yelled at him and went into the living room.

I turned back and saw that Mr Johnson had retrieved the children and I realised they'd probably seen me with my arms around the bodyguard's neck. Not cool – I'd now have to do some pastoral work, get them onside. They were attentive, clean looking kids, dressed in t-shirts, jeans and sneakers. The file had said the boy's name was Sam – the younger of the two. He was dark-eyed and thoughtful looking. The girl – Joanne – was the ten-year-old and she had a more confident, bossier thing about her. I asked them to sit. 'My name is Mike, I'm from Australia too,' I said. 'I'm employed by your insurance company to ensure nothing bad happens to you.'

'Daddy, who are these people?' said Joanne, and the mum said *Shhh*, and pulled the girl to her.

'You guys ever seen bullies at school?' I asked.

'No,' said Joanne, too quickly, and Sam put up his hand.

'Yes,' said Sam, quietly. 'I've seen them.'

I saw the parents look at each other in confusion.

'How do you think we should deal with those bullies?' I asked him.

'Beat them up,' he said, wide-eyed and not looking away.

'And what about the victims of the bullies?' I asked.

'Save them,' said the boy.

'That's a great answer, Sammy,' I said, and pointed to the bodyguard and personal assistant. 'These people wanted to bully your family, and my friends and I are here to save you.'

'Really?' said Sam.

'Yes, and you know what? I can do my job if you help me out – you want to help me, Sam?'

He nodded and smiled, and I roughed his hair. He was on board.

'Is there anyone else in the house?' I asked, turning back to the Johnson parents.

Mr Johnson shook his head. 'Maid starts at eight.'

I nodded but I wasn't going to take his word for it. Having subdued the personal assistant and bodyguard, Rich lifted his thumb and I gave him the nod: he ran from room to room, checking the house.

'Send the maid a text, if you wouldn't mind,' I said to Mr Johnson. 'Tell her she has the day off.'

Johnson picked up his iPhone and started tapping. I had their attention so I kept going. 'These employees of yours were about to kidnap you, and we have intercepted them. We're all in a lot of danger because they are part of an organised crime group that do this professionally.'

'Shit,' said Mr Johnson, looking up. They were listening to me properly now that the initial adrenaline was out of their systems, and I got a good look at the two adults. He was in his late forties, going bald, and with an office-dweller's body. She was about forty and the looker of the duo – brunette, pretty, and looked like she used the gym.

I addressed the kids, because sometimes it helps to be an adult who's not the parents, giving the orders. 'I need you to do exactly as I say, okay, Sam, Joanne?'

The kids nodded.

'Okay, you have one minute to grab one bag each,' I said. 'Mr Johnson, you have to get all passports, credit cards, visas – anything that'll get you into another country.'

'Where are we going?' he asked.

'I'll tell you soon,' I said. 'One minute, one bag, passports, money, credit cards. Okay? And no phone calls. Stay off your phones.'

I clapped my hands and Mr and Mrs Johnson and their kids took off.

I leaned back and looked through the doorway – in the hall, Intel was tagging and bagging the bad guys while Rich cleared the house room by room. The assistant and bodyguard were bound and had duct tape over their mouths. Intel was zipping up the body bags they had been loaded into.

Rich bounced to the bottom of the stairs and gave me a thumbs-up as he moved to help Intel.

The Johnson family came back down the stairs and into the living area with an assortment of bags and backpacks. They were acting fast, and I could see Mrs Johnson making an effort to be controlled in front of her kids. Some people never muster that strength – I was encouraged by her performance.

Rich and Intel grabbed an end each of the body bag with the bodyguard in it, and I saw his body shimmy a bit as they carried him to the security car. I asked Mr Johnson if he was ready and he gulped and said yes, so I led the family to the lead car, which still had MG in the driver's seat.

'All four of you across the back seat,' I said as I opened the rear door. 'Adults first, one child in the middle, smallest on Dad's lap.'

They put their bags down on the ground where I pointed, and piled into the lead car, while I stored their bags in the cargo area of the car. Mr Johnson's phone dinged – a text arriving. 'She's taking the day off,' he said to me.

'Good,' I said, and realised a new option was open to us.

MG was scanning like a machine: because of his military service, he was highly attuned to choke points. He was wired and wanted to be out of that driveway.

Intel and Rich had the bodyguard stashed in the cargo area of the security car. I could see his legs kicking under the black vinyl: he was scared and uncomfortable but it wasn't life-threatening. I wasn't going to kill him. As Rich and Intel moved back into the house to get the assistant, I pulled them up.

'Sorry, fellas,' I said, having decided on a slight alteration. 'There's no one in this house and the maid is taking the day off. Let's leave the bad guys here, okay?'

'The place is filled with things they can use to break free,' said Intel.

'So let's find a room with nothing in it,' I said.

They pulled the bodyguard out of the car and carried him back to the house. Doug caught my eye from where he was standing beside the gate, covering all of us. 'Okay, mate?' I asked.

'Yep,' said Doug.

The Johnson family settled into the back seat of the 4x4 and I shut the door. 'We'll be out of here soon, it's all okay,' I said to Mr Johnson. He nodded but couldn't meet my eye.

I walked to Doug and we watched Intel and Rich jog out of the house. 'They're in the study,' said Rich as he got into the security car driven by Frank. 'They're both bagged and the door's locked.'

'Okay, boys,' I said, and signalled for my drivers to turn and head down the driveway. Doug hit the manual gate switch and the steel door started sliding sideways. I followed the cars as they edged impatiently towards the gate, handgun pointed at the ground and my eyes on the walls around the compound. As the Pajeros left the compound and emerged onto the street, Doug hit the gate button on the wall. We walked into the new morning sun, and saw an empty street as the gate whirred its way back into place. I slipped into the passenger seat of the lead car, and told MG to move it. Looking at my G-Shock, I saw it was 7.50. The pick-up had taken nine minutes – now we had to get to the airport, and that distance felt like a lifetime.

9

At this stage of a gig, you feel as if every eye is on you – as if everyone in that city is looking straight at you and is about to stop you in your tracks, blow a whistle and call the cops. This is the most paranoid part of the job. I'd made the decision to leave the assistant and bodyguard wrapped up in the house for both pragmatic and legal reasons: pragmatic, because an empty house is as good a holding facility as any, and means you don't have to transport your captive around the city, potentially interfering with the exfil timing. Live bodies can cause dramas – if you had me in one of those bags, I'd be causing trouble, believe me. And there're legal considerations, too: in most countries the cops and courts see a big difference between the big mean whiteys who swoop in and save a family from local kidnappers, and the big mean whiteys who are driving around Rawalpindi with some kidnap victims of their own. We'd be locked up for that. But helping an Aussie oil executive and his family to leave sunny northern Pakistan in a hell of a hurry? The local cops might not be so concerned.

That still left a criminal group run by Guardal Alpha. These people might already have had surveillance in place around the Johnsons' house. And on hearing that their kidnapping deal – potentially worth millions of US dollars – was disappearing, they could easily decide to repossess the Johnson family.

I'd swapped weapons with Intel and I now had an AKM (sort of a newer, sleeker version of the AK-47) secreted alongside my left leg, against the inside of my door. MG was beside me, saying little and driving smoothly but quickly, not wanting to draw attention to us. I had some snacks and drinks left over from our stay at the dirt-floor garage, and I offered them to the kids. They both shook their heads and I didn't blame them. There would be time to relax and eat, but it wasn't now.

The traffic was building and we stop-started across the big boulevards of Islamabad, and suddenly we were on the IJP Road, heading south. Now we were in the midst of trucks and buses and the throng of Pakistan getting to work in the morning. Crowds stood at bus stops and the pavements were a sea of man-dresses and sandals. This was a modern, well-resourced society that in many respects still looked like the birthplace of Jesus. MG hooked left, off the modern infrastructure of twenty-first-century Pakistan and into Rawalpindi, with its crumbling roads, dung-fire haze and choking smell. Pindi had been around, apparently, for at least 2000 years – maybe 3000 – and had been home to Buddhist, Muslim and Sikh dynasties, hence the overburden of temples and mosques. And no one in that time, it seemed to me, had thought to clean it. I'm no snob, and I try not to judge. But let me put this into perspective: here's Rawalpindi, part of the capital of Pakistan, and it has a leprosy hospital.

It was almost 8.30 when we turned into a street that would lead us out to the airport and the traffic slowed us to around twenty kilometres per hour. I twisted in my seat and smiled at the family under our care, but I was looking through the rear window, at the security car. I wanted them close by, and they were right there. As per my requirements, the security car was driving on the lead car's bumper so that if there was a stoppage or obstacle that we deemed dangerous, the security car could come forward very quickly and simply knock out the obstacle. If the obstacle was a person – usually one with a firearm – then too bad. They get a pie in the face and the lead car can keep driving. This is why we're picky about our vehicles in-country. Pakistan is a nation of tuktuks and Suzuki vans powered by sewing machine engines. I can't use vehicles like that in these gigs. I need heavy, strong vehicles that can take the hits. And I can't go straight to the Hertz depot and hire a shiny new Land Cruiser. That's when intelligence people see you're in-country and operating, and in Pakistan the ISI are deeply connected to the big crime groups – in fact, those big crime organisations are the ones funding the Taliban, creating a drugs-for-arms trade. So I go dark when I work in places like Pakistan. I send in someone like MG as the advance guard, let him infiltrate, find a private seller and keep it all in cash and informal.

So there we were, driving through the streets of Pindi, our stomachs churning. We were all feeling it – just clock-watching, legs jiggling with impatience. The locals were staring and I was trying not to stare back, when I suddenly became aware of a ringing sound. I looked out my window and saw nothing.

'Tango, my side,' said MG, using the American military term for a terrorist. I looked behind his shoulder to see a motorcyclist pulling up to the driver-side rear window. He was late teens, wearing a Manchester United t-shirt, riding a Yamaha 125cc trail bike.

'Shit, are you kidding me?' I said reflexively, before I realised that I wasn't really calming the Johnsons. As I tried to free my AKM to aim it, the rider's arm shot through the gap at the top of the window and was feeling around for something to steal. This vehicle had no air-con, so we were ventilating with the cracked window. The wife screamed, lurching away from the spider-like hand, and MG couldn't swerve – there was too much traffic. So I unbuckled, twisted around, and thrust the stock of my rifle at the thief, hitting him on the forearm but in the process jamming my finger between the rifle and MG's seat, with a lot of force. I saw stars and I could feel my face going purple with the strain of keeping down a yell. Fuck, it hurt! But the thief backed off from the Pajero and I could see him swerving to miss the headlight of our security car.

Settling back in my seat, I tried to control my breathing and ignore the pain in a finger that I may have come close to breaking. A bead of sweat popped over my right eyelid. I just had to stay calm. We were eight minutes from our ride home and I had to show some starch, just make it look routine. The looks on the faces of those kids as I swung the assault rifle at the thief? They weren't relaxed, and I needed to get all of us back to a state of composure.

We stopped in traffic and I had an idea: I'd find a radio station on the car stereo, and maybe I could have a laugh with the kids. I pushed the 'scan' button on the radio, and at each station there was either a rattle of Urdu (or Pashto) or it was a blast of the local music that has so much treble that it sounds like fingernails on a blackboard. The selections were terrible and I made some faces, asked Joanne if this was Justin Bieber? I got the kids laughing, at least, but as I ran the options on the radio, MG's Texan twang rang out loud and clear.

'Tango, your side Mike.'

The fuck?! I looked up and over my shoulder, and the motorcycle thief was back, this time on my side. He was up against the side of the Pajero and at the very moment I saw him, Mr Johnson also saw him and started yelling, trying to punch the rider away from his daughter sitting on his lap. By now I'd had enough of this city, and I start muttering at the motorcyclist as I lifted up my AKM and pointed it out the window.

'Mike!' came MG's voice as he gripped my bicep with his spare hand. 'Not here, buddy.'

I paused, realising what I was about to do, and pulled the rifle inside the car. Then MG started a game of cat and mouse with the motorcyclist, speeding up and slowing down, not letting the bike have any room. At one point the motorcyclist was so boxed in that he was forced up onto the footpath. But he stuck with us, and we had pandemonium in that car for a solid minute of our lives as the children yelled out whenever the rider came into view. Just as things reached the point of farce, MG found a side street, boxed the motorcyclist in and finally pushed him down the narrow street. The whole scene would have lasted no more than ninety seconds but the stress and the drama it caused was immense. This is the crucial point of the whole gig – keeping your subjects safe and calm as you exfiltrate – but the cabin fever of that garage and the ugly undercurrent of danger was getting the better of me.

I took a couple of deep breaths, wiped the sweat off my brow, and composed myself. Then I turned and looked at the two children in the back seat. 'Gee, why doesn't he just go shoplifting like every other kid?' and that got a laugh. Then I looked at Joanne, and I said, 'Imagine having that bloke as your brother? You'd never have to guess where your toys went.'

We had a giggle and I could see that the gesture was appreciated by Mrs Johnson. The whole morning scene had probably hit her the hardest, and the idea of the proximity of these thugs – living in her house and being around her children – was sinking in. There was probably another wave of fear and distress to come when she started thinking about the bodyguard and assistant too much, and I needed her to stay calm for another five minutes.

The approach roads to Benazir Bhutto International were jammed – it was not the ideal time to be making this trip, but our schedule had been largely dictated to us. MG got off the boulevard and we spent a few minutes stop-starting with all the family traffic going to the airport before we veered away onto a commercial road that led around the side of the precinct into the freight hubs.

'They have a security gate for the freight depots?' I asked MG, and he told me there were none on the maps.

We tucked in behind a big yellow DHL truck and when it swept into its hub, we kept going into a less salubrious area. We slowed, turned off the main trucking road and now we were on a narrow, potholed street that ran alongside some crappy warehouses.

'What's this?' I asked, not too loud.

'Should be just down here,' said MG, slowing. He pulled up in front of Punjab Air Services. My heart was sinking: it was a run-down freight warehouse that looked abandoned. And even if it was used, it had an underworld look to it. If this place was in Sydney, it would owned by the Serbian mob. There were three enormous roller doors side by side, which obviously opened to truck bays, but they were all closed. A standard door entrance was on the right of the façade, with floor-to-ceiling windows around it and a *Punjab Air Services* sign in red and white above the entrance.

I couldn't see the tarmac for the line of buildings, but my instructions from AAA Freight Corp were clear: the charter jet would be waiting at Punjab Air Services between 9 and 10 am. That was the window and this was the RV.

And I didn't like it. 'You ever worked this place?' I asked MG as I scanned the building, looking for clues.

'Nope,' said the Texan, also scrutinising it as he fished for a smoke.

'No one home?' I asked under my breath. 'Or is it that no one's expecting us?'

MG shrugged. 'Who called this?'

'Charter,' I said.

MG nodded and I made a decision. 'Let's do it.'

I got out of the car and opened the back door so I was beside Mr Johnson and looking at his whole family. 'This is the part where we stay calm, stay together and do as we're told,' I said, as friendly as possible. 'Our ride's on the other side of that building – we're going to walk through in a close formation, and I'll tell you where to stand and what to do, okay?'

They all nodded and said yes, and I turned to Mr Johnson. 'You have those passports?'

He nodded and patted the backpack beside him. On the other side of the Pajero, MG took a security stance, his right hand touching the Makarov pistol holstered across his stomach on the stab vest. Frank, Intel, Rich and Doug now surrounded the lead car, Rich tucked in close so passing traffic couldn't see the AKM.

'Okay, Mrs Johnson,' I said softly. 'Grab your things, take your son by the hand and please walk to my friend,' I said, pointing at MG.

When they left the car I said to Mr Johnson, 'Please take your bag and your daughter and follow your wife.'

They shimmied across the back seat of the Pajero and walked the two paces to MG. By the time I'd shut the doors and walked around the car, my crew had an outward-looking circle around our subjects, and I could see Rich scanning the roof line of the freight depot with his rifle. It didn't feel right and all of us were trying to work out what was up. With my crew encircling the Johnson family, I walked to the entrance door of Punjab Air Services and knocked. There was no reply so I pushed the glass door and it opened.

'Hello,' I called. There was no response. Inside was a stand-up reception desk with a computer screen on it. But the foyer didn't turn into offices – it immediately opened into a warehouse. I could see boxes stacked and a shipping container. It was lit by panes of glass in the ceiling, from what I could tell: the lights weren't on.

I called again, and still no reply. Now my pulse was banging in my temples. You know what it felt like? Like a B-grade film director's vision of a warehouse ambush. That's what I was looking at. Yet on the other side of this ambush-waiting-to-happen was our ride home.

I turned back and saw my group. I had to make a decision. There's a temptation when you're suspicious about a venue to go check it out with a colleague and leave your subjects somewhere else. It's a temptation you have to overcome because the potential danger you might spare them by having, say, me and Rich go and clear the building, is not worth the extra hazards you create by splitting the group. When you're exfiltrating the subjects, you have to stay together. You need a full-strength crew to deal with any bad guys, and in any event the subjects need to feel us all moving together. The herd is a calming influence – ask any horse.

I inclined my head at MG and he led the group over to the entrance. He leaned in the door with me.

'Anyone home, Mike?'

'Not that they're saying.'

MG's pistol came out of its holster and I told him the charter was on the other side of the building and that there was supposed to be a customs person to stamp us out of the country.

'Really?' said MG. 'In here?'

I shared his doubt but there wasn't much I could do. Our ride was through this building and I wasn't going to postpone. I was getting on that charter, and so were my subjects.

'You lead,' I said as a large jet came in overhead to land.

As MG pushed into the building, I held the door and Rich walked through first, swapped firearms with MG, and then ushered the family through.

'Stay close, stay bunched up,' I said. 'Hold Rich's belt – hold each other's shirts.'

We crabbed through like a ten-person centipede, out of the foyer and into the warehouse space. I confirmed there were no lights – only diffused sunlight from clear ceiling panels. The place was a shambles, and it was muggy and airless. I'd had dreams all my professional life, of how things would end for me. And the dream setting was always a place like this: a rat-trap, an ambush, one moment of complacency . . .

'Hello,' I called again, the sounds of planes taking off and landing messing with my hearing. 'Anyone here?'

We inched forwards among the stacks of boxes and pallets of crates. Most of the cargo writing was in subcontinent dialects. There seemed to be a roller door open ahead which accessed the airside, but my main concern was the lack of wriggle room in that warehouse. I couldn't see more than twenty feet in front of me – there was always another stack of boxes interfering, and the shipping container we had to walk around was the perfect place for someone to shoot down from.

We walked into an open space among the freight consignments and now I could see onto the apron through the open roller door. A plain white Falcon 900 was right there, its three engines still whistling.

'Hello, can I help you?' came a Pakistani voice, and I almost leapt off the ground as MG spun around, rifle pointing. Appearing between two stacks of cartons was a middle-aged local with an Errol Flynn moustache and Brylcreemed hair. He had a credential around his neck and he looked friendly, but he had something in a pouch on his hip.

'Easy,' I said, looking at MG, who was aiming up as I moved towards the man. 'Easy, mate! Name's Mike,' I said as I reached him. 'You're expecting an outbound party?'

'Certainly, Mr Mike,' he said, cool as you like. I could have kissed him. 'Do you have your passports?'

Keeping our defensive posture around the subjects, it was quickly obvious our official was accustomed to arrangements like this and people like us. The weapons didn't faze him one bit. I brought the official to the family and he said, 'Passports open at a blank page, please.'

Mr Johnson handed the passports to each family member, and they opened them and got them ready. And then our new friend with the lounge lizard mo reached into his holster, and, as MG tensed, the man drew out an ink pad and a stamp.

By now I had bullets of sweat trickling down my cheeks and a heart rate going crackers in my temples. I was completely wired on anxiety and Red Bull.

'Fuck,' I said, laughing with relief. 'It's a fucking stamp pad.'

As I caught a look from Mrs Johnson, I tried to make it right. 'Sorry, kids, that was a mistake. I mean, it's a blimmin' stamp pad.'

The kids smirked, but not with as much of a smile as Mrs Johnson.

The man went from passport to passport, whacking the ink and then generally aiming the stamp at the passport page. He didn't look at a single passport photograph. Then he stamped Intel's passport and ended with me. I stowed the Makarov in my shorts belt and held my passport with two hands, to give the man something to hit. He grabbed a big lick of ink and hit my passport with the stamp, throwing so much ink that it dripped down the page and off the paper. Through the whole drama I didn't take my eyes off his; I was heaving for breath, and – now I look back on it – probably dehydrated.

'Have a good flight,' said the Pakistani, and he disappeared again, into the mountains of freight. The look of relief on my face must have been very obvious, because Mr Johnson turned to me as he collected his kids' passports, and said, 'Well, that wasn't so bad, in the end.'

'No,' I said, the adrenaline still buzzing. 'That wasn't too bad for a lesson in modern art.' I held up my passport, which now had a dark blue, wet stain down one entire page, with a wet smear at the top which was indecipherable as a customs and immigration stamp. That got a laugh from the children, and they held up theirs too, rolling their eyes and wondering what the hell that was all about. And even as the giggles lingered, I grabbed the Makarov and led them through the open roller door and onto the tarmac. The involvement of children in these jobs is inevitable and regrettable, all at the same time. Short of having a degree in psychology, there isn't really an operating manual for rescues: some kids are mentally hardy and others go to pieces. Just like adults, actually. I do what I can to keep it light, maintain morale and obscure the brutal truth. Sometimes I strike up a rapport with the kids, and things roll along nicely – as it did with Sam and Joanne. But it's not always like that, believe me.

My crew followed us, in a V formation, weapons at the ready. This game is all about choke points, and also about Murphy's Law: just when you think the gig's over and you can relax . . .

We all knew that trap and the guys kept their game faces on while they escorted the family to the air stairs, which were down. I could see two faces up in the cockpit. One lifted his hand, disappeared and reappeared at the head of the stairs. I climbed them, identified myself, although the co-pilot made no attempt to do the same. These charters are a no-names operation, and unless there's a medical emergency on board, the pilots do not interact with the customers.

'Usual rules,' said the co-pilot, wearing whites so bright that they needed a warning sign about looking at them with a naked eye. 'There's food and drink in the fridges and the cupboards. There's a microwave and there's a shower and bathroom at the back.'

'Okay, thanks,' I said, knowing there was also a bedroom and double bed in the rear of the cabin.

Me and the boys must have looked like shit, because the aviator winced slightly. 'And if anyone wants to sleep in the bed, they must shower first, okay?'

I assured him that was okay, and the co-pilot walked down the stairs and asked the Johnsons to leave all their luggage on the tarmac and enter the plane, find a seat and buckle in. This is for the charter company's operational security, by the way – it isn't because there's porter services attached. I nodded at the family and they did as they were asked. As Mr Johnson disappeared into the cabin, the co-pilot followed him with the bags, which would be stowed in the interior baggage compartment. I turned to my crew. Only Intel and I would be making this leg of the trip into Sydney for the hand-off. MG and Rich would drop Frank and Doug at the airport, and those two would enter the building separately. They would take different flights: Frank into London and Doug to Karachi and from there onto a connecting flight to Singapore and Sydney.

MG and Rich would take the cars into the bush, burn them, break down the weapons and dispose of them, and leave the country as tourists. I wanted this to happen before dusk. The whistleblower on the whole thing would be the Johnsons' maid, who might take the day off or she might decide she needed something and drop into the house from her granny flat out the back, and discover the bodyguard and assistant struggling around in their black vinyl sleeping bags.

Intel climbed the stairs and I handed my Makarov to Rich – he'd destroy it along with the other weapons. Then I shook each of my crew by the hand, thanked them for their help and assured them that the money would not be far behind. They knew I was good for it, and as we farewelled one another, the co-pilot said 'Okay' from the top of the air stairs, and I turned, walked up the stairs and ducked into the leather and mahogany security of the executive jet.

I slumped in one of the leather seats and buckled in. I was accustomed to this sort of aircraft, but not because I could afford it. The cabin door was pulled shut and the engines' revs came up. I closed my eyes and leaned back, feeling like I could fall two miles into that chair. Through the windows, my guys were disappearing back into the freight warehouse. They were going to complete the mission, and for the first time in nearly three weeks, I relaxed.

10

There was something pushing into my face. Something quite painful. I opened my eyes and I was looking along carpet, under a bed. My phone buzzed on the floor beside me. I had no idea where I was. Sitting up, I picked up the phone and felt the headache hit.

'Hello,' I croaked, my throat stuck together and dry.

'Mike?' It was Liz's voice. 'I'm at the airport – where are you?'

I groaned at my stupidity. I was now eye level with a triangular cardboard sign on a writing table. It said, *Grace Hotel – Sydney*.

'I'm in Sydney, love,' I said, wincing at the pain of talking.

I stood up. I was fully clothed and I smelled like a distillery. I was in a hotel room and my travelling backpack was on the bed. I slapped my pockets – force of habit – and felt my credit card in one pocket. The left pocket of my jeans was filled with receipts. Throwing them on the bed I saw an evening of drinking, gentlemen's clubs and taxis. My head felt like it was going to eject and seek alcohol counselling.

'I was picking you up, remember?' she said.

'Sorry, love,' I said, feeling really remorseful.

I sat on the bed, my memory a blur. We'd delivered the Johnsons to the insurance guys at the private jet terminal of Sydney's Kingsford Smith Airport at around 3 pm local time, having stopped once to refuel at an undisclosed location (I suspected Denpasar). Intel had left to sign something with a lawyer. I'd gone and checked into the Grace, getting rooms for Intel and Doug, and when Doug arrived at Sydney International about two hours later I'd shouted the guys to a night on the piss. Judging by the receipts we'd been all over the city, from Newtown to Pyrmont to Bondi.

Liz wasn't too hard on me. She knew the downside of this world of mine and she knew I don't usually party after a gig. In fact I usually like to hide away for a few days, do surveillance-detection on my trails, see if anyone's tapping into my email – that sort of thing. What had happened last night I honestly put down to a week of drinking Red Bull causing some basic dehydration. I didn't like Rawalpindi and had felt spooked the whole time I was there. And when I decompressed in Sydney, I'd gone overboard.

I don't make this point to excuse myself. I screwed up, leaving my wife waiting at Tullamarine Airport in Melbourne while I slept it off on the floor of a Sydney hotel room. But the thing to remember is that I work in partnership with my wife, and that means I'm trying to get home after a gig and I'm open about everything I can be open about.

Liz was my second wife. In my previous life, working intel for governments, I was married for the first time, and because of the burden I carried and the security orders I operated under, I couldn't be open with my wife. If I'd missed an airport pick-up I'd have been more likely to say that something had come up in Perth, or I'd had to fill out forms in Brisbane. That was how folks in my world had to roll. And it gets to you after a while.

So where does someone like Liz fit in? People like me have to be realistic. You get a good woman who can handle your life and your endless shit, and you have to play your part. As Wife Number Two, Liz got Improved Version 2.0 of me; Wife Number One was also an intel operator for a government agency, and she got Mike Daly Version 1.0 – phone calls from places I couldn't name, whispered conversations that ended with *Gotta go*, missed birthdays, forgotten anniversaries. Not to mention the time I turned up from a two-week gig, four weeks late . . . minus the toenails in my right foot. Try selling that to the missus. You can't say, *A Middle East government's secret police operation got the wrong guy and before they could work out their mistake, my toenails were gone*. It's hard to have the conversation, so you don't have the conversation. You come up with a story, make it plausible and move on. Don't ever talk about those toenails again, and if you really have to, make sure it's a light, suburban vignette about heavy things falling on feet – not about pliers and meaningless questions. And so you sink further into a hole dug by lies.

Liz was my chance to get it right. Because she'd worked in major emergency and trauma wards for many years, she had high levels of mental control and stamina and I'd decided to trust her with simple versions of the truth. So, one of the first things I did when we became intimate was to tell her the true story about my toes. And you know what? She handled it, and I handled it, and we've had good communication ever since. So yeah, my work still took me out of the country and occasionally I'd go dark for two or three weeks. But no more lies to my wife. I was exhausted and dehydrated, and a few drinks with the boys had put me on my ear. Guilty, your honour.

I signed off with Liz and then I wanted to know more about my night. As is no doubt clear by now, I'm a little paranoid about op-sec, and I could remember almost nothing. For professional reasons I had to know how I got into this room.

I dialled 9 on the room phone and when the person at reception answered, I asked if everything was okay. The woman handed me over to another person – a man – who called himself Gary.

'Hi Gary, do we know each other?' I asked.

'I took you to your room this morning, sir,' he said. 'You fell asleep on the foyer sofa.'

'How did I end up on the floor?' I asked.

'We rolled you off the porter's trolley,' said Gary. 'You were too heavy to get onto the bed and we couldn't wake you.'

Feeling the early stages of someone about to take the piss, I thanked him and signed off. I stripped and headed for the shower. Did that gig really happen? Sometimes I wonder this when I'm back in normal surrounds. The surreal combination of starting the day in a dirt-floor garage in Rawalpindi, and ending it eating carpet in a Sydney hotel, was too weird. At least I wasn't in a Pakistani prison, or being hunted by the largest criminal organisation on the subcontinent.

Like I have after so many other gigs, I decided to park it all in the bottom drawer of my mind. I'd clean up, get some lunch and then get on the phone to Si and see what's going on. It was now all behind me – I was back in civvie life, and now I was a different kind of contractor again. I was back to the hi-vis and the nail-bag.

As I stepped over a pile of my clothes to get in the shower, something caught my eye. It was my cargo shorts – the ones I'd been wearing when we lifted the Johnson family. As the hot water hit my back, I started laughing, like a kid. Couldn't contain myself.

The gig was behind me, but Pakistan had left its mark. Or should I say, a Pakistani customs bloke had left his mark – a bloke with the worst stamping technique I've ever seen. Streaking down the front left leg of those shorts was a long, dark blue ink stain that looked like a mark of Cain.

PARIS AU GO-GO

1

My world is a global club with a tonne of IOUs floating around at any given time. These IOUs accumulate in a serious way because when someone does a favour for me, they could be saving my life or at least sparing me a visit to the cellar. I do other operators the same favours – and if they're calling me and asking for information or asking for an introduction, it's only because it's serious. In most parts of life, the real owner of a car that started parking in your street, or the beneficial owner of a Malaysian company, is immaterial. But for people like me, it might be crucial. It might be the difference between a nice night's sleep in a hotel, and being dragged into a van at two in the morning, with a black hood on my head. Just about every dangerous or near-death event in my career could have been averted by better information, delivered in timely fashion.

The tradie networks operate in a similar way to the intelligence contractors. If you need something done quickly – Cash Quickly – and a fellow tradie answers your call on a Thursday evening or a Saturday morning, then you're in the network and you're on the hook. They answered the bugle call and saved your lily-white, and you'd do the same for them. But the great difference between tradies and intel contractors is their spending habits: Aussie tradies don't buy retail. It's just not our culture. But when you're working in-country as a different kind of contractor, everything is retail. It's how you blend in.

The house I was building, which Si had looked after while I was away, was due for the roofing crew to come in and they were going to complete it in a one-day blitz. This was an ace team of Maoris who you don't find in the Yellow Pages. They're used by the trade to get houses capped quickly, because having the roof on usually cues another payment and we builders, we like those progress payments. And fast, in-demand roofers? They like that cash.

The guys were due to roof my house in early November, and the milestone was going to trigger a payment to me and put me on the home stretch for completion in December, and therefore the finish payment would come to me before Christmas. These Maoris were known as 6 am starters and I was ready on-site that Monday morning at 5.45, taking the tarps off the frames and getting set up. I had a Thermos of coffee, but I was without my labourers, Hoodie and McKenzie: I was letting them start a week later, while I got the roof on and bedded in any problems with guttering, downpipes and stormwater connections – all the usual pottering around.

But 6 am came and went, and then 6.30 and 7 am, and pretty soon I was into the phone, trying to track down James, the roofing crew boss. No response – just voice mail. It was strange, because I was paying these guys cash and they were going to do in one day what most roofing contractors do in two or three. Leading up to Christmas and New Year, they'd want that money – I knew they did because I wanted my money too.

But they didn't show, and soon I was drifting down to the local McDonald's for a stack of hotcakes, a coffee and a hash brown. My builder mate, Si, got out of his Land Cruiser and wandered in around 7.30, already covered in concrete dust. I waved and he brought his breakfast over and joined me.

'Know where James and the Maori roofers are working?' I asked him. 'They were supposed to be roofing my place this morning.'

'Beats me,' said Si. 'Can't find 'em?'

'No-shows,' I said. 'All I get is voice mail.'

'That doesn't sound like them,' he said, making a face. 'James is usually Mr Reliable.'

He pulled out his smartphone and scrolled through his contacts, hitting a button.

'Robbo, you old mutt,' he laughed into the phone, giving me a wink. 'How's the King of HardiePlank?'

Chuckling, Si held the phone away from his face as Robbo – a florid-faced, always-stressed builder – took the bait.

'Shit, take it easy, old man,' said Si, cackling. 'Happy birthday to you too, my brother.'

I couldn't hear what was being said, but Si eventually cut through and said, 'Mike's looking for his roofing crew, James's guys, the Maoris.'

'Yeah, *that* Mike,' said Si, winking at me. 'The little fella.'

There was a pause and then Si was hanging up. 'One of his guys on-site is a New Zealander – knows the roofing blokes, he'll call soon.'

We ate as we waited and I could see the wheels turning in Si's head. 'If you can't find these guys, I have someone else for ya.'

'Who?' I asked, not feeling confident. I wanted the roof on that week. I wanted the Maoris.

'Really pro bunch of guys from up Romsey,' said Si, one of those Aussies who talk slow and think fast. 'Davo used them a few weeks ago, over on that Box Hill job. Remember the heritage hoo-ha and the fucking council and he needed it done before the Friday?'

'Okay,' I said. 'But Romsey? That's a two-hour drive . . .'

Si's phone rang and he answered, said, 'Yep, yep, cheers,' and hung up. 'He's texting you the number,' he said to me.

'I have James's number,' I said, a little annoyed.

'Nah, mate. This one's in New Zealand, one of those Funga places,' said Si.

My phone trilled with a text notification, and I copied the number into my phone and called it.

A woman answered almost immediately in a thick New Zealand accent.

'Hello, is James there, please?' I asked.

She simply put the phone down and I could hear her screaming in the background. Footsteps padded up and then James was speaking. '*Kia ora.*'

'James, Mike Daly, from Melbourne –'

'Fuck, Mike, I'm so sorry, my bro,' James said, and I could tell he was remorseful. 'We got stopped at the airport, they sent us back, man!'

'What?' I asked. 'Who sent you back?'

'Aussie government, cuz,' he said. 'Wouldn't let us through immigration in Melbourne, said we had – you, know – criminal records and that, and turned us around!'

'What?!'

'They kept us overnight, my phone went dead and when we got back to Auckland I headed to my sister's in Whangarei, but my mate had my charger. I'm here with no phone and this one has a tollbar on it.'

We had a chat and he said sorry a million times and when I hung up, I asked Si for the number of the Romsey roofers. It wasn't just that I wanted the progress payment, I had all the other tradies booked to come in once the roof was on and I didn't want a traffic jam of things not getting done because I couldn't get the roof on. And remember, this was the serious lead-in to the holidays when you have to get things done. Because from around 20 December to the end of January, most tradies are relaxing in a camping ground, drinking beer, catching fish and burning steaks. They don't want to work in the hottest part of the Australian summer so they squeeze an extra effort into the weeks leading up to Christmas. If you get it wrong, you're dealing with a skills shortage from the beginning of November to the end of January, and having lost my roofers I couldn't afford to get caught up in that.

The Romsey crew were young – Jaso, the boss, was all of twenty-five – but they were keen for work. Jaso drove down that day, took one look at the roof and asked me what the Maoris had quoted. I said $9000 and he didn't even blink, said he'd do it for the same, but cash is king. 'Sure,' I said, and they started on Wednesday at 6 am.

I felt bad about telling them the Maoris' rate, because the standard rate was closer to $14,000. These youngsters were going to do half their dough in diesel just driving to and from Romsey. So when they started I looked after them by bringing in food and coffee, and even though the roof was a bit tricky I vowed to help them finish it in two days – make it worth their while. They were fast and moved across the roof like spiders, but there was one overhanging piece of battening that wasn't quite going in, right up at the apex, and there was a young bloke struggling to line it up while the others loaded up with roofing tiles on the ground. So I climbed the ladder, picked up the roofers' Skilsaw, and tried to help this roofer trim the batten, in the spirit of the thing. And I misjudged my angle, and instead of taking off a corner of the batten I basically amputated my left forefinger.

Liz saw the whole thing because she'd just pulled up on-site to get me to sign something from the bank, so she was just in time to see a geyser of blood erupt from my hand. I must have been in shock because according to her I stood there staring at a finger flopped back 180 degrees on itself while blood shot out in a jet. I remember staring at it like an idiot, thinking, *Shit, really!?*

The youngster I'd been trying to help was so fast and fit that he skipped to the edge of the roof, jumped straight off it onto the ground, grabbed a t-shirt from the truck and scooted back up the ladder to me. I was still staring at the bloody mess, claret pouring off my elbow and onto the floor below. Because of Liz's work in emergency, she didn't get upset but calmly told the roofer what to do with the t-shirt. But she was clearly annoyed with me for doing a young man's job on the roof, and when he'd stopped the bleeding with the t-shirt, she shouted to him, 'And if he gives you cheek, shove it in his mouth.'

You get days like that in the trades. Just like in my other work, really. You plan and you plan and it all makes sense on paper, and then one small thing screws you up. Liz didn't see things with so much philosophy. Nurses who work where she works have seen too much and I guess they keep a lid on their emotions so they can do the job. But boy, they let fly with the ones they love.

'Are you *kidding* me?!' she said, as we weaved through traffic for the hospital. 'What the hell were you doing up there?'

I'm sitting there in the passenger seat, thinking maybe this isn't the best time to ask her to keep in her own lane.

'Trying to help the boys,' I said, my right hand under my left elbow, trying to catch the blood. 'Just wanted the roof on.'

'They didn't need help,' she said. 'You had no business being way the hell up on the top of that house!'

I didn't see it that way. 'I wasn't really on top of the . . .'

'I was there Mike!' she said. 'Don't bullshit me. I saw the whole thing. Now look at you – you'll be lucky to keep that finger.'

The trip through A&E, reclining on a gurney and being wheeled into an operating area, adhered fairly much to this theme: my wife regaling the medical staff of what a dumb-arse her husband was.

And so it was that I was lying on the lounge two weeks later, air-con crispy cool on poor old Mike, sitting there with my bandaged hand, skin full of antibiotics, head filled with painkillers and the Foxtel remote my only connection to reality. The Taiwanese surgeon at the hospital was a microsurgery specialist and he'd stitched my finger back on to where it was supposed to be. He reckoned there was a good chance of it knitting back – my job had been to watch closely and report any darkening in the flesh. After five days, I took the bandage off to have a look and the flesh around the scar was dark-green turning to black. I'd gone straight back to the surgeon, who'd done a 'scraping' of the wound and now I was dealing with the pain of the original wound *and* the scraping. The drugs were great, but you slice through a bone and it aches as if the pain is deep inside, and trying to get out. But it was growing back, the surgery had worked, and I could bend it a few millimetres. And I'd tapped my builder mate Si to help out around the site, so I could take more of a management role.

Liz wandered into the kitchen-lounge area and I asked if there were any Crownies left in the fridge and she said, 'Not for you, there isn't,' which meant I was going to have to wait till she left for the night shift. I think women are more caring than men, but that doesn't mean they like doing it. And that doesn't instantly make men grateful patients.

I'd just found something on Fox Sports – the re-run of an AFL game – when the phone went. Picking it up I saw it was from 'Henny'. That would be Danny Hendon, a mate of mine from the old days, when we did government intel work. He'd moved on to managing security for major global sports events and now worked high-level security in Canberra. It was a little hush-hush, which didn't concern me.

I picked up on the third ring.

'Big Unit, you clear?' he said, no preamble.

'Clear, mate,' I said, 'how's Frogland?'

'Fucked,' he said. 'Fucking fucked.'

I'd talked with Henny a couple of time over the past week because he'd been scouting Paris ahead of the Climate Conference, due to start in two weeks' time. He had a complete list of our Prime Minister's movements at the UN conference and his job was to drive the routes, walk the corridors, lie in the hotel beds, sit at restaurant tables and stand in front of bathroom mirrors. He'd even visit the toilets along routes and venues, give them the once-over. He had to understand where the PM would be for every minute of his three-day visit, and know where the threats would come from.

'French still being French?' I chuckled. Fuck him, I thought: the bastard is lurking about in Paris while I'm trying to complete a house, with a finger that may or may not grow back. If the worst he can say is that the French are annoying him, well he could hand out some slaps, do some hard diplomacy.

'You remember Manny Maroun?' said Henny, ignoring my gibe.

'That money guy?' I said, leaving off any mention of Hezbollah.

'Yeah,' said Henny. 'Had a brother in Bathurst, for murder. Ahmed Maroun?'

'Sure,' I said, watching a Dockers full forward bump off some flying defence from Carlton. The Maroun brothers were a decade in my past. I didn't get it.

Henny continued. 'Arkie turned up in Turkey. He was making these ISIL dickheads legit for Europe, selling them passports and shit.'

'Europe?' I said. 'Jesus!'

Henny said: 'Turkish intelligence got hold of the prick, roughed him up. They have enough to throw him in a dungeon for life – he's fucked.'

'So, what do you need?' I asked, padding to my kitchen and cracking a Crownie.

'You hearing anything?'

'About what?'

'Europe, Paris, France?' said Henny. I could tell he was stressed.

'Only the ISIL refugees,' I said, referring to all the Syrian and Iraqi fighting-age males who were drifting into Europe as part of the massive refugee flows. 'What else?'

There was a brief silence and I let it go. There's some things best unsaid on phone calls, and I guessed he was thinking about it.

'Ahmed is singing to the investigators, keeping himself out of Turkish prison,' said Henny, voice lowered. 'He's talking about a terror cell in Paris, and there's fuck-all going on in Paris except this climate thing. So . . . you know . . .'

Yeah, I did know. I sat on my sofa and turned off the TV. I knew Henny wanted me to reach into some of my old networks, rattle some cages and perhaps some teeth as well. See where monkeys would swing. But I was no longer in Sydney and the old Hezbollah and Hamas networks I used to monitor in Western Sydney now belonged to a younger, nastier generation who thought the Hezbollah commanders were old and soft. It was all Twitter and ISIS now.

'I'm not plugged in to that stuff, mate,' I said, staying arm's-length.

'What about all that XBox shit?' he asked. Henny was referring to the online gaming networks I'd broken into a few years before. Terror cells were communicating through the voice channels that operate between XBox and PlayStation players in different states or countries. When they hooked up to play *Call of Duty* together, they had a VoIP connection so they could talk. But that was a lucky find – in reality, it was almost impossible to search for those conversations because they're not saved on a hard drive. I shared that win with the Federal Police but the AFP intel guys still needed to know where to look and then they needed to listen to these gamers' conversations. Very helpful but also very difficult.

'I'll ask around, mate,' I said. 'Let you know.'

We signed off amicably, but he'd wanted more and I'd ducked him. The truth was I was still active, but me breaking back into Sydney's al-Qaeda and ISIS scene? That wasn't what Liz had signed up for. Liz came back into the kitchen, and I hid my beer.

She was all readied for the night shift at the hospital and before she left she reminded me of my meds and told me to stay off the booze.

'Yep, cheers,' I said, as she leaned over and kissed me.

'And that includes the one you're sitting on,' she said. 'See you in the morning.'

I gave her another kiss, asked her to be careful, but my mind was on Turkey and Paris and a Sydney thug who was coughing up what he could to stay out of the dungeon.

I didn't want to be back in, but the problem was I'd never really left. I'm called a GNE in my world: Good Not Evil. I like to help – it's what motivates me. So I turned on the footy again and I was watching the game, but in my mind I saw a map with Syria over on the right, and Paris on the left, and I wondered what new hell Henny had been mumbling about. He'd always been a worrier, I told myself; always dwelling in the column labelled 'what if' . . .

I came out of a deep, beer-assisted and painkiller-softened sleep, aware of the phone vibrating on the bedside table, the eerie greenish screen-light of the old Nokia beaming out in the darkness.

'Fuck me dead,' I groaned as I reached the phone and looked at it. The number started with +4420.

London! Didn't they have a world clock?

I answered it. Dead air crackled as I rubbed sleep from my eyes and squinted at my watch on the bedside. A shade after 6 am.

A voice came through, English middle-class but not poncy.

'Hello,' said the man. A man I knew.

'Yep.'

He paused. 'Is that the Contractor?'

2

I went to the kitchen and turned on the coffee machine. Something told me this was going to be a long day.

'Yeah, Charles,' I said. 'It's me.'

'Got a job, needs to be done now,' said Charles.

Charles was a security manager at Arcadian Underwriters which, like Allardyce Insurance, was a large London insurance company that underwrote the life policies of expat executives. I dealt with him on a semi-regular basis – sometimes for full gigs, other times for intel, and occasionally for a reference on another operator.

'What's up?' I asked, grabbing the remote control on the kitchen counter and firing up the TV.

'Seen Paris?' he asked, and I paused because for a split second I thought he was asking me that literally, but before I could respond I was watching CNN footage, and Paris was in chaos.

'Fuck, mate,' I said, confused. 'I'm looking at CNN . . .'

'So am I,' said Charles, not quite doing the stiff upper lip as he usually did. 'Paris is fluid.'

I watched the ticker running along the bottom of the images of people hurrying through the streets, bodies on the ground, police looking stunned, and heard a panicked voice-over from a reporter, obviously in the thick of it, obviously not enjoying it. The ticker along the bottom was counting deaths – they were up to thirty confirmed.

'Bunch of armed terrorists, moving around central Paris,' said Charles, back to the London Met cop he'd once been. 'They've killed a lot of people and they're still going.'

'Holy shit,' I said, not even thinking. Was this what Henny was worried about? Had he picked it early while I'd just fobbed him off?

'We have a client who needs a lift. Hotel chain executive – he's insured for US$11 million.'

'You don't have anyone in Europe?' I asked. I was flattered he'd rung, but it was six in the morning and I was standing in a house in Clayton.

'French national police have closed all the roads and rail into Paris,' said Charles, impatient but polite. 'There're roadblocks all over the city, and the French just closed the airspace. No one's getting in or out while the terrorists are still loose. It's a lockdown.'

I nodded, still unable to take my eyes off the footage from Paris. 'What's the gig?'

'The client needs to be extracted, now. First choice London but I'll accept Manchester or Glasgow.'

'Numbers?'

'Four,' said Charles. 'Client, wife, two kids aged nine and fourteen.'

'Condition?'

'Safe, for now,' said Charles. 'I spoke with the client five minutes ago.'

'Enemy contact?'

'No, but the wife is having an anxiety attack . . .'

'They locked in? Is there a safe room? Escape protocol?'

'They're locked in a bathroom. They're in a second-floor apartment on the Avenue Montaigne, it's in the eighth . . .'

'I know where it is,' I said, moving into my office. On a previous government job, I'd been assigned to run personal protection for a minister who, rather than stay at the Commonwealth-supplied hotel in Paris, insisted on staying with a wealthy friend on the Avenue Montaigne. The security detail's apartment was fairly impressive in itself and that street would always conjure up images of wealth and power for me.

'Number?' I asked.

He gave me the names, street numbers and the client's mobile phone number – an incredibly important piece of the puzzle. By the time I stopped writing on my legal pad, I'd decided to accept the job. I had an idea how to get it done. I opened my laptop and told Charles to verify the engagement.

'Charles, let's make it my normal quote, but – mate – if we've got restricted airspace over Paris then even Air Force One will have problems landing there tonight.'

'Yes, I know,' he said, and he almost laughed. 'That's why I'm calling you.'

Rule Number One: if someone says *That's why I'm calling you*, then the gig is going to be tricky.

'Include a rider for the aviation expenses,' I said, opening my email system. 'My quote covers US$70,000 worth of flying but if it goes over that – it won't be by much – it's from your end.'

'Done.'

I said, 'I'll know in half an hour if I can get it done.'

'Writing it now,' said Charles. 'I appreciate this.'

The email landed three minutes later. It was a form letter of engagement, with Charles's signature. It included a few details and the expected outcomes, and tagged on the end was my rider about exceeding the aviation budget. Most important for this work, I checked that my bank account numbers in the British Virgin Islands were all correct, and the fee – US$375,000 – was clearly marked. When I worked for Charles, I had an up-front payment from Arcadian of half of the total quote. That was my starting fee, and by the time I'd found the bank website portal and input my numbers, the start payment was in my BVI account.

I attached my e-signature, and returned the letter immediately. I was working again – now all I needed was to infiltrate a city in lockdown on the other side of the world. And I was still in my PJs.

How hard could it be?

3

In this world, I'm called a specialist. That's how the intelligence agencies, insurance companies, police forces and militaries refer to me, with possibly the word 'private' thrown in or the word 'intelligence' planted at the front. It doesn't mean I'm a soloist. It's all a team and it's all teamwork. I learned that when I first worked for the government in Australia; even if you're the most elite and highly trained operator, you'll get precisely nowhere without good people around you. And when I say that, I mean above you and below, not just beside you. There's no point in being churlish because someone is above you in the food chain, and you don't get points for talking down to the person you employ. There's no such thing as 'just' in my world; there's no *He's just a driver*, or *She's just running comms*. Every person plays their part because every part of the puzzle has to work smoothly. The team is crucial and if I don't think I have the personnel to complete the job, I don't take the job. I have come to rely so heavily on trusted, competent people that I have a standing policy on payment: I declare the total quote to the team and split what's left after the expenses, evenly between the people working the gig. Everyone knows where they stand and they all stand on the same ground.

By the time Charles had received my signed engagement letter I was working the phone and sketching on my legal pad. I break my gigs into five pieces: you get each piece right and you give yourself a chance of winning. If you try to mix the elements too much, you either miss details or get lost in them – both of which are disastrous. That's when you enter into 'hope and a prayer' territory. I don't run those gigs, which is one of the reasons I have a top-drawer stable of people to call on.

My pieces are always these: People – to do the gig; Transport – the means to move the people on the ground; Movement – the passes and permits required so my people can be where they have to be; Logistics – the planes, the choppers, the fuel, the pilots and airspace clearances; and the Exit – the ability to get the whole team out of there if things go pear-shaped.

To have good people rely on you, it pays to be clear about the last item, first. All the best people with special forces backgrounds want to know there's an exit before they see anything else, so you might as well have your plan ready. My planning was already running through entering Paris by air, a personal security detail (PSD) that would travel across Paris to Avenue Montaigne, lifting the client and four warm bodies, and then return to the airport, and the exfil to London.

Each phase had its own risks and required different resources. I also had to have a Plan B on each piece. Not only do I need a way to make it work if small things go wrong, but the people I work with – former military, intelligence and law enforcement – all expect a Plan B if they're to trust you.

I sketched it out and decided on a private jet into Paris–Le Bourget Airport, carrying two of my best operators. They'd pick up a nine-seater vehicle of the type kept on stand-by by police forces and dignitary security operations. In France this would be a Mercedes Sprinter van (perhaps an Iveco), with darkened windows and seats in the back. Most important, this vehicle would have to have the internal security stickers used in France – colour-coded circular stickers that run down the left-hand side of the windscreen, allowing police, military and intel to know which arm of government you are operating from, and what clearance you've been given.

My guys would use the vehicle and stickers to negotiate their way through the Paris roadblocks and, having reached the apartment building, the family would be assembled with what they wanted to carry. They'd be taken to the airport and the private jet would fly them to London where they'd be met by Charles's team from Arcadian.

I pulled one of my prepaid burner phones from my desk, tore open the packet and fired it up. My first call was into Lyon. A nice part of France, but for my purposes also the headquarters of Interpol. I had a good contact there and if I was going to do this gig, I wanted as much intel as I could on what was happening in Paris. My mate Zac – a Canadian special operations cop who I'd met in Indonesia and who was now high up in Interpol – picked up. He was in no mood to talk.

'Fuck, Mike,' he said. 'I'm *really* fucking busy.'

'Won't keep you,' I said. 'Tell me one thing – the airspace: is it a civil or military lockdown?'

He sighed, and I could hear him shouting to a room, first in English and then in French. Several voices came back and then Zac was in my ear again. 'Military.'

Before he could hang up, I asked him for some numbers. He yelled at me, and when he'd calmed down, told me to call back in half an hour.

'Gotta go,' he said, and he was gone.

The panic ringing in my ears, I called Dubai, where the key to the whole thing was sitting in a private hangar on the southern end of Al Maktoum International Airport. The owner of this precious piece of hardware – a Gulfstream V – was AAA Freight, who'd helped me out during my Islamabad job and many times before that. I was owed a favour by the CEO, but how big a favour? There was a catch with what I was going to ask him, and that was the controlled airspace over Paris. How many owners of a Gulfstream V will charter it into an area that's been shut down, and has fighter jets and drones in control of the skies? There was only one answer to that, and it was the tail numbers and the call sign. The air traffic control tower at Le Bourget would be under military orders, and when the ATC declined to let my Gulfstream land, and I instructed my pilots to give them a tail number, it would have to be a number from hell: a sledgehammer. Something to override their orders.

I put it to the CEO of AAA Freight and he whistled low and told me Paris was no-fly.

'I couldn't get in there, Mike. I couldn't land, and even if I could, would they let me take off again? In Paris? Christ, have you seen the news?'

Well, at least he was talking to me. 'What if I could get you a government tail number?' I asked him, and now there was a big pause at the other end. This aviation company ran 'clean' planes – with no tail numbers – and they were used to spelling them out to air traffic control. But what I was suggesting was risky given the situation because the French were ready to shoot someone out of the sky.

'*Can* you get me a government tail number?' he asked very slowly, 'without getting me arrested?'

'I can, mate, but I don't have it yet,' I said. 'So here's how we have to play it: I need you to be wheels-up in half an hour. You'll be flying with two of my guys and I'll relay the tail number and a call sign to the pilots when I get them. Can do?'

He didn't like it, but like I say, he owed me, and he said he'd get on it.

'I'll get us fuelled and ready,' he said. 'What's the turnaround?'

'Two hours on the tarmac, then into London City Airport.'

He agreed and I rang off.

My next call was to an aviation firm I use in Melbourne. I needed to be on a plane to Dubai, with a couple of my special people, because Dubai was going to be my Plan B for the exit and my base of operations. I lined that up in a forty-five-second call, with no paperwork.

Then I called MG, who was back in the United Arab Emirates. He'd get in touch with Rich. I wanted these guys as a team to do the lift in Paris and bring my clients out to London. They were both smart, cool and battle-tested but it was also crucial that my guys in-country be able to operate without their own firearms. Trying to bring weapons into a country, or carry them around when you're a foreign national, is asking for trouble and you don't generally do it. MG and Rich could disarm you and turn your weapon on you if you aimed at them. They'd probably also travel with small devices that looked like one thing but could be used as a weapon. And in any event, if I could get a van with the agency stickers on it, there would be a driver in the deal and he or she would be armed.

It was going to be a bad environment in Paris and I needed a couple of people who could stay calm while the client's wife had a panic attack. I had a contact, Jo, who would have been ideal for the job, if she hadn't been working on a full-time contract in Kuwait. She wasn't just tough and smart, she was also excellent with emotional people. Every intel operator comes at their profession from a distinct angle, and Jo's was psychology – just don't ever call her Jolene. Using her real name was a trip to the mat.

But with Jo busy, I was hoping MG and Rich would be good for it and not too annoyed by the Pakistan gig we'd recently completed.

'MG, it's Mike,' I said when he picked up. He sounded sober, which is a good start in this business.

'Hey, it's the Big Unit,' said MG in a long Texas drawl. 'What's cookin', man-dress man?'

'Yeah, well you picked my frock, so cut the humour,' I gibed at him. 'I need you on a bird into Paris right away,' I said.

'I'm in,' he said, just like that.

'Can you get hold of Rich?' I asked.

'Sure, I can get him,' said MG, slow but assuring. 'What's the job?'

'You seen Paris?'

'Fucking mess,' said MG. 'All fucked up.'

'I need you to pick up a client, his wife and kids, put them on a plane and fly them to London.'

'They hurt?'

'No, mate,' I said. 'The wife's having an anxiety attack and the insurance company wants them out of there now.'

We agreed to terms and he took the gig without asking another question. He said he'd be at AAA's hangar inside twenty minutes, with Rich, and I believed him.

Now I needed numbers for that plane and a vehicle for my team. I took a breath – I needed this part to work. I scrolled through my contacts and called a number in The Hague, head office of Europol. I had a good relationship with a Spanish police-intel guy called Juan and I was sure he'd help.

'Hey, it's the Aussie,' said Juan when he heard my voice. 'You like what you're seeing on the TV?'

'Looks like hell, mate,' I said. 'Juan – I need a van, for Paris. It needs all the stickers.'

'Where?' he asked. Juan was a well-dressed, compact bloke who'd grown up in Madrid. You see us next to each other, we look like Fred and Barney, but we'd always worked together well.

'Paris–Le Bourget,' I said. 'It needs to have enough stickers to get through the roadblocks and not be held up by the cops.'

He asked me where the van had to get to and when I told him the Avenue Montaigne, he made one of those long Spanish *ooooh* sounds that essentially meant I was nuts. Did I mention the Avenue Montaigne? Long before there were gated communities and leafy suburbs in the New World, there was Avenue Montaigne, which sits just north of the Seine in the part of Paris where the diplomats and ambassadors, the bankers, politicians and billionaires live. For centuries it's been a sort of European hub for the rich and powerful and traditionally an area that France's security services protect very seriously. One of the ISIS attacks had occurred to the east of the Montaigne neighbourhood, at Les Halles shopping centre, and that attack site was right over a major Metro station, on the line that rode due north to the Stade de France, where a suicide bomber had detonated at a McDonald's. So if the terrorists were moving around on the trains it wouldn't take much to leap on a Metro train and go west, into the area where my subject was hiding. And if they were moving around in vehicles, from the Stade de France they'd quickly get onto the Boulevard Périphérique, the periphery road that circles Paris, and get off wherever they wanted to do their killing. The Avenue Montaigne was convenient to the western curve of the periphery road and I knew where the major roadblocks were going to be.

'Is there going to be a problem, Juan?'

'Paris is a problem, right now, Michael,' he snapped. 'Avenue Montaigne is going to be very difficult.'

'Impossible?'

Juan snorted. 'I have the vehicle.'

'Driver too?'

'Yes, a driver. You owe me.'

'As always, brother,' I said, and wished him luck.

Now I needed those tail numbers. Without them, Paris would remain no-fly. There was no polite way to do it – Interpol would be busy for the next week. There would be no good time to call. So I got back to Zac in Lyon, told him what I needed, and why. We tossed it back and forth, and I could tell he just wanted me off the line. He asked me some questions and then he laid it out.

'I don't know the insurance firm or this executive you're rescuing from Paris,' said my buddy. 'But I know you, Mike, so if I do this it's on you, okay?'

'Okay, Zac,' I said.

'If the shit flies, it'll be landing on me, man. And then I'll talk to *you*.'

I told him I got it.

Zac laughed. 'We good?'

'We're good, mate,' I said, and breathed out. And then he read out a tail number and a call sign, and I jotted them down on my pad.

Having finished with him, I called my chief executive at AAA Freight.

'We're a go,' I said when he picked up.

'That's just as well, because I have two of your guys on board, asking for coffee.'

I laughed, and then told him how it was going to work. 'I can't give you the call sign or tail number until you're about to be challenged by Paris tower.'

'Why?' he asked.

'Because they're Interpol numbers, and we're flying on their rules.'

I hadn't wanted to push my luck with Zac, so I hadn't asked the question. But I suspected the tower at Paris–Le Bourget would be treating that Gulfstream as if it carried a foreign dignitary, and any mistakes with that would cause a lot of embarrassment for me and my allies.

As they say in the classics, *Don't fuck it up, Mike.*

4

It becomes obvious when you look at an operation like this that making it run smoothly relies on not only good contacts but having a few favours in the bank. The whole tradie network in Australia operates on favours and good deeds – hey, it's a deadline-driven business and lots of weird stuff happens between the architect's drawings and lock-up. You need an army of people to call on and many favours waiting to be returned, or even small jobs that won't yield any profit. Intel work is not so different. Just apply it to a globally dispersed community of GNE operators, trying to deal with bad guys and threats and needing all the help they can get. Most of my credit in the Favour Bank was deposited there from gigs in South East Asia and the Pacific. That's my chosen theatre of operations and that's where I've been able to help out Americans, Canadians and Europeans over the years. It might work like this: imagine you're a Canadian crime fighter, part of Ottawa's child-sex tourism taskforce, operating out of Bangkok. You have to perform a sting and you have to have some locals onside, and you have to be able to do what you're doing in – say – Cambodia, without one layer of law enforcement stopping another layer from doing its job. Every time you try to spring your trap and catch these paedophile tourists, a certain bunch of cops tips off the criminals. So you're getting frustrated, and then someone says that you should have a chat with an Australian dude called Mike, because this Mike character might be prepared to make some calls, dip into his extensive South East Asian contact book, and make it so that the corrupt cops stay out of the road for a few weeks so that you can spring your trap.

Do you see? Here's another example: perhaps a Europol investigator is in Asia, trying to link Indonesian money men to Jihadi terror cells in Spain and France, and he can't get his investigation any deeper than the official level. So someone gives him a card with an Australian mobile phone number on it, and the person on the end of that call has a fairly good list of the always-shuffling Bahasa names and which corporate entities they are linked to. And once you realise that Indonesians change their names and operate under many aliases, the job becomes easier for you. You look great back in The Hague, and when that Aussie puts in the occasional call to make *himself* look good, then you give him the time of day.

That's why I have the hide to ring some of these people and ask them for impossible favours. I don't overplay or over-ask, by the way. The Favour Bank is a fragile economy and everyone can only take as much from the well as they put in. But contacts or not, running a gig in Paris from Melbourne is not easy. At one point I had three phones and two laptops on the job, trying to keep the balls in the air and the mission on the move, and my injured finger was aching.

The first priority is always to have your ground people connected so that you retrieve real-time ground intel and you have a chance to respond. I was watching the CNN coverage on TV and scrolling through Reuters and other feeds on one of my laptops, and cross-referencing what was going on with a tourist map of Paris. When MG and Rich landed and picked up the van, I wanted to be able to give them the best route through to the Avenue Montaigne.

MG always travelled with his BGAN satellite phone so I knew I could talk to him once the plane was in the air. He also travelled with a small laptop, so when Charles from Arcadian Underwriters sent me a biography package of the family to be lifted – complete with names and photographs – I sent it on to MG and then called him.

'I've got pics coming through to you now,' I said. 'Stand-by for the van pick-up. We have a driver.'

'Got that, Unit,' he said, and signed off. He'd plug the sat phone into his laptop and download his email, and then he and Rich would have some faces to go with the names and descriptions.

Then I used my other burner phone to call Juan at Europol. 'How are we with that vehicle, Juan?'

'Got the van, Mike,' he said. 'But I've lost the person who was going to drive it out there – we're very busy.'

I sighed, maybe too hard. Juan was doing his best. 'What if I find a driver?' I pushed.

'Won't work,' said Juan, with Spanish politeness. 'It's in a security garage. The driver has to be authorised – they won't sign it out to one of your guys.'

He could hear my stress and told me he was on it – he'd know for sure in half an hour.

So Plan B had to kick in. I found a number for the Hertz desk at Le Bourget airport and dialled it on my main mobile phone. I was put on hold as I heard keys in the door and Liz wandered in from night shift. She saw my set-up and instantly knew I was 'on'. Rather than go to bed, she blessedly asked if I wanted eggs.

'Please,' I said as the other burner trilled. I picked up.

'Mike, it's Juan,' said my Spanish buddy. 'Just got a driver – the van's on its way to Le Bourget, but he's not happy.'

'I owe him,' I said, clicking off the Hertz number on the other phone.

'No, I owe him and you owe me,' said Juan. He told me where the van was going to park and rang off.

I rang MG on his sat phone and told him the pick-up arrangement for the van. 'You're on a Europol job, okay, mate?'

'For you? Anything, Mike.'

I grabbed another coffee, and I slurped while Liz drank coffee at the kitchen island.

'Okay, Mike?' she asked.

'Yeah, honey,' I said, giving her a wink. 'We're sweet.'

'You on a plane?'

'Fifty–fifty,' I said. 'See how we go.'

I stood and stretched, thought about a shower and canned the idea. I took a deep breath and considered painkillers for my finger, but decided against those too. Then I thought about the most important conversation of all. I was going to brief the subject – the insurance company's client – and like all the people in my world do, I was hoping to God he wasn't a muppet.

5

Forget all that shit where special operators talk to satellites and talk to operations centres and talk to radios and talk to their cufflinks. Don't get me wrong – that whole technology rigmarole is real, and having superior comms is always an advantage when dealing with the bad guys. But actually, most of the special ops, tactical ops and intel worlds come down to humint – human intelligence – the ability to enlist another human to your cause in a few seconds.

Whether you're a SWAT negotiator with a big city police department, a CIA interrogator at Guantanamo, or an Australian Commando doing hearts-and-minds in a village in Afghanistan, the first few seconds of interaction are crucial. The way you carry your body, the props you use (positive like a cup of coffee; negative like a nightstick), the eye contact you give, the first words you use, the first question and the second and the third. Some of the best female interrogators use clothing and scent to establish the mood; SWAT negotiators like to use background music; soldiers go for humour and common interests, like sport.

It doesn't matter which approach you take; if you need someone to be with you – not against you – you have to establish control and authority from first contact. It's an art, and one we are trained in and practice. I was trained by foreign government agencies and an Australian government organisation. I'm good at wrapping instant control inside a warmish affinity. Which is what I was going to do with the client, let's call him John Smith.

Of course, I didn't have body language and eye contact to work with on this occasion. There were no props I could wave around to make him feel safe or calm. All I had was my voice and my words, so I had to use them carefully. I had to take control and – in the same sentence – tell this guy that he and his family were safe, and that they must do exactly what they were told. Try that balancing act when there're terrorists running in the streets shooting AK-47s and there's a very loud, very anxious woman standing in the bathroom with you. And try that when your subject is an English CEO, used to earning a gazillion dollars and having his every command followed.

A bad guy? You give me a van, some zip-ties and a body bag – and I'll deal with your bad guy. But now, the subject is the good guy – I can't tag him, bag him and drag him. Yet it's his behaviour and propensity to freak out that is most likely to bring the gig undone and bring danger on my guys. You don't see this too much in the movies, but in my profession we know that delays and poor choices are usually what get us shot, and bad guys and good guys are equally capable of bringing these circumstances upon us. In other words, the muppet who flips out can hurt you just as much as the terrorist waiting in ambush.

I made the call. Mr Smith picked up on the second ring and I heard, 'Hello.'

He sounded like a child at the end of the hallway. A child with a plutey English accent.

'Mr Smith,' I said. 'This is Mike Daly, I'm picking you up on behalf of Arcadian, your insurer.'

'Yes,' he mumbled. 'Are you here?'

'No, mate,' I said, sensing I needed to keep this light to start with. 'An hour away, but we're all good my end and none of the shooters are near you, okay?'

Mr Smith hissed and groaned at the same time.

'How's everyone? Let's run through it – John, right?'

Making the subject account for his people isn't just information gathering, it's an important way to get the subject focused on what he can *do*. If you can get a scared man to start focusing on the welfare of the people around him, eight times out of ten it gets him floating down my channel. The other two times? You might have to smack him, let him sleep through the gig.

'Yes,' he said, clearing his throat. 'It's John, and um . . .'

He was looking around – I could tell by the way his voice slipped off the phone mic. I could hear someone talking in the background, an adult woman, and she didn't sound happy.

'Yes,' he said. 'We're all okay.'

'Linda's going to be fine, just a bit of a shock, right, John?' I said, trying to stay light with the wife trouble. 'You hear gunfire and everyone reacts differently. Bit of anxiety is quite natural. Fight or flight, nothing more.'

'Yes, um, it'll be fine.'

'She got some Mogadon or Xanax?' I asked. 'She take anything for that?'

'Well, yeah,' said John. 'We have Serepax but she can't keep it down.'

'Normal for this sort of thing,' I said, watching CNN on the telly and imagining a bathroom occupied by four people and the smell of a woman's vomit. 'Get her to sit down, head between her knees, breathe in through the nose, out through the mouth. Count the breaths in groups of twenty, and then get her to repeat that – can you ask her to do that, John?'

I heard him talking to the wife, and I shovelled scrambled eggs into my mouth while the Paris police told CNN there were now more than eighty confirmed deaths and hundreds with injuries.

They were saying the attack at Stade de France came from a suicide belt. It was developing into a highly volatile situation and I felt the stakes rising. It's one thing to read the intel about terrorists; but it's different – believe me – when you're dealing with people who are caught up in their madness. There was no way I could help the public who were being killed by these fanatics, but I could sure as hell help the Smith family.

John Smith came back on. He was actively helping – a good sign.

'Nice work, John. You got food, water, something for the kids to do?' I said. 'David and Susan – they'll have something to talk about at school.'

'Couple of bottles of water and some biscuits . . .'

'What kind?' I asked.

'Spekulatius, the Dutch ones.'

'Nice, mate, well played,' I told him. 'Sugar up – bulk down. You a former soldier?'

He breathed out. 'No, Mike – but I'll have to use that one in the office. They'll laugh at that.'

'Tell 'em that Mike from Australia said you manned up, mate. Stood on that fucker's foot, made him look into your eyes while you smacked him senseless!'

Now I got a laugh out of the guy. 'Okay, Mike,' he said, the stress leaving his voice a bit. 'I like it.'

'Listen, John,' I said, lowering my voice. 'You're staying calm so I'll need to bring you in on this.'

'Yes? What do I do?'

If you're trying to enlist someone quickly, this is gold. A person in danger, asking *What can I do?* is delivering themselves into my hands, and that's what I need. Not a hero or a genius who read something on Google. I need the person to say those words, because once they have, I'm in control and everyone is less likely to be in danger.

I took him through some of the basics: stay away from the windows, don't answer the door, leave the internet and mobile phones alone. And I asked him if everyone was holding it together. If someone is blabbering and panicking – and by that I obviously meant the wife – isolate them from the herd. Don't expel that person, but quarantine the non-panickers from the threat of infection. In the background I could hear a constant babble – clearly the wife chattering at the kids – and I was giving John permission to stop that chatter and put the kids in another corner.

'Give them something to do, John,' I said. 'Tell Linda to concentrate on the breathing – not the talking, okay?'

'Um,' he said, lowering his voice, 'yeah – you know.'

I did know, and told him to use touch to calm her: hold her hand, stand so his shoulder touched her. The basics that most husbands have no idea about.

'John, you'll be running the op from the inside, you're my inside guy,' I said, to get his mind off Linda. 'You good for it?'

'Yeah, sure,' he said, and I decided to believe him.

Then I told him the code word for my guys, the code word that means 'Open your door': *Alchemy*.

'No one else, John, you got that?' I said. 'I don't care if it's me outside that door, and I'm saying *It's Mike – let me in*. You sit tight, you hear me? The only person who comes through that door tonight is an American who will call himself MG, and when you ask for the code, he'll say *Alchemy*.'

He said he understood.

'And John,' I said, keeping it friendly. 'MG is proven in battle, he's a top professional. Do as he says, okay?'

'That's fine,' said John, letting out a breath he'd been saving. 'Christ, this is a mess.'

'My guys are the best there is,' I told him. 'When MG arrives, from that moment on, he's running the show, okay?'

'Yep,' said the Englishman. 'I understand.'

'I need you to be ready to walk out – no one goes back in the apartment. Once MG is at your door, the group stays together. Got that?'

'Yes, got that,' said John.

'There are four of you, John, and you're responsible for everyone staying in one pack. It's the wolf pack, okay, John, and you're the alpha.'

'Okay, got it.'

'Everyone will need their passport, and, John,' I said, 'I want you to take every mobile phone your family has, turn them all off and put them in a bag. The only operating phone will be the one you're on, and no one else uses it, okay? There's going to be no texting or Tweeting on this operation. No calls to friends, no posting to Facebook.'

'Okay,' he said, and I could sense the executive in him re-emerging. He paused, and then asked me, 'What's the plan?'

I expect this response at some point in these gigs. The people we work with are paid a lot of money and they lead thousands of people. They have egos. At some point – once I've built up their confidence and brought them on board the Mike Train – they're going to try the chief-and-Indians bit, and I welcome it because it's my chance to reinforce that this is my show.

'You don't have to know the plan, John,' I said. 'That could put you and your family in danger. Your job is to be ready to walk out the door – passports and one small bag each – and to do everything MG tells you to. That's all you have to know. When you're safely back in London, we'll have a laugh about it, but for now, MG is the boss.'

Before he could come back at that, I asked him what Linda's favourite drink was.

That took him by surprise. 'Um, wine, New Zealand sauv blanc, I guess.'

'Okay, John,' I said, trying to keep it light. 'You tell her to do one more cycle of the twenty breaths, then you go into the kitchen, pour her a glass and give it to her. Don't tell her what you're going to do – just give her the glass, okay?'

Liz stood in front of me and pointed at the coffee machine. I gave her a thumbs-up. Down the line I could hear John walking to the kitchen and opening the fridge, and I could hear Linda, the wife, yelling at him.

'Stick with it, John,' I encouraged him. 'This is her reward.'

He delivered the glass of wine while I finished my scrambled eggs and he handled the situation perfectly, lots of 'Well done, darling,' and 'I'm proud of you,' followed by, 'Mike says if you can't keep the Serepax down, you're allowed wine.'

'Doctor's orders,' I said, and in the background I heard her say, *Well, thank God for Mike.*

Some people don't need drugs or an expert's assurance about their children's safety. They need a glass of wine, and don't tell them one's enough.

John came on the line about thirty seconds later. 'Shit, Mike,' he said, and it sounded as if someone had loosened the vice around his head. 'That fucking worked!'

'Okay, mate,' I laughed. 'You've got your own mission, before MG gets there. As I said, should be around an hour. So, passports first, then phones handed to you – all turned off, all in a bag; then turn off the internet and then you pack four small bags. You only pack what each person can carry, okay, John?'

'Yeah, sure,' he said, and I slammed it home. 'One bag each – MG is not a porter, with me, John?'

6

During the Paris shootings, one of the most locked-down information sources was the tactical mapping. The French National Police and Paris Police were operating and deploying from real-time computer mapping that gave the tactical commanders a clear view of the battleground. There would have been hundreds of operators in emergency call centres and scores of police stations around Paris, all taking calls from the public about new sightings, the sound of gunfire in the street and new outbreaks of violence. The police themselves were also calling in the latest fatalities and numbers of injured as those terrorists ran through the city. The police built maps of where the violence took place, how many perpetrators there were and what they were using. And the massive stream of intel gave them a bird's-eye view of where it was all headed and a chance to get in front of the violence.

I wanted access to this information because my mission depended on getting my guys across Paris – from Paris–Le Bourget to Avenue Montaigne, and back again – without delay or incident. I was fairly certain that the Europol-supplied Sprinter would get us through. The fact we had a Europol driver was a big bonus too. Those two factors took 90 per cent of my worry out of that part of the gig. But that left 10 per cent: that's where a senior person stops the van and doesn't like the fact that a Europol person is driving soldiers with foreign accents around Paris while there's an armed uprising happening. And then maybe this senior person wants to make phone calls; or the shooters are moving through an area my guys want to drive through, and the roads are blocked for everyone, and the Europol driver is not apprised of the fact.

You can imagine why I'd like to have that mapping on my laptop, live from the tactical operations centre in Paris. I'd be able to steer my team around all the roadblocks and away from all the action.

Perhaps, in the back of my mind, I was also concerned about the possibility of actual *engagement*. I employ smart, specialist operators who can stay calm and do their job without being distracted. But people like MG and Rich? Yes, they're clever, personable people, but in the end, they're special forces operators with significant combat experience and if an ISIS maniac comes at them, these people of mine won't turn the other cheek. And I didn't want that. I wanted my team to run to timetable, not be given an excuse to pull a quick side mission against these shooters.

I thought about it for a few minutes, wondering who would represent the widest authorised use of the police intelligence mapping of Paris that night. I'd probably used up my bonus points with Juan at Europol, and now I owed him. Likewise Zac at Interpol. It wasn't so much that I now owed Zac – it was more to do with him telling me to get lost because he was insanely busy. I didn't want to disrespect that.

So I sipped the coffee Liz had handed me and flipped through my address book. I had a good contact at Scotland Yard; I'd done some specialist weapons training with her at a three-letter agency, back in the day, and she'd told me to give her a call whenever I needed help. I'd done just that a couple of times, but it was always for the obscure, factual crosschecking, not an actual 'favour'.

The entire Scotland Yard anti-terror and intelligence operation would be arced up because of Paris, and it probably wasn't the right time to pull a rabbit out of that hat.

So I flipped further in, saw Stan's name and decided to call him. I called his mobile number, thinking he could be anywhere in the world, given his job, and he picked up on the second ring.

'That the Big Unit?' came this low rumble, as though a bear was on the other end. 'Fuck me, I'm sorry, officer, I did it, I did it, please . . .'

He was taking the piss, making fun of my front-on style when it came to breaking from the van and getting my hands on a bad guy.

'You behaving yourself, Stan?' I said. 'Not drunk, are ya?'

Stan whooped with laughter. Like most people he calls me Big Unit, but he's an inch taller and ten kilos heavier than me.

'You watching Paris?' I asked.

'Only game in town,' said Stan, and he reeled off a few names of the people he was with. 'It's a cluster, dude.'

'You watching the French cops' live feed?' I asked. 'By any chance?'

Stan chuckled. 'Oh boy, you're not actually *in* that shit are you, buddy?'

'No, mate,' I said. 'But my guys are flying in, doing an extraction.'

'You can land?'

'Maybe,' I said. 'Listen, mate, the hardest part is going to be moving around Paris. I need some ground intelligence.'

Stan laughed even harder. 'Oh, man,' he said as he calmed down. 'I don't think the French would appreciate what you're suggesting.'

'A quick peek?'

'It's a closed system,' he said. 'We access it but I don't think we can . . .'

I heard him asking someone else in the room and then he came back on. 'No dice, buddy, but I can talk you through it. What are you after?'

I told him my guys were driving in a van from Le Bourget to Avenue Montaigne. I was committed to having the Gulfstream on the deck for two hours, max, and wanted the best way through, avoiding both security services and ISIS shooters.

'Okay,' said Stan. 'Got your map ready?'

I leaned over the Michelin map I have of Paris – one of about seventy travel maps I have of the major cities. I've been collecting them for years, because when the crap starts, I like a big piece of paper I can spread out – Google only works to a certain point and then I need paper and a pen.

'Looks like they're closing the off-ramps from the A1 and N1 into the Stade de France precinct and the on-ramps from it – got that?'

'Yep,' I said, putting crosses on the points where the sports precinct connected into the major north–south arterial road. 'Anything else?'

'The Metro line that comes down from the Stade de France into the middle of Paris is closed,' said Stan.

'Any other roads?'

'Looks like all the north–south bridges over the river are shut,' said Stan, concurring with someone beside him. 'Think they're bringing in troops from the south side of the river. In the north – is that 10th arrondissement? – they've shut Rue de la Chapelle to traffic at Boulevard de la Chapelle, and Boulevard Saint-Martin has a roadblock on it, at a point where about five roads come together. This making any sense?'

'It's useful,' I said, making my crosses and small signs. 'What about 8th arrondissement, mate? Avenue Montaigne?'

'Looks open, but there's a big police build-up down the river end of the Champs-Élysées. I wouldn't come into the 8th from the south, over the river, but you could probably get in from the periphery road, west of 8th arrondissement. That okay?'

'Thanks, mate,' I said. 'I know the airspace is in lockdown, but have they kept the access roads open, to Le Bourget and Charles de Gaulle?'

'Looks like they're massing security people . . . apparently it's military and police at Charles de Gaulle. Road into Paris looks jammed already . . .'

'There another way?' I asked, wanting to break something. A windscreen full of security stickers could get my guys through roadblocks, but if the roads from the airports into Paris were clogged with traffic, it was going to be a long night.

'My buddy here's telling me the traffic's jammed inbound to Charles de Gaulle.'

'My guys are coming into Le Bourget,' I said. 'How's it looking?'

'Not too bad.'

I let out a sigh. 'You around, Stan?'

'I'm going nowhere.'

'If someone needed a heads-up?'

'Give them this number,' said Stan. 'We'll guide 'em in.'

7

Because of the situation in Paris, I wanted to be closer to the action, and I wanted to be on the ground to run the Plan B exfil if we couldn't get back to Le Bourget Airport, or if having got back there we couldn't take off. Then it was going to be a cross-country drive to an airport in Italy or Hungary – or maybe Denmark or the Netherlands – and we'd try to fly the family out from there.

So I had also had a private jet at Essendon primed to take me to Dubai if needed. But the further we got into the Paris job the more I had to concede that I wouldn't be leaving my living room. My role was to coordinate the whole thing, pull the strings, ask the favours, make it all happen. It didn't matter where I was, and in fact operating from home gave me advantages. I was the puppeteer and I had to stick to my role.

At 10.20 am my time, I took a call from the pilot on our Gulfstream. 'Paris tower accepted the numbers,' he said. 'Cleared for landing.'

I reminded him of the agreement with AAA Freight, and he agreed to remain on the ground for two hours from the time he let down the stairs.

Then I called MG. 'We okay?'

'Sure, Unit,' he drawled.

'You'll be picked up. The driver will need the address, but, mate, you're in control, okay? You assert that early.'

'Roger that.'

MG rattled off a stream of *Roger that*s as I went through the arrangements, and finished on my last advice. 'Access code for the subject is *Alchemy*. Your name is MG. He won't open for any other combination.'

'I think we're landing,' said my Texan colleague. 'Anything else?'

'Yeah,' I said. 'Good luck.'

*

On my first check-back with Stan in Washington, he told me I was in luck. 'Cops are telling everyone to stay in their homes, no rubbernecking,' said Stan. 'Looks like they're obeying and staying off the roads.'

'Any new roadblocks?'

'Yep, but not on that western side of the city,' he said. 'Just don't try to cross the river.'

I was about to hang-up and Stan said, 'You said Europol, right?'

'Europol van and driver,' I said.

'Last time I rode in one of those vehicles, there was a dashboard cam with a wireless signal,' he said. 'Might come in handy.'

I thanked Stan and immediately called MG. 'Mate, there's a dash cam in your van. If you can work out how to stream it, let me know?'

He agreed, hung-up and I made a call to my guys at Essendon Airport, telling them I wasn't going to need that extra charter jet. I made another coffee, took a big drink of water from the tap, and got back to my map. I could see a line heading from the north of Paris – at Le Bourget – down to the periphery road, that hooked southward and would take the van to the west of Avenue Montaigne.

The phone buzzed and I picked up. It was MG, in the van. He read out to me a web portal and a pass code – repeating from a heavy French accent in the background – and I tapped the information into the browser on my laptop. The screen in front of me was black for a few seconds and as I told MG it wasn't working, the vision of Paris at night, through a windscreen, burst into my kitchen.

'We're on,' I said, and now I saw how much traffic there was on the freeway heading south. It was heavy, but it was moving. And even though I could see a lot of cars parked on the shoulder, and people out of their cars, I allowed myself a small amount of optimism that the team might actually make it back to the Gulfstream, with the family, in the allotted time.

'What does the driver say about the roadblocks and the traffic?' I asked.

'His name's Christian. He drove through this to get here,' said MG, his Texan accent strangely reassuring. 'He says that there's roadblocks on the off-ramps to the Stade de France, and once we're past those it gets clearer.'

'He's getting live traffic updates?' I asked.

'Sure is,' said MG. 'You scored big with this one, Mike. How's the dash cam?'

'Excellent,' I said.

I followed the progress of the van and my team, south for Paris. The traffic moved quickly but lining the freeway were parked cars, with people wandering around, pointing at places and events I couldn't see. At one point it looked as though the van was moving faster than every other vehicle on the road and when I caught a flash of blue and red reflected on a car window, I rang MG's sat phone.

'You don't have the emergency lights on, do you?' I asked.

'Yeah, Mike,' said MG with a low chuckle. 'Didn't I tell you that?'

The cheeky bastards were flying through Paris with a set of police emergency lights flashing out of the grill of the van.

Now I relaxed and got off the phone, allowing MG and Rich to do their jobs. The vision through the windscreen was one of controlled pandemonium. As the van took an off-ramp into the 8th Arrondissement and onto the Avenue de la Grande Armee, we came face to face with one of the biggest roadblocks I've seen. And I've seen a few. From the vision in that camera, I'd say thirty paramilitary police stood at their bollards, across the enormous boulevards, all of them toting automatic weapons. They were flagging a lot of drivers through and many were being pulled over on the other side of the roadblock, and interviewed. The van driver slowed for a few seconds and then was driving at a decent clip past other traffic, down the Grande Armee, towards the Arc de Triomphe. In the distance, hanging over night-time Paris like a shroud, were the thousands of strobing red and blue lights of the police and other emergency services. An ambulance flashed past on the other side of the boulevard, going way too fast. Half a minute later a fire truck blasted past our van, going the same way, sending traffic surging to the right lanes to let the vehicle through.

The van driver speared off into a street to the right, and now we were into the cafés and restaurants and shops that make this some of the most expensive real estate in Europe. It was eerily dark and I realised the shops and eateries were closed or had their blinds pulled down. The flashing emergency lights from the van now filled the more confined space and I also saw that no one was on the streets. I looked away and had a quick look at CNN: a live music venue called the Bataclan was being emptied out by police and ambulance and there appeared to be a lot of bodies in the building.

Another two minutes and the van was parked in front of a large, baroque Parisian apartment building. It was 11.08 Melbourne time. The phone went and I picked up: MG, asking if I wanted to do the talking.

'No mate,' I said. 'John – the father – is primed to hear you at the door.'

I knew that MG was being polite but both of us knew that he had to be focused and in total control when he met this family, and he didn't need any distractions.

'I'll put them on when we're in the car,' said MG and I thought I heard something in the background.

'What's that?' I asked. It sounded like the van engine about to blow.

'Gunfire,' said MG. 'These tangos must have some ammo to burn, but don't worry – they're ten blocks away.'

He signed off. To the right of the van's dashboard I could see two men in Columbia-style action clothing move to the large glass and wood doors at the building entry. One of the men – MG – pushed at a button and I could see him lean in to speak to it. The door opened and MG disappeared inside, leaving Rich at the entry, standing on the footpath. I'd been in his position many times before. This is a time of hyperawareness; you scan the street and the passing vehicles like a robot. Any parked car starts to look suspicious. A third man, who I guessed was Christian the driver, joined Rich. He wore a short windbreaker over Levi's jeans and it was obvious that he was armed – a 9mm on his right hip.

My TV showed more carnage, and the live shots of Paris gave me a slightly disjointed view of reality – my guys were in there, right now, and a few blocks away the shooters were still moving around. At 11.12 my time, MG emerged from the apartment doors and held his body flat against the open door, allowing the four Smiths to crawl as one outside their sanctuary. John Smith held the younger girl under his arm, and Linda – the mother – had the older boy under her arm (or was he holding her up?).

Rich moved in on their other side so, as they came out of the doorway towards the van, they were covered by my two guys.

They disappeared from the camera's view and then the vision rocked slightly as they piled into the car and then the emergency lights were flashing again and the van was winding its way through the anarchy of Paris.

The van had been going for five minutes before the phone rang. MG was on the other end. 'Mr Smith would like a word,' he said, and handed me over.

'That you, John?' I asked.

'Yes, hi Mike,' he said, the stress still strong in his voice.

'Everyone good?'

He breathed out long. 'I think so. We're just going along with the plan, and these guys are doing a good job.'

'Wife and kids?'

'Everyone's pretty good,' he said.

'You brought the medicine?'

'Umm . . .' he said, and then the penny dropped. 'Oh, yeah. Yes, I brought some with us, in the backpack.'

'Good for you, John,' I said. 'Now sit tight and do exactly what MG says – he's got himself out of much worse scrapes than this.'

'Thanks Mike,' he said, and we left it there.

At midday, my time, MG called from his seat nearest the cabin door on the Gulfstream. 'We're taxiing,' he said, as though he were narrating a child's story.

'All clear?' I asked.

'Looks like it, but I've never seen a couple of civvie pilots more motivated to get in the air,' said MG. 'We got some white knuckles up the front.'

'The airline will let you backload to Dubai,' I said. 'But you'll have to wait for their Go. You and Rich may as well get to Heathrow and hop on a commercial – save the receipt and bill me, but you're flying coach, you know that, right?'

'Aw, come on, Big Unit – you got me all used to the high life. Don't do that to me, man.'

'Call me when you hit London,' I laughed. 'The person you hand over to is Charles, from Arcadian. I've sent you his pic.'

'Got it, seen it,' he said.

'Your payment details are the same?'

'Roger that,' said the American, and he rang off as the engine noise rose in the background.

*

I shuffled off and took a shower, had a shave and got dressed. The Gulfstream would be at London City Airport in twenty minutes. I wanted to be fresh and ready to debrief with Charles from the insurers. But before I could call him, he called me.

'Mike, wow,' he said, straight in. 'That was impressive.'

'Subjects all okay?'

'Better than okay,' said Charles. 'This company is a major client and there was no one else I could get for this job. I'm very happy with this.'

I could hear the sounds of doors shutting, voices speaking: airport sounds. 'The missus okay?' I asked.

'Ha!' said Charles. 'She's had a few – high as a kite and very happy.'

8

The costs always go out before I split the money, but Charles and Arcadian were so happy with the Paris job that they promised to pick up the full AAA Freight bill – US$85,000, not just the $70,000 rider.

The aftermath of these things is exhausting. I usually have a big adrenaline let-down, and this gig was no different, even though I wasn't 'there'. I slept deeply for two hours in the afternoon, and when I arose I made a list of everyone I had to call back and thank. Most of the operators in my world rely heavily on networks of like-minded and suitably motivated people. We help out the good guys where and when we can. We're like a global club, and the price of belonging is being prepared to give, and always acknowledging. You don't have to be silly about it, but you do have to take the time to acknowledge that the person who helped you may have created a career headache for themselves, or it just might have been a really bad time – as it was for my buddies at Europol and Interpol. Acknowledgement is a big thing for the people who risk their lives and never have their pictures in the paper. The Americans even have a system for it – their 'coins'. These are the size of a Silver Dollar, are usually made of pewter, brass or steel, and have the agency name and insignia embossed on one side, and the name of an operation or the general or intelligence director you helped out. They are given with a handshake. Acknowledgement of your part in something bigger is a sort of nod to the fact that when some of us act for a safer world, we're being non-ironic.

So I always put back in, and make my calls, give a debrief, tell them how crucial their help was to me. I don't have my own coins to hand out so I make a point of touching base with people when I'm in their country. I absolutely seek them out and shout them lunch or take them for a few drinks. Maintaining a network isn't just important for my business, it means we can all do our jobs that much better. And given the adversaries we face, it has to be that way.

Before the European morning started again, I put in a call to MG.

'How are things?' I asked.

He yawned. 'Boarding in fifteen minutes. BA's got premium economy – might stretch out, get hammered in the sleep position.'

'Thanks for this, mate,' I said. 'You had no reason to take it at such short notice.'

'Well, not much in our world is truly planned, right, brother?'

'Thanks again, mate. You'll be paid in a few days. Can I talk to Rich?'

A Scouse accent came through the line. 'Aye!'

'Rich, Mike here, mate.'

'Aye!'

'Thanks for this, mate. All went okay?'

'Like a dream, Mike. Very smooth.'

'Your details still the same? Same numbers?'

He confirmed, I thanked him again and suggested he have a few drinks for me on the flight.

'Fucking aye,' he said, and signed off.

That evening I wrote my report for Charles, sent my final bill with it, knowing the balance of my BVI bank account would shift considerably in the next forty-eight hours. I divvied up the money on a legal pad, and it came to just under US$90,000 each. MG had an account in Singapore and Rich used a bank in Tel Aviv – they were in my system. You might think that US$90,000 is a lot of money for less than twenty-four hours' work – and of course, in comparison to most jobs, you'd be right – but in the first place, who else do you call for something like this? You can't go to the phone book. Secondly, these are the people who put their bodies on the line and take all the shit that the insured person wants to avoid. And, as MG and Rich knew, for every gig that was over in twenty-four hours without incident, there were ten that dragged on and were filled with discomfort, danger and confusion.

In the middle of this administrative end of the gig, I took another call from Charles in London.

'You made me look good, Mike,' he said as soon as the pleasantries were done. 'You up for another one of those?'

'Yeah, sure,' I said.

'Good, because I owe you.'

'Don't say it too loud, Charles,' I said. 'The angels will hear.'

MAN ALIVE

1

In the mid-2000s I was doing a lot of work for a number of organisations that happened to be based in Sydney, so I would often fly in from Melbourne and be living and working in Sydney for two weeks or more at a time. Through mutual connections I was introduced into the wonderful world of zoos, via a large zoo's logistics and security person, who we'll call Roger.

After we'd known each other for a couple of months it became obvious that he was from my world. We knew some of the same people and he'd once worked in intelligence, so when he lowered his voice to discuss something with me, I knew what it meant and he knew he could trust me, and vice versa.

You might wonder why former and current intelligence people would have anything to do with a zoo. Zoos are fun places for outings with the family but they're also a full-time, 24/7 management project. They cover large acreage, they have thousands of places where bad guys can illegally enter, hide and engage in wrongdoing, and of course, you have around 1000 animals locked up in there that would otherwise be wild. And by wild, I mean they'd frighten the life out of you if they weren't sitting in a cage, eating a banana. And that's before we include the real wild animals who cause chaos around a zoo. Zoos all over the world attract a known cohort of humans, who – due to mental illness, drugs or alcohol – think it's a good idea to jump a fence and join their favourite animals. Some have just seen *Gorillas in the Mist* once too often and have missed the point that the scientist in that movie spent decades getting to know one colony of gorillas. She didn't get drunk at the pub and decide to climb into the gorilla cage at 2 am because she wanted a hug. Because she'd get a hug all right.

One of the first gigs Roger pulled me in on was in early 2005, when the zoo had a problem with someone living in the grounds, stealing food and making a bit of a nuisance of himself. Roger brought me in to assist when a female employee was scared witless by the appearance of a man down near the chimpanzee enclosure, and then later the administration block was broken into and food and a computer were stolen.

Roger asked me to help him and so I took some days off my contract work to see what I could do. I spent a couple of nights in the zoo, just stalking around, and I established a pattern of life. I worked out that the guy was hiding in the tortoise enclosure at night – and having a good old munch on the hungry tortoises' vegetables – and moving around the zoo grounds, picking up what he could. At one point, I believe, a chainsaw went missing. At this time the tortoise enclosure was built to accommodate twice as many animals as they had, so one part of the sleeping quarters was not being used. I concluded the guy was bunking in the unused one. I noticed that he tiptoed back to the tortoise sheds around 6.30 am, when the employees who started at 6 am were moving down the zoo to get started on their day. Our fugitive – or whatever he was – was onto it, and timed his homecoming fairly tight. He was cocky.

One of the zoo workers was a woman aged around forty who we'll call Julie. She came from a New South Wales Police background and she had a good strong presence about her. She was one of the employees who started at 6 am, and I took her aside and I told her what was going on and what I planned to do. Because I wasn't employed at the zoo, and was doing Roger a favour, it wasn't legally prudent for me to apprehend the stowaway myself. And I didn't particularly want the paperwork or the embarrassment for Roger, should the subject decide to arc up, requiring me to incapacitate him. Julie agreed, and we were on.

That night I camped in the bush of the zoo's parkland and stalked the malingerer, carrying my overnight snacks and bottle of water. As the first light of the rising sun created a red line on the horizon, I ensured the subject was elsewhere and I slipped down and secreted myself in his unused tortoise shed. I looked down at my watch: 5.58 am.

The basic plan was that Julie – rather than make a cup of coffee at the admin and staff block at the main entrance – would walk straight down the campus, towards the water, as soon as she got to work. I suggested she wave a torch and maybe be talking loudly on her mobile phone. Be obvious, make a ruckus, move this idiot along. I had her walk down the pathway near where he lurked – at the picnic grounds – and sure enough, at around 6.04 am, I heard the hurried scraping of feet and a light panting sound and I peeked through an air vent in the tortoise house. A shadow was coming along the staff service path, racing for the rear entrance of the house: the one the public doesn't see.

I waited . . . and waited . . . and as he got to the building, I flung open the reinforced steel door as hard as I could. Really threw my shoulder into it. The door came to a sudden, shuddering stop and there was a sound like a watermelon being dropped. I walked around the door, and a heavily tattooed man was lying unconscious on the pathway.

Julie came up the path with her torch about twenty seconds later, and checked his vital signs. Once she'd done that, I slapped him awake and put some zip-ties on his wrists.

As I pulled him to his feet and handed him over to Julie, he said, 'What the fuck happened?'

'Ever hear the one about the tortoise and the hare?' I asked.

'What?' he shouted, up in my face, like I was the stupid one.

'You're in a zoo, moron,' I said. 'Learn your fucking animals.'

2

So I wasn't totally unknown to the zoo system when I took a call from Roger's boss in November 2005. I was at home in Melbourne, going over plans for a series of retaining walls going down a hillside, on which I was being asked to build four attached townhouses. I had to quote for the job but I didn't know if I really wanted to do it. I didn't like the plans – they looked fine on paper, but I'd walked the proposed site with an engineer mate of mine and neither of us was convinced. It looked like it would turn into a stop-start job, which meant I'd lose money.

Roger's boss asked me if I knew Roger, and I told him I did. He said that Roger had been seconded to a sister zoo at Dubbo and had a couple of security concerns. Roger had suggested to him that I be retained on contract to look into the matter, and this boss told me that he'd had a look at my CV and decided to give me a go for two weeks if I could fit it into my schedule.

'When do you need me?' I asked.

'I need you at Dubbo immediately,' he said. Tourism is big business for Sydney and New South Wales, and the executive government does not like people messing with it. Which was how I came to be on a flight into Sydney that afternoon.

As I cabbed into the city to meet Roger's boss and sign the paperwork, I called Roger and asked what was going on.

'We've got someone living in the grounds,' he said. 'Police are not that interested and we don't have the people to do this sort of work.'

What went unsaid, of course, was that I did do this sort of work.

'Okay, mate,' I said. 'I'm on my way.'

I booked a week at the Cattleman's Inn in Dubbo and signed out a zebra-striped Suzuki Vitara from the Sydney zoo vehicle pool. I had a few errands to do in Sydney and I had to touch base with my networks, see what other intel was available on this job. So with a bit of messing around I didn't head west until late in the evening. These were the drought years west of the Great Dividing Range and it was an eerie drive through dried-out country with no stock, and the full moon illuminating it like a scene from a horror movie.

I drove straight to the zoo, on the edge of Dubbo, and arrived at Roger's house at 4 am on the dot. I prefer to get straight into a gig, and see it for myself. The research, interviews and intelligence work will all come along in good time, but the first priority is to be there. I dressed in cargo shorts, a polo shirt and baseball cap with the zoo logos on them. I had no idea who was watching us or if this homeless person was being helped by a staff member. So in the first instance I decided to slide into the safari-style zoo not as a cop in a white Commodore, but as a zoo employee sent from Sydney on assignment.

Roger met me at the door and put on a pot of coffee. I drink coffee at all times of the day, and my morning caffeine is taken in a container the size of a milkshake cup. We sat at the kitchen table and I asked Roger about the gig.

'For the past month, we've had a few strange incidents,' he said. 'The elephants were getting hungry because the food left to them overnight was going missing. This guy likes bananas in particular.'

I nodded. 'Any security cameras?'

'Not enough to cover the whole zoo,' he said. 'It's just too big. There're a couple of cameras around the admin building, but our unwanted guest seems to know where they are and steers clear of them. I think he's familiar with staff movements and rosters too.'

'So, he's been up to the offices?'

'Yeah,' said Roger. 'Out the back of the restaurant is a dumpster where the uneaten and out-of-date food is dumped. We know he's been in there, too.'

'How do you know?'

'Because the manager might throw out a whole tray of chicken rolls, and in the morning two or three have been taken out of it. It's not an animal doing it.'

'Anything else?'

'Feed bags from the elephant house were found behind the rhino enclosure, jammed down in between a couple of bushes, with a little bivouac over the top, like a hidden bed.'

'Recent?'

'Few days ago, Mike. There were fresh chocolate milks and pie wrappers found around the bedding.'

I thought about it. It didn't sound like the guy was doing any serious damage, but with the summer holiday season about to begin they obviously wanted him gone. 'Okay, so on the phone you described this person as homeless. What does that mean?'

'It's what the police have called him – I suspect they're saying that to make management feel calm.'

'And, what do you think?' I asked, knowing that Roger didn't bring me out here for a homeless person.

Roger leaned back in his chair and looked at the ceiling. 'I think that someone's been going into my fridge,' he said, 'and it's freaking me out.'

3

Roger showed me around the zoo parklands as the dawn came. It was a large property, around 300 hectares, with animal exhibits you could drive up to and watch from your car. I saw lots of buildings and houses, stands of bush and lakes, and many, many options for a homeless person to camp out and not be detected. Roger showed me the elephant enclosure, the various food storage buildings and the vet hospital. Then, at 8 am we drove back to the massive entry gates of the zoo. When I got out of the car, the sun was in the sky, the temperature had hit thirty-five and the flies were like a moving blanket. We parked in the employees' car park and walked to the admin section and into the general manager's office.

It was an informal chat: the three of us in that room were the only ones who knew who I was and what I was doing there. The general manager didn't want visitors being annoyed by a homeless person, especially given the 'Roar and Snore' overnight sleep-outs that were popular at the zoo. They also had a big 'glamping' safari camping ground with four-star tents and a restaurant. Basically, they didn't want bad publicity. Zoos are not unlike theme parks or cruise ships: they can measure their bookings by the number of negative stories about them in the media.

I understood the problem.

The general manager was a little embarrassed when he said he didn't want violence used in this operation. I didn't know what Roger had told him about my work at zoos, but this person wanted things to be sorted calmly.

'If it's okay by you,' I said, 'I'll make an intelligence assessment, and based on that material, you can call the police or a security firm. Okay?'

He seemed very happy with that, so Roger and I left, grabbed a coffee at the café and went on another tour. We got in his zebra-striped zoo 4x4 and went for a drive around the park. We stopped at the dumpster bins, and I saw how they sat out the back of the café and restaurant. Easy pickings for a motivated individual. We spent much of the morning visiting the sites where some sort of find or incident had occurred. The elephant feed-bag bivouac was nicely placed on higher ground – behind the rhino area, and bordering the glamping section. That bedding was set up so the guy could observe the zoo's administration area, but it was low enough in the grass and bracken to keep him hidden and keep the sun off during the heat of the day.

The picnic areas where he'd been sighted, or where he'd used the coin-fed barbecues, were interesting choices. Responding to some noises one night, Roger had found still-hot barbecues at 5 am, at the Savannah picnic grounds over the road from the macaques' lake.

The elephant enclosure was also interesting. These large, powerful animals don't like people sniffing around, especially when they have their calves with them. Roger showed me the big canvas feed bags that this homeless person was using, and he'd obviously had to go right into the elephant house, to the area where the keepers store the fruit and vegetables, to get the damned things. The guy we were tracking was resourceful and brave.

We sat down at the Streets kiosk at the top of the park and had an ice-cream in the shade.

'What's really going on here, mate?'

Roger was silent for a while. 'My milk jug always has less in it than when I left.'

'Another employee bludging?'

'No,' said Roger. 'My place is too far out of the way just to take a glass of milk. There're other things too: my bread and vegemite. I mean, when you live alone you *know* how much bread you've used, right?'

I nodded. If this homeless person was hitting the restaurant dumpsters then he was probably raiding fridges in the houses. I'd noticed that Roger's house wasn't visible from the main admin area and the homeless man probably felt secure there.

'You talked about this guy knowing the routine, or the rosters,' I said. 'What's that about?'

Roger shook his head. 'This is going to sound too weird.'

'Try me,' I said.

'I was on the phone in the house one day, and I was rearranging the times and the protocols for feeding the elephants. I wanted to change the timetable a bit to catch him out.'

'Yeah?'

'Yeah, so now he's still taking the elephant food, but he's out of there half an hour before the *new* times.'

I thought about that. It was not good.

'Swear to God, Mike,' he said. 'I think this bloke's spying on me.'

4

We headed back to Roger's place and in the clear light of day I saw there was a 'lawn' around the house – or a dusty, brown drought-affected version of one. As we walked up to the house I could see this would be an attractive proposition to a loiterer wanting someone's food. The doors used basic locks inside the door knob – locks that even inexperienced thieves know how to pick. Entry would not be a problem. The set-up of the house was accommodating to a thief: the back door looked out onto the koalas, and the boundary of the wolves' enclosure was adjacent. From a vagrant's perspective, it was located so you could hide among the bushes and come out when no one was around. Once Roger was working, the malingerer could go in and help himself, undetected.

It wasn't until I was almost at the house that I realised we could easily have been watched by our unwanted guest. From here on in I'd blend into the pattern of life, which clearly our adversary was observing. I didn't want to alert him to why I was there.

Inside the house we had a look around. It was a plain, three-bedroom prefabricated place, but comfortable and air-conditioned, with a TV set and Austar box in one corner. Dubbo is in the heart of the Western Plains, which means baking hot in the summer and cold at night in the winter. I wondered what else the trespasser was doing in the house, apart from taking a man's Vegemite and drinking straight from the milk jug.

But this was an intel gig, remember. I just wanted to collect the data and let the zoo make their own destiny with it.

Now that Roger had got the fear of being spied on off his chest, it was obvious my buddy was a little creeped out. I could see why he wanted me out there. If someone was actually listening in – and I wasn't totally convinced – we could start with seeing if Roger's phone was bugged. I'd take it with me at the end of the day, and I'd run some software on it that I had in my laptop. I'd soon know if his phone was compromised.

The other idea was that our thieving vagabond was sleeping under the house, and when Roger stood in a certain place to make calls, he could hear what was being said. But when we had a look under there, there was no sign that anyone had been there recently.

Roger's fear was that the guy was inside the house while he was, maybe hiding in a wardrobe, and that was how the intruder knew when to come out and grab the food and drink. I didn't buy it – a person who goes to such lengths to avoid detection is not going to hide in a wardrobe while you're in the house. Why? Just so he can hear your phone calls? But I was sure as hell intrigued. I'd done some casual tracking around the house, looking for sign: a footpad that led into the bush, a broken bit of tree or shrub, where a person has pushed through too often and it's turned into what looks like nothing to most people, but is a footpad to me. Human hair on a tree twig? A thread of clothing on a branch? Footprints in the undergrowth?

I didn't see anything like that, and also no foot trails through the dust around the house. If a bush-person was coming out of his hide and straight into the house, it would be evident to me. I'd know it.

Roger had to get back to work and I headed back to the admin section to do some paperwork. I wanted to glean information from the zoo staff, in their own words. While I was tempted to interview them, I didn't want a bunch of Chinese whispers being told to me – all of it third-hand. If they had to write it down they might think twice about recycling rumour as fact. I was given a PC and I quickly wrote a questionnaire that would form part of the 'survey' from the special operations person – Mike – up from Sydney. In the end it came to around twenty questions, such as, *Have any items been inexplicably moved from your work station in the past month?* That sort of thing.

I'd also travelled west with some other gear, which was still sitting in my borrowed car: one was a 'sniffer' box that detected radio frequency (RF) transmissions being made, even if they were in latent or 'sleep' mode. I would run this over Roger's house if he really wanted but I didn't think he was being bugged by a homeless person who was sleeping under elephant feed bags.

I ran off fifty copies of my survey on the admin section's printer and asked the general manager's executive assistant to find a way for every employee to get a copy that day.

I hadn't slept for around thirty hours by this time but I still had some energy. So I grabbed a few sandwiches and a drink and turned my attention to the maintenance staff. These were the people who moved all over the safari park and I judged them to be the folks most likely to see people coming and going. I had an idea in the back of my mind that perhaps one of them was playing a joke on Roger, with the food in his fridge. All intelligence work, in the end, comes down to people, and you have to have that aspect ticked off before you get too immersed in technology. Often, it's the client who is made happiest by blinking lights, PowerPoint presentations and diagnostics. Me? I like to talk to people, bring them in close, see what their eyes do when they speak. When I was first inducted into this profession by a government employer, I was on an operation in which a Lebanese-Australian pizza shop owner in Sydney was being fitted up as part of a ring of white-collar criminals who funded some black-list mosques and prayer groups. Part of the evidence for his involvement was the theatrical and quite wild anti-government spiels he would make over the phone to his friends.

I got a job at one of his pizza shops, and as I got to know him I realised he was an illiterate Lebanese business owner who made up for his insecurity and lack of education by mouthing off about the government and the tax office. Some of his associates may have been dodgy, but they were also accountants, solicitors and mortgage brokers – slightly more accomplished than him, or so he thought. I wasn't convinced that he was involved in tax fraud or funding of terror. One night when the news was blaring from the TV in his pizza kitchen, there was a story about a souk being blown up in Iraq by a suicide bomber, and he went completely crazy, throwing things around the kitchen. I asked him what was up, and he told me – with tears of rage – that these terrorist 'animals' had wrecked his own country and now they were destroying the rest of the Middle East. He told me that any person who put a bomb in a souk would not be allowed into heaven. Allah would not allow it. And then he poked me in the chest and said, 'This is a great country. We must never allow these terrorist scum to live here.'

When the fraud ring was wound up, the pizza shop owner wasn't among those charged, and when asked about the funding of the mosque, the real conspirators had no idea why the pizza shop owner was even being mentioned. He had nothing to do with it.

So getting in front of someone is always the best first step, and I intended to do that with the maintenance staff. I also had a chat with some of the restaurant and hospitality people, because it was possible one of them was bringing some dropkick out with them a few times a week, and leaving them in the car, but the person was wandering around the zoo being a nuisance. I know, I know: that didn't explain the warm barbecues and the food stolen from the dumpster. But I was starting at zero: I didn't even know how many homeless people we were dealing with here. Was it one, or a couple? A family?

I finished up with my interviews and some staff were helpful while others seemed a bit insulted. Oh well, can't be loved by all the people, all the time. What I did have now was a list of sites that our homeless person was visiting: the elephant house, the picnic ground barbecues, the stores building, restaurant dumpsters and the vet building.

But I was also intrigued by Roger's house. He'd told me he'd heard what sounded like a possum in the roof, so after I'd sent out the survey and talked to the maintenance people, I grabbed a ladder and went back to Roger's. I climbed the ladder on the side of his house, checking to see if the thief was shimmying in along the electricity wires. I thought it highly unlikely but it also occurred to me that a possum mucking around on his roof had no tree to transport it there. While I was pondering all this, Roger's cleaner turned up with her mop and vacuum cleaner. She said hello and seemed friendly, so I decided to come down off the ladder and have a chat, see what she knew.

Her name was Carole, and she was a middle-aged Dubbo woman who cleaned all the staff houses. I asked her if she'd seen anyone creeping around, acting suspicious. She shook her head, and asked me what I was talking about. I told her we thought there might be someone accessing Roger's place unlawfully and stealing his food. She laughed and said she'd offered to bring him groceries each week, to make sure he had something to eat. But she couldn't help me and I thanked her and went outside to bring down the ladder and approach this from another angle. I don't like to fail – I don't like bad guys getting away with it. So now I was getting in deep. It felt personal.

As I was getting the ladder into the back of the Vitara, Carole came out into the sun and the flies and said to me, 'Maybe you should ask David.'

I had no idea who she was talking about. I'd only been here twelve hours and it could have been anyone. 'Who's David, love?' I asked. 'He work here?'

'No, he's Roger's friend.'

'Roger's friend?'

'Yes, Roger's friend from Sydney who was staying with him last week. A nice fellow.'

'Okay, Carole,' I said. 'Thanks for that.'

I returned the ladder to the maintenance shed and walked back to the admin building where I grabbed myself another coffee. Roger was on the phone but I plonked myself down in the chair in front of him. By this stage I was feeling tired – I'd been on the go too long, and now that I could see people getting ready to go home, I was also winding down. Roger signed off his call and I told him I'd sent out the survey and interviewed the maintenance and hospitality people, but that I'd like to have a chat to his friend David, from Sydney.

'Why?' asked Roger, genuinely confused. 'What's David got to do with it?'

'Wasn't he staying with you last week?'

'Where?' spluttered Roger. 'Here?!'

We looked at one another. 'Mate, just to be clear: David, your friend from Sydney, didn't stay at your house last week?'

Roger's face screwed up and his palms pointed to the ceiling. 'Mike, what are you fucking talking about? I haven't seen David for almost a year.'

No, I thought, *but I bet you've been talking with him on the phone lately.*

I stood up, my mind spinning. Now I was sure I had an actual sighting of our creepy homeless person.

5

Carole had left the zoo by this time, and headed back into Dubbo. And with all the privacy crap that employers have to live by these days, management couldn't give me her address. But the reception woman, who knew Carole, said she was probably heading for a café in town that her sister owned.

I leapt in my Suzuki and gunned it, heading into Dubbo. The café was on the main street, and I found a park, went in through the multi-colour plastic strips and saw Carole behind the counter, helping to shut down the place. It was past 5 pm by now and all the chairs were on the tables, and there were mops in buckets and what have you.

'Oh, hello,' she said with a big smile.

'Hey, love,' I said. 'How about I order a coffee, and you talk to me for five minutes?'

She said she'd help me out, so she made my coffee, brought it over and we grabbed a table. I kept it quick.

'This arvo you told me about this bloke, David? Roger's friend?'

'Yes,' she said.

'Tell me how you met him.'

She poked a finger at the table. 'I was cleaning the house last week, and I was trying to get into Roger's bedroom.'

'Trying?'

'The door wouldn't open properly,' she said. 'I pushed it once and it just wouldn't open. And then I pushed it again and it came back to me.'

My blood was running cold as she told me this. 'And then?'

'I poked my head around the door and there he was.'

'David?'

'Yes, he asked me if I could hand him a towel – he'd just got out of the shower.'

I took a breath. 'Shower?'

'Yes, he was dripping wet.'

I stayed calm. 'So you got him a towel?'

'Yes, and I asked him what he was doing in here, and he said, *Oh I'm David, Roger's mate from Sydney – I'm staying with him for a few days.* Is everything okay, Mike?'

'It's fine – did he say anything else?'

'Not really. He got out of my way, and I vacuumed the bedroom.'

'What did he look like?' I asked.

'Medium height, quite muscly,' she said. 'Oh, and he's a black-fella – but I guess you know that?'

I got some more details from Carole, about the man's face and any identifying scars and tattoos, but I was so freaked out I couldn't finish my coffee – which, believe me, is very strange. I thanked Carole and asked for her number, in case I had more questions.

I got back in the car, punched the air-con to full, and rang Roger. I told him I'd be back at the zoo at sparrow's the next morning but there was something he had to get started on.

'I want you to give Carole a paid holiday for a couple of weeks, okay? That woman is not to enter any house at the zoo until I clear it, swear to God.'

'Sure,' said Roger. 'Um, is everything okay?'

'We'll find out,' I said.

6

I was under a lot of pressure to keep all of my investigations to myself, but after Carole's revelations I thought I had to get the police involved. The typical intelligence approach is to collect information about a person without them knowing. But this homeless person had been alone in Roger's house with a cleaner, and I thought it had gone beyond me just collecting the information. I thought it was dangerous.

I called the Dubbo police, but I couldn't get through the sergeant at the desk. 'We know about the zoo,' she said. 'We're on it. Sorry, who are you again?'

It was like that, so I did it another way. I went through some police intel people I knew in Sydney and explained the situation and what I was looking for. To the best of my ability I gave a description of the man, as given to me by Carole. She'd been pretty good with his facial shape (round) and his body type, height and age. So I got the people in Sydney going: who was outstanding? Who was wanted? I just needed a sense of it. A bad, cocky Aboriginal man – muscular, resourceful and able to stay ahead of the cops.

I got a call back in less than half an hour, when I was back at the motel. My guy had come up with a name of a bad dude, wanted in central-western New South Wales. But he censored himself by saying that the last sighting had been in Lightning Ridge, more than 300 kilometres to the north.

'Well, try me,' I said.

The name he gave me was Malcolm John Naden.

'What's he done?' I asked.

'Wanted for questioning in relation to murder,' said my contact.

I didn't like it, immediately, but as it sank in, it somehow sounded right.

'You got a picture?' I asked, and he said sure. And because this was 2005, we were still using faxes, and I gave him the number for the fax at the Cattleman's business centre. I didn't want this material being seen by the staff at the zoo – well, not yet.

I paused. A person implicated in murder? Roaming around in a zoo where people sleep overnight? I was buzzed and a little shaken. My contact told me he'd send the pic in the next five minutes. I went down to the fax machine and waited. And when it came through, he'd been kind enough to attach several extra pages on Malcolm Naden. In all eleven pages came through.

I took a long shower and after a steak meal and a beer at the Cattleman's restaurant, I lay on my bed and watched TV in the air-con. The weather woman said Dubbo had reached a high of thirty-nine degrees at 3 pm. I believed every degree of it. I moved to the table in the room, and cracked a VB from the fridge. Sitting, I flipped through the faxed pages, looked again at the old picture of a young Aboriginal man with a black beard and crazy dark eyes: he was wearing a flannelette shirt, black track pants and some sort of a hat, perhaps a cap worn backwards. He was standing in a humpy or a caravan. It was an indoor shot, flash-filled, and quite crowded.

His sheet said he was born 3 November 1973, and his last place of residence was in Dubbo. A former abattoir worker. In January Naden's cousin Lateesha Nolan had gone missing, in Dubbo, in suspicious circumstances. Naden was interviewed; no charges were laid. Nolan was still missing.

The second sheet detailed another incident in Dubbo, this time in June: the partner of Naden's cousin – a woman named Kristy Scholes – was found murdered in the bathroom of Naden's family home, and when the detectives went to see Malcolm Naden about it, he was not to be found. He'd been on the run ever since, wanted for questioning over the murder and sexual assault.

I dropped the page, sipped on the VB and felt the air-con on my neck. The initial gig was to collect the facts, write an intelligence assessment for the zoo, and then go back to Sydney.

But I wasn't going back to Sydney. I was going to catch this creep.

7

The café opened at 7 am and I was there at 7.01. Carole opened up and she recognised me and we exchanged smiles.

'Mike, my favourite man,' she laughed. 'You got me two weeks off, and they're paying me!'

'Never know your luck, Carole,' I said. 'Wondering if you could look at some photos for me?'

'Sure,' she said.

We went into the café and sat at one of the tables while the coffee machines heated up. I pulled four photographs from my file, of Aboriginal men aged twenty-five to thirty-five. Three of them I'd printed from the internet at the Cattleman's.

'That man called David, at Roger's place?' I asked. 'Can you see a likeness of that man in any of these pictures?'

Her hand went immediately to the one of Malcolm Naden. 'That's him, right there.'

'Sure?' I asked. 'It was dim in that room.'

'I was a metre away from him, Mike,' she said, like I was simple. 'We had a conversation. That's him right there. Why, what's he done?'

I took the other three pictures away, so only Naden's picture was in front of her. 'On a scale of one to ten, Carole – where one is *I'm not very certain* and ten is *I'm 100 per cent certain* – what ranking would you give this picture that it is the man you saw in Roger's house?'

'Ten,' she said, without hesitation. 'That's the man I spoke to.'

After thanking Carole, I jumped in the car, headed back to the zoo, and called my boss in Sydney – the person who had allowed me to be assigned to Dubbo.

'Where are we on our homeless person?' he said before I even asked him for more time or resources.

'We're getting in deeper,' I said. 'I think there's a chance we have a criminal in this zoo, but the zoo doesn't want a big song and dance about it.'

'Got a name?'

'An idea about a name – nothing solid yet.'

He asked me, 'What do you need?'

'I'll probably need more than two weeks,' I told him. 'And when the time comes, I'll need a way to get the local cops moving. They're not interested in this.'

He hissed. 'I'll sort it but you play nice out there. No fucking ripples.'

'Always nice, boss,' I said. 'Always nice.'

When Roger and the general manager arrived for work, I hustled them into a meeting. I told them what I had but admitted I didn't have enough facts to say that I absolutely knew we had Naden in the zoo. The response I got from Roger and the head of the place was that if the police didn't think Naden was in the grounds, they preferred me to continue to work under the radar and find him without too much noise. They certainly weren't ready to make a big drama with the police.

So I had this idea – if the police wouldn't stalk Malcolm Naden, I would. I grabbed one of the large tourist maps of the zoo from the kiosk, and I got in my car and headed back to town. They have some good camping shops in Dubbo, so I ducked into one on the main street and bought a small backpack, a lightweight sleeping bag and roll-up groundsheet. Then I found a Lowes Menswear shop and I bought a large black hoodie, a pair of black trackie pants and a black cotton bucket hat that they were selling in their schoolwear section. I already had my black Hi-Tec boots.

I came back to the zoo and spent the tail end of the afternoon moving from employee to employee, going through their survey replies. Most of the stories were genuine and they had a few things in common: reports of articles of clothing and footwear being lifted (or no longer being where they were left); food stored for the animals being low on weight or count when it came time for feeding; and food for human consumption disappearing. There were two 'sightings' of a person moving through a part of the zoo where visitors would not be. But they were fleeting and there was no facial description to go with them.

When my interviews were done, and the employees were going to their cars and leaving for the day, I parked my Vitara in one of the maintenance sheds, grabbed my bag of camping gear, and signed out one of the zoo's weapons: a Remington 870, a pump-action shotgun. This was a weapon intended for use on escaped animals. I had no intention of shooting an animal. I was going to spend a night in the zoo.

*

There was a gentle slope down from where I sat among the trees, through a copse that opened into the Savannah picnic grounds. I had a half-moon and it was a warm night, and I was comfortable on my ground mat. Loosely arranged over my black clothing was an assortment of hessian bags, which I called my homemade ghillie suit – the foliage-covered suits worn by snipers to avoid detection. A good ghillie suit doesn't have to be a $500 item from a Qstore. It just has to break up the human silhouette, especially around the neck and head.

The Remington lay beside me on the ground but I didn't feel too bad about being out in the bush. When I was growing up in regional New South Wales, pig-hunting was a sport and one that we'd pursue all weekend, sleeping rough and following big groups through really isolated country. I fired my first rifle when I was eight, had killed many pigs, deer and goats before I entered high school, and without boasting I don't think there's any terrain I've heard of that I'd be unable to survive in. The social circles I was brought up in were big into rugby league, boxing and hunting. That was the world of my family and friends, uncles and cousins. Like many boys from the bush, by the time I was in high school I was pretty confident of taking on just about anything. Many of us went into the military and the police, went farming or went into the trades. Me? I did a chippie apprenticeship and ended up working in intelligence. There's a big stretch between those two occupations, I guess, but at the base of it all was the confidence I got from moving around in the bush in the dark as a kid, whether catching a brumby or stalking a deer.

Now I was back, in a safari zoo, stalking a possible murderer and rapist. I had a night-vision sight with me: like half of a pair of binoculars, which enhances your vision at night. But in truth I didn't plan to use it much because I prefer to let my eyes acclimatise to the darkness.

I found myself thinking about Naden's movements, and I rewound all the way back to that first morning when I'd turned up at Roger's house, before we'd headed to the zoo admin area. I wondered if my presence had spooked him. If he was as resourceful as I suspected, he may have watched me and not liked what he saw. The question now was whether he was still in the park, or whether he'd moved on.

I leaned towards him being in the park. You see, I'd only been stalking around in the zoo's bush for a few hours that night when I picked up what I thought was a footpad. I'd followed the faint path and up ahead – maybe 200 metres – a bunch of macaques had started up with irritated chatter. I couldn't prove it, but I had a very strong impression Naden was in front of me. Now I was waiting along this footpad, and it was almost three in the morning, and I had nothing to show for it.

As the sitting and waiting seemed to be getting me nowhere, I decided to investigate another aspect of Naden's nightly movements. As I'd crept into place in the middle of the zoo, I'd taken a roundabout route that followed a very vague footpad across the southern part of the parklands, through trees and scrub between the eastern-most picnic grounds and an animal habitat. It was hard to track at night but the footpad seemed to lead to the boundary fence. I decided to see if this footpad-to-nowhere yielded anything new. I was careful about my movements because Naden was wanted for violent crimes and he'd been in the park for long enough to have superior knowledge of the place. So I carefully picked my way through the trees – virtually pausing at every step – and after half an hour of following what I believed to be a footpad, I came to the fence – the southern boundary.

I crouched down and looked. The footpad was worn with use here, so my guess was that Naden moved around the zoo along the perimeter fence, where no one was watching, probably ducking under the fence at points that would bring him out where he wanted to go. After less than twenty metres following the footpad I found a large concrete culvert, which went under Camp Road, the road bordering the southern edge of the zoo, on the other side of the fence. On the zoo side of the fence the culvert continued as a ditch into the trees. I lined up with it and tried to look through the culvert, but the blackness was too great and I couldn't see a thing. But now I believed I was looking at one of Naden's hidden routes, which would take him into farmland on the other side. By the fresh look of the footpad down the side of the fence, this was an option he'd been using in the past few days.

I sat among the trees for twenty minutes, shallow-breathing so I could pick up the slightest human movement. I decided there was no one in the culvert and slowly and carefully got on my stomach and crawled through the gap under the fence, and stealthed to the culvert. I climbed over the low wall that held the grille, and walked into the culvert. It was dry and dusty, and I walked to the other end, checked for company, and came back to the middle, where it was pitch-black – I couldn't see my hand in front of my face. I slid to the ground and sat there, the Remington across my lap. I controlled my breathing and waited. And waited . . .

Fatigue must have caught up with me because I fell asleep for a few seconds and awoke to movement. Someone was entering the culvert tunnel from the non-zoo side, and they were in no hurry. I held my breath and brought up my shotgun. It was so dark I couldn't see a thing and my pulse banged in my temples. My lungs screamed for air as the shuffling noise got closer, and closer. Finally, I could feel breath on me and I could smell a man who hadn't had a shower for a while. I suddenly got the flash of his eyeball glinting in the dark. Then I couldn't take the suspense anymore and lashed out with the shotgun, saying, 'You're busted, mate.' As I did that, the barrel of the gun struck him in the face, and there was a grunt and a kerfuffle and he shouldered past me and bounded away. The penny dropped. As I listened to the hopping sounds of my adversary's retreat, I marvelled at how human-like a kangaroo can look when it's very dark and she's very close.

I sank to my knees, cold sweat pouring down my forehead and my heart doing all sorts of gymnastics. I gasped for breath, my body racked with panic and relief. Small moans came from deep in my stomach and I sat there for a good ninety seconds trying to compose myself. I was mentally fatigued.

That was it. I called it a night.

8

The next day I had a re-think of what I'd been doing the previous night. I had been out in that country, and I estimated that all the points I knew about, where Naden had slept or used a barbecue, or taken food from a dumpster, were about fifteen minutes' walk from each other. This meant that Naden was always close to either food or cooking facilities or a place to sleep. He was actually an efficient and logical person: he seemed to have split up the eating, sleeping and cooking sites so that if one of them was busted he could move on to another and the whole operation wasn't blown. I was also very interested in the service roads around the edges of the park, and the fact that the zoo was bounded by three major roads, one of which was the Newell Highway. But before I looked at the other routes in and out of the zoo, I wanted to have a closer look at the culvert on the southern boundary – my kangaroo culvert.

The episode with the kangaroo had been frightening and I'll tell you now, I'd been shit-scared. That big dark eye, suddenly apparent in the darkness, right in front of my face? That was life-long nightmare material, right there. To this day, every time I get a flash of that moment, I have a shudder down my body.

But once I'd calmed down I had a think about it. I'd been very focused on sign and using my skills with footpads and tracking, but really, this was about catching a man – not an animal – and I had to engage with him in terms of what he was: crafty, intelligent and egotistical.

I told the general manager that I needed to organise some security patrols, and he authorised a budget and told me he'd get on it. I wanted to tell him that I'd select the security people and brief them, but in the circumstances it was probably easier to let him hire them and I'd brief them.

The next night I slept late and walked the perimeter fence, starting at around 3 am. I stalked up the footpad to the southern boundary that I'd found the night before, gun out in front of me in case I ran into Naden. This was all conducted in overcast conditions and no ambient light. It was inky out there.

When I got to the culvert, I crawled under the fence and duck-walked along the channel that led to the culvert. I reached into my backpack and pulled out a cold can of Coca Cola, and I placed the can of Coke on the low concrete wall in front of the culvert and withdrew back into the park. If our intruder was Naden and he thought he was outsmarting everyone, I thought I'd taunt him and see what happened.

I had breakfast back at the zoo restaurant, and hooked up with Roger. I told him about the Coke can, and we went through into his office. I wanted a bigger map of the zoo which included all of the details from the local council and the water board. Roger unfolded one but he wouldn't let me have it. So I went over this huge thing and drew my own external gateways and culverts onto my tourist map.

I drove to the southern boundary, keeping an eye on the fence. About two kilometres along that road, there it was: the channel that led under the chain-link fence and into the box culvert that continued under the road. Another 100 metres along I found the road that turned right off the highway and led to the farm operating on the other side of the culvert.

I could see that the farmer was at the drive shed fiddling around with a tractor, so I drove down and introduced myself. We had a yarn and I said I was interested in anything strange that might have happened lately. Any thefts, anything weird?

He said the dogs had gone off a couple of times, in the early hours, but they did that for roos and wombats. He thought someone had been in his shed, and his missus thought a pillow and doona had been stolen, but he thought the items might just have been misplaced somewhere. I asked him if I could look at the culvert from this side of the road, and he said, 'Help yourself.'

I didn't want to mess with the bloke's gates so I left the car by his shed, climbed a fence, and walked across a large paddock, through a creek bed and up a slight rise to the culvert. There were footprints going each way from this side of the culvert, and they were fresh. I estimated the sole imprint was from a trainer, probably a Nike. I walked across Camp Road and dropped down into the culvert on the other side.

I saw it immediately: the Coke can was still on the low concrete wall. But it had been opened and put back exactly where I had placed it in the early hours. I pulled out my handkerchief and picked up the can by the rim.

Half-full!

Naden was taking the piss.

9

After five days of this, we had security patrols doing loops of the zoo at various hours of the night. But I still had nothing I could seriously take to the police, so I had to see if I could catch our target on the zoo property. I had made some fruitless attempts to try to track him at his unofficial entry points to the zoo. I uncovered four bivouacs, some of them very recent, and the security guards were still finding still-warm barbecues at the picnic grounds in the early hours of the morning.

The worst of these occurred like this: I had staked out the Savannah picnic grounds for a few nights, making passes at it as I stealthed around Naden's known haunts. But on the subsequent night – when I didn't stake out the picnic ground – the security guards did their rounds at 5 am and found a still-hot barbecue. This time it was still cooking. The coins still had some life in them.

The young guard was a bit freaked. 'You have to see this, Mike,' he said, and I headed over.

When I got there I asked what was up, and he pointed. The coin-operated barbecue had bacon and sausage on the hotplate, and a halved bread bun, toasting. And then I saw the taunt: on the brickwork beside the hotplate was a can of Coke. Opened.

I reached for it, and even before I touched it I knew what it would feel like: it was half-full. By now I was sure this was Naden, and I was certain he was in the zoo grounds. We had a pretty good surveillance on the dumpster behind the restaurant, so the only other way Naden was getting what looked like fresh food and beverage was by stealing from the public – which I doubted – or he was being supplied by friends and family.

I figured Malcolm Naden had us under surveillance and that he had taken a personal interest in me. I'd been going 24/7 on this gig for ten days by the time we found the Coke can beside the cooking barbecue, and so I went back to the Cattleman's and slept. It was a Sunday and I needed to rest. I emerged around 1 pm and decided a proper lunch was in order. I'd been given a voucher for 'Buy one meal – get one free' at Dubbo's Commercial Hotel, so I rapped on Roger's door – he'd become freaked about his house at the zoo and was also staying at the motel – and suggested we grab a bite to eat at the Commercial, have a few cold beers, watch some cricket on the big screen and wind down a bit.

He was up for it and we found an outside table in the beer garden and settled in. We sat back, ate our cheeseburgers and fries and got some rounds of beers going. It was a blisteringly hot day but I was finally relaxing.

At around 4 pm, a group of six or seven Aboriginal men walked into the beer garden and sat at a table near us. Almost as soon as they sat down the comments and insults started, about the 'dirty cops' and 'white cunts' who were harassing a relative of theirs. I said something along the lines of, 'Ask Kristy Scholes about what harassment means,' and one of them said, 'Mal never did nothing, you lying cop cunt,' and before the discussion could get too heated, security was out in the beer garden trying to get rid of these people.

I can look after myself in a fight, but we were outnumbered and we weren't in that frame of mind. These people had come from nowhere with the intention of getting into it. They put up an argument with security but then the ringleader got up to leave and another followed him, and they started moving towards the exit. At least, I thought they were leaving – but then the ringleader made a lunge towards our table, grabbed it and up-ended it. The beers went everywhere and we leapt to our feet. The ringleader was collared by security, but he tried to poke me in the chest, and said something like, 'You're dead, cunt.'

I say he *tried* to poke me in the chest. I intercepted his wrist and twisted down slightly, which I can assure you would hurt. I saw the rage in his eyes and then the bouncer had him and was dragging him to the gate.

The whole thing was over in less than three minutes, but it kind of wrecked the day.

10

I spent all the next day at the zoo, first having the culvert beside the main entrance welded shut so no one could get through it. Then we laid fishing line across some of the main footpads – it wouldn't trap him, but I'd know if he'd been using that trail. By evening Roger and I were bushed. And hungry. So at around 10.40 pm we left the zoo and headed for Dubbo KFC. We were almost there when Roger got an alarm alert on his mobile phone.

We U-turned fast and zipped back to the zoo, where the alert was telling us the breach was in the admin building, right at the main entrance. I told Roger what I was thinking as we drove: the zoo would be black, so he was to let me out in the darkness before he drove the extra 150 metres to the building with the alarm. We got to the main gate, where he slowed and let the Commodore roll just inside the gateway. I got out and it was a still, warm night, and I stalked to my left, along a cycle track, through some trees and past the hire centre where visitors can hire bikes for the day. I crossed the main car park in pitch-blackness. It was dark and quiet and very still. Roger continued motoring to the admin building, and as he slowed to a stop, he hit his high beams. Right in front of me, beside a large LPG tank against the admin building, a man stood up.

It was him.

I was unarmed, and so stunned that all I could do was say, 'Malcolm, it's me.'

He was looking away from me at the time, at the car, but he quickly turned back. I don't know who was more scared – him or me. But we were three metres from one another and the way our eyes locked was primordial. The look we shared was one of mutual homicide – I was ready to kill him, because those eyes told me that was the only way he would allow himself to be caught.

My heart was in my throat, and he was out of there. I mean, this guy was quick. He ran straight into the bushes, and although I didn't have my shotgun with me, I gave chase into the bush. I had my two-way radio with me, and as I went further into the darkness I decided I should let Roger know where I was. I triggered the radio but I was panting so hard into it that Roger couldn't hear me.

'Get, here, now,' was the eventual command that he heard, as I gasped it out. Have I said that adrenaline hits me really hard?

He joined me in the bush and we gave chase through the parkland and came out in a large picnic and eating area where there were scores of tables and chairs and folded-down umbrellas in the middle of them. We had to check each one. We ran further along the entrance road, and then Roger said, 'There,' and I followed his finger, and there was a shape of a running man, now on the other side of the lake, disappearing into the bushes.

Roger called the Dubbo police and the desk sergeant sent out a patrol. Two young female constables turned up and when they'd heard our story they told us that everything was under control and there was no evidence that Malcolm Naden was in the zoo. Roger argued with the more senior of the two, and she phoned her sergeant and told him we'd just seen Naden, and so the commander in charge of the night shift came on, demanding to speak to Roger. He proceeded to give my buddy a total bollocking. So I was standing there, watching where Malcolm Naden had run, hearing this police officer's voice bellow out of Roger's phone, telling him that Naden wasn't in the zoo.

But he was. I had now seen Malcolm Naden, face to face, in the zoo. To say I felt frustrated was an understatement.

We spent most of the night cruising the property, looking at the usual spots. I was ropeable, and I decided on a way to cut through the police attitude.

The following morning I swooped by the café and asked Carole if she could help me out at the zoo for half an hour. She said yes, and then I rang Dubbo Local Area Command and managed to get put through to the Dubbo detective handling homicides. I stated who I was and the male detective asked me if I was a police officer.

'No,' I said, and I introduced myself and continued, 'I want to report a sighting of a man wanted for questioning over the murder of Kristy Scholes – Malcolm Naden.'

He was sceptical until I told him I had two people who could identify Naden.

He came out with his offsider, and when he saw the picture I had of Naden, he wanted to know where I'd got it from. I told him it came from a fax machine. Then I turned to Carole, showed her the picture and asked her again to rank the image – on a scale of one to ten – in terms of likeness to the person she'd interrupted while cleaning Roger's house.

She said, 'Ten,' and now the detective asked her a few more questions, and got his notebook going.

I put up my hand too, and said, 'This man,' stabbing at the picture, 'was standing right there, beside that LPG tank, at 10.45 pm last night. I was three metres from him, I called his name and he looked at me. That is the man.'

Now the detective, who knew all about Naden, wanted to dust Roger's house and get a fingerprint ID. He wanted proof. I asked him if the forensics person could come out in plain clothes. 'I believe Naden has that house under surveillance,' I said.

The forensics guy arrived in a plain car and in plain clothes, in the afternoon, after the detective had left. I called Roger and he came over from the admin block. The forensics man took a full set of Roger's prints. He scanned them into his laptop, and now they had a record of what Roger's prints looked like.

Next, we stood back and he dusted the surfaces around the house: kitchen, bathroom, living area and bedrooms. And when he switched on the blue light that illuminates the prints, we saw there were fresh prints *all over the house!* The forensics man showed me where Roger's prints were. But the majority were fresh and unknown.

I stood staring and the forensics man asked if I was all right. Roger was pale with shock. I remember him mouthing, *What the fuck*, over and over, as he moved around this house he'd lived in for the last eight months. He was not in a good way.

They input the unknown prints into their system and there was a match: Malcolm Naden.

Naden's prints were all over the toilet seat and the cistern and the flush. They were around the bathroom sink, and yes, on the stand where the toothbrush and toothpaste was stored – I shit you not, this creep had been using Roger's toothbrush!

Naden's prints were all over the shower stall and on the towel rail.

But the worst of it was back where we'd started. In the kitchen.

Roger, the forensics guy, and I – we stood and looked at the fridge and pantry door. They were covered in hundreds of this person's pawprints. But what we were looking at was fingerprints around the pantry door handles, which was to be expected, but also fingerprints on the top of the pantry. I was confused, but then the forensics guy said, 'Look at this,' and opened the pantry doors. The Naden fingerprints led up each of the pantry's shelves, all the way to the ceiling. He'd been using the pantry as a ladder. But a ladder to where? We all looked up and saw fingerprints all over the trapdoor that led to the attic. We gawped, jaws to the floor.

This fucker was in the ceiling? *Seriously?!*

I struggled to get my head around what kind of psychosis or mental illness we were dealing with here. But as sick and weird as I felt, I didn't want to take one more step on this gig without a firearm in my hands.

I ducked out in the heat and pulled the shotgun from the boot of my Vitara, which I'd parked just outside the front door. I usually relied on a handgun in these situations, but I had to side with my American law enforcement friends on this point: if you don't know who you're dealing with, but you suspect they are off the charts of your comprehension, there is nothing more effective than a load of double-aught shot into the gap between you and the bad guy.

I pointed the shottie at the manhole and gestured for Roger to grab something. He came back with a broom, and the forensics guy brought through two chairs. I stood on one chair, just under the manhole, and Roger stood on the other, holding up the pointy end of the broom.

I nodded, and Roger pushed the cover upwards, and I leaned into the widening gap, muzzle-first.

My heart was beating up in my mouth and sweat ran down my back. We were all stressed out and ready for anything. I couldn't see Naden in that hole, so I whispered to Roger, 'Push it back,' and he gave the manhole cover a heave and flipped it back. Now there was some light in the attic.

'Come out, Malcolm, we're armed and the place is surrounded,' I said. 'If you want this to be peaceful, give me two knocks on the wood.'

There was silence, except for our panting. I thought Roger was going to have an infarction. His breath was rasping.

I slid the reload slide back and forth, which makes a distinctive sound. 'I'm serious – you knock twice on wood or I start shooting, Malcolm.'

Slowly, I put my foot on the kitchen bench and stood up, raising my head higher into the attic. The Remington 870 had a tactical flashlight clipped on the underside of the barrel, giving me good light in that dark space. I looked around 360 degrees and no one was up there. But in the middle of the attic the flashlight picked up a sheet of plywood covered with a doona, a pillow and some empty water bottles. And as if to confirm we were dealing with a cheeky bastard, some magazines.

I pulled my head down and told the others it was clear. I didn't know what to say to Roger, so I avoided his eyes as I stepped down to the kitchen floor. All of us in that room were gasping for breath, and a little wide-eyed.

Roger took my place in the manhole, and we listened to a muffled roar. 'The cunt took my *Men's Health* magazine?' he yelled. 'Who is this fucker?'

Indeed. The Naden legend was just beginning.

11

We left Roger vomiting in his toilet. I had crawled up into the attic and grabbed the doona and pillow, which I stuffed in a black plastic garbage bag I found under the kitchen sink.

I got in the car, maxed the air-con and left some rubber on the road as I pulled out and headed back to the farm at the southern boundary, on Camp Road. I pulled up just as the school bus took off, and a child – maybe eight years old – was walking up the tree-lined drive. I let him get into the house before I drove up.

I knocked on the door and a woman in her late thirties, wearing shorts and a singlet, opened the door. The wife. I introduced myself as being from the government in Sydney, and told her I was trying to track a fugitive who was wanted in connection with major crimes. She asked what she could do, and I said her husband had told me that she'd suspected a break and enter in her house, and that several items had been taken, but that her husband had thought the items might just have been lost.

'Yes,' she said. 'Bedding, mostly, and some food.'

I asked her if she could identify what was stolen. I went back to the car, pulled out the garbage bag and poured the contents onto the bonnet.

'Wow,' she said. 'That's our doona and that's our pillow.'

'Okay,' I said. 'I have to keep these for now. I'm trying to get a handle on this bloke. Is there anything else he took, or was trying to break into?'

*

I worked most of the night from my motel room, and when I arrived at the zoo at 8.30 the next morning, I placed my intelligence report with Roger and the general manager. It simply stated that investigations into the 'homeless person' living in the zoo revealed it was most probably Malcolm Naden, aged thirty-two, from Dubbo, who was wanted by police in connection with the disappearance of Lateesha Nolan in January, and the sexually motivated murder of another woman, Kristy Scholes, in June. Both women were related to Naden. I wrote that Naden had been third-party identified from photographs as being inside Roger's house, and that his fingerprints had been found all over the interior of Roger's house. The doona and pillow found in the roof belonged to a farm up the road, which had experienced a break and enter more than three weeks earlier. I recommended that for the safety of employees and guests, the Dubbo detectives be notified immediately and the investigation be handed to them. I said I was available to assist the police in whichever way I could, and I would not decamp to Sydney until the police and the zoo were satisfied with my debrief.

The general manager was a little freaked by the information, and wanted to speak with Roger, alone. So I grabbed a coffee from the restaurant and chilled out. I'd put it together, but I hadn't caught the bloke. I'd been close but I hadn't got my hands on him. The idea that he was hiding in my friend's roof, reading his magazines, irked me. There was no doubt he was dangerous. It was clear from the way the detectives had worded their sheets on Naden that he and no one else was being looked at for the disappearance of one woman and the murder of the other.

Roger came through about twenty minutes later, looking for me, and when he sat down he had a look of mischief on his face. 'Boss phoned the detectives, they're on their way,' he said.

'And?' I asked.

'And he wants you to do an extended handover to the cops,' said Roger.

'Extended?'

'He thinks the zoo needs its own interests looked after, so . . .'

I frowned. 'I'm due back in Sydney.'

'. . . so he just called Sydney and they're giving you another week out here.'

I winced. 'You have no idea the phone call I have coming today,' I said.

When the detectives arrived, I gave them everything I had. We took a walk into Roger's house and we went through the sequence: the dusting, the hand tracks to the manhole, and the revelations from Carole. I told them about the night he'd stood in front of me, I showed them the faxed picture, told them where they could find Carole, and I produced the items I'd been collecting: Coke cans, elephant feed bags, food we'd found cooking on the barbie.

They were excited by the finds and I felt we were now in good hands. These blokes really wanted to take this guy down and I was also happy that there were no egos involved. I had stumbled on Naden – I hadn't been asked to find him. So they just wanted a brain-dump from me. From my perspective, I suggested the detectives keep it plain clothes and low-key, at least for the start of the search for Naden. If we made it seem like everything was business as usual at the zoo, I argued, perhaps he'd feel comfortable staying in the grounds. Even if he knew his hide in the roof had been discovered, he might stay in the zoo, which gave us the best chance of catching him.

The lead detective sympathised with my approach, and it was one he agreed with, but he said the commander for Dubbo would escalate the operation because Naden was wanted in connection with a murder, and because thousands of tourists a week went through the zoo. So while the detectives started interviewing the staff, and making their maps of where Malcolm Naden had been sighted, I was back into meetings with the zoo management. The first thing to go would have to be the 'Roar and Snore' sleep-outs, because once you know that someone like that is out there, you can't allow the public to sleep in his domain. My suggestion to the management was that they tell people that the overnight camping in the zoo was booked out – sounds a lot better than letting them know there's a sex-murderer on the loose.

Yes, it would ease the burden on the zoo's reputation, but I was also going into op-sec mode. I was aware that Naden was part of a large family group around Dubbo, and he obviously felt safe and supported around this area, which was why he stayed here even with the New South Wales Police searching for him. I had no doubt that news of Naden being in the zoo would leak, and when challenged by the media, the commander wouldn't lie about it. But until that public acknowledgement, I wanted the chance to move quietly around the zoo and catch this bloke.

I had been introduced and more or less seconded from the government, so I tried to take basic matters offline with Roger, who would be working with the police from here on in. He was going to increase the security guards' patrols around the park, by night and in the day. And the New South Wales Police special operations command was bringing its specialist tactics group to the zoo. These were the paramilitary cops who carry assault rifles, use dogs and infrared cameras in helicopters to track down criminals and terrorists.

They had a good reputation: and besides, with the cops now riding into town, I felt freed up to go dark and really breathe heavily on this sleazy fucker.

12

Do I need to point this out? If you're a man who hurts women, I'll hurt you if I can get away with it. Everyone has some childhood pain to live with and I live with mine. And in living with it I carry a lifelong problem with rapists, wife-beaters – that sort of person. As a big-boned teenager, I was rather unsophisticated in how I dealt with this anger. I'd walk up to the problem and attack it. That didn't end well for me or the victim, and it was probably my sister – getting me out of the bush and into Sydney – who smoothed me out, made me think with my brain rather than just with my fists.

The rage I have about people like Naden was something I self-managed for many years, but when I met Liz, I caught wind of some of the dropkicks she had to deal with in her emergency services job, and I didn't like what I was hearing. She told me to back off and leave it, and I promised to stay out of it. 'It's just part of the job,' she said. 'A lot of these people are on drugs and they have no impulse control.'

So I was Good Mike for many months, hearing these stories, and barely containing myself. And then one morning she came home, and she'd been roughed up by some druggie jailbird, and when she'd tried to calm the bloke, he'd used spitting to resolve the matter.

Now, I love this woman, so I kept my word. No violence against people who offend against Liz. But over the next week, I asked around, got CCTV footage from a security guy, managed to access the desk logs, found this character's name, found a car rego so I found an address, and what do you know? About two and a half weeks later, the guy moves out of his apartment, out of the suburb and out of the city. Gone. I simply got inside his life, and inside his apartment, and inside his internet, and with some of the pictures I sent him I got inside his head. And I didn't lay a finger on him. Didn't even speak to him.

So the same day I got the detective in and we found Naden's prints in Roger's house, I saw a chance to get more personal with Naden – I really wanted to take this guy down, and the inevitable police involvement gave me the chance. We were now into December and it was getting hot – high thirties hot. The police operation quickly set up a base at the zoo's admin block, and it now didn't concern me too much that Naden thought he was toying with me. Clever, egotistical criminals want to engage with their pursuers and beat them. And the more they engage, the greater the chance that they'll make a mistake.

The holidays got moving and a heatwave hit us. By now I was constantly getting sightings of Naden, and reacting to food thefts, because we'd so effectively shut down his food supply that he was having to be brazen in how he fed himself. I got a bead on him and where I thought he was basing himself – in the 'sanctuary' precinct of the zoo, far from the admin buildings. I spent many long, hot hours backed into the wombat holes up there, sipping on water and waiting for Naden to walk by. I generated a lot of sweat and some beautiful bed sores, but no Naden.

On 21 December the zoo had its Christmas dinner for the staff, and I remember that day well because by the time we sat down for a turkey lunch it was forty-five degrees Celsius in the zoo, and we were huddled in that air-conditioned restaurant area like our lives depended on it. Someone cracked a cold VB for me, and my mouth was watering as I poured gravy all over the turkey. And just as I was about to tear into this meal, my phone sounded and I picked up. It was one of the doctors from the vet block: there had been an attack on an animal at the turtle enclosure and then she'd seen Naden running into the bush beside the vet building.

I hurried down there, the baking heat taking my breath away. At the turtle enclosure the staff were quite upset: someone had torn off a turtle's head and sucked its guts out. I saw the dead animal and asked some questions, then I jogged down to the vet block where the doctor showed me where she'd seen Naden run into the bush. I went to my Vitara, took out the shotgun, and one of the security guards and I hurried into the bush, on his tail. We were too late, of course. He had this place wired, and now – to show us how annoyed he was with the food being cut off – he was killing animals and eating them.

The next night I was in Dubbo with Roger, getting a KFC feed after a long day chasing Naden leads, and while he was getting the bucket of chicken I dropped in to have a chat with the police. It was 9 pm, and once I was in there, they wouldn't let me go. The Special Operations Group was inside – thirty or forty of them – and they had photos all over the walls. It was obvious they were building up to a big push. They were finally taking this thing seriously but now I was being sidelined – they didn't trust me to leave the building and not tell everyone what was about to happen. I was told I had to call Roger and ask him to come down to the police station, and once he was in the building we were locked in. The snipers in their ghillie suits left before midnight to be in place by 2 am, with the main group to follow by 5 am. I negotiated with the police when Roger reminded them that there were around 1000 animals that needed to be fed at the zoo. So the police agreed that I could call two feeders and they'd be allowed in during the police operation. When the main police contingent left for the zoo, Roger and I were allowed to accompany them and we met the two designated feeders at the main gates. Each feeder had two snipers assigned to them, and were driven from one enclosure to another, where they had to run to the enclosure with one sniper, feed the animals and run back to the police van before going on to the next.

The New South Wales Police closed the park at 6 am on 23 December, and chaperoned the glampers out of there at 6.30 am. They were not happy, I can tell you. The police came in with a hiss and a roar, combed the whole place, positioned snipers around the property, but produced nothing. The person running it said the operation in the zoo was successful in that the known Naden sleeping sites had all been vacated, but they couldn't find the fugitive. So now the police threw a lot more resources at it: twice the manpower, dogs, infrared camera–equipped helicopters and a line of people sweeping the zoo. It was so hot during this operation that the police German shepherds could only work for twenty minutes at a time before they had to be taken into the air-conditioning. In one incident, I let the police dog handler and his dog into the food stores block and we saw a manhole cover in the ceiling pulled back slightly. The police officer lifted his dog up and we pushed it into the ceiling, allowing the animal to search for Naden. Until this time, there had actually been no sighting of him, except by Carole – four weeks earlier – and then by me. There was still a residual question not of *where* he was in the zoo, but *if* he was still in the zoo. Now, after the turtle incident, a hundred police combed the zoo and at the end of it, the police announced the place was clear.

By now the media were on to this and it was high-profile enough that the pursuit of Naden was a fixture in the nightly news bulletins. The rural ABC Radio feeds, in particular, were asking people to watch out for an Aboriginal man trying to hitch a ride, access vehicles or find money, clothes and food. The entire assumption of the police, the zoo and the media was that Naden was now on the run.

I was mentally exhausted after this gig, and I was going home.

13

Back in Melbourne, I had things to do. But even as I recharged the batteries after such an exhausting gig, I continued to get phone calls on my mobile from the staff out at Dubbo. Keepers were having jumpers and jackets go missing. The elephant house was still being raided, with bunches of bananas simply disappearing. And the zoo campers were back in the grounds, the business becoming heavier as the holidays ground on.

I tried to drop it. The Naden gig had messed with me and I needed to decompress from it. I was even switching off radio reports on Naden if they came on in the car. And then one day I was assigned to go to – of all places – Dubbo, because a world-famous comedian and a very high-profile Australian philanthropist who gives to the zoo were going to be staying in the camping ground for a week. My job was personal security detail – I had to keep them safe.

I flew into Dubbo where I picked up a brand-new BMW X5. I had to wait for a few hours, until these two celebrities flew in on a private jet, and then I drove them to their glamping tents at the zoo. Almost as soon as I was inside the zoo, the staff were telling me their stories of strange items going missing, and food being pilfered from the animals. The Dubbo police had officially 'cleared' the place and the media still had stories of Naden on the run. But the people who worked there were adamant: Naden was still in the zoo.

So for the next week, I drove or walked directly behind the comedian and philanthropist wherever they moved in the zoo or in Dubbo, ever mindful of this suspected murderer who'd lived in my friend's ceiling. Because my charges insisted on sleeping out in the glamping section of the zoo, I had to protect them. So before they slept the night there I sealed every tent except the ones they were staying in and I checked the tents every day. And every night, I pulled on my ghillie suit (which I'd kept) and I kept vigil in the long grass around the occupied tents. The police may have moved on, but I listened to the employees, and if there was a chance Naden was around, he wouldn't be getting near my clients.

I got very tired because I was working around twenty-two hours a day, and one morning I came in from my watch, very early, and grabbed some breakfast from the chef, and as I was sitting, this very famous comedian I was guarding came in and sat down. I leapt up and took my food to the kitchen and made a few comments that mimicked the lines this man had made famous on TV. He obviously heard it because he called me out, insisted that I eat with him, and then said, 'And you got it wrong – it goes like this,' and performed his famous walks and speeches for about two minutes, at 6 am in the restaurant of the zoo's camping ground. All the kitchen staff came out to watch. It was amazing, hilarious, unforgettable.

He knew how tired I was and I think he appreciated my efforts.

On the day I took them to the airport at Dubbo, I walked to the BMW, and guess what can of drink was sitting on the bonnet?

Yep – and it was half-full.

*

I kept a handle on the Naden story, over the months, as people from various task forces would call me to get background on random things. They chased shadows for months and then years. And yes, Naden did move on from the zoo. He was sighted at Lightning Ridge, in northern New South Wales. He was tracked to Kempsey, and to Condobolin, and then into the dense, isolated bush country of Barrington Tops National Park, between Scone and Gloucester. Police thought he was jumping on cattle trucks to move around.

He shot a police officer when they closed in on him, and when the police finally tracked him to a cabin deep in the bush in 2012, he tried to run again and was only stopped by a big police dog, who got him by the foot and broke it. When they brought him into the courts, he pleaded guilty to murdering Lateesha Nolan and Kristy Scholes in 2005, and to an aggravated sexual assault in 2004.

He got a life sentence plus forty years and it's unlikely he'll ever be free.

And that was my zoo experience – all done. Or so I thought.

TALKING TO ANIMALS

1

I was sitting in an office in Sydney in early 2006, at the tail end of a gig. I was finalising paperwork, about to do a debrief with my handlers, before flying back to Melbourne where I had a house project that had slowed somewhat. I was keen to get back there, light a fire under some of my employees, and move the project along.

Across the office from me a New Zealander walked in, sat down and started having a conversation with another person who worked about two desks away. I didn't pick up much of the conversation, but when the word 'zoo' was mentioned, I guess I pricked up my ears and tried to listen in. I didn't get much and I forgot about it. But in the afternoon, after my debrief, I got a call from my employer. He was with the New Zealander and he wanted me upstairs. So I went upstairs and walked into the office.

'You hear all that?' asked the New Zealand bloke, who I'll call Terry. 'You seemed interested.'

'I heard the word *zoo* and then you guys started whispering.'

'I'm doing a project with the zoo,' he said. 'I'm told you're the person who can help.'

'Sure,' I said. 'What have you got?'

He told me that a consortium of two large zoos – one in

Melbourne, one in Sydney – was saving a group of eight Asian elephants from their cruel lives in Thailand. Five were going to a new enclosure at Sydney and three were going to Melbourne. One was an unwanted circus elephant and the others came from logging camps in the Chiang Mai region.

'Sounds great,' I said. 'What's the catch?'

'We're experiencing some sabotage, court actions and threats,' he said. 'Animal rights people. It's organised – some of it's with lawyers, but some of it's plain nasty.'

I didn't understand. 'Aren't the elephants being saved?'

'Well, yes,' he said. 'But the activists think the elephants should stay in Thailand.'

My employer leapt in. 'I don't care who's got the halo,' he said. 'The government wants those elephants here, and you're the zoo guy. So we're helping the zoo, okay?'

And with that I was seconded to the effort to save those elephants – both from the loggers and the activists.

*

In my world many of the people with so-called 'expertise' in a certain field have just washed up there. They did one gig in which they had to, say, find internet hackers or counterfeiters, and because they succeeded once, they go through the rest of their careers with a 'hacker' or 'counterfeiter' flag on their list of competencies. Mine now included 'zoo', although tracking and catching a bad guy who's living in the zoo grounds requires a very different skill set from running an international counter-extremist operation. I started from the disadvantage of not even understanding how you would save an Asian elephant from a logging camp by insisting it stay there.

Anyway, I was the Zoo Guy now, so I went for a quick coffee with Terry. I liked him immediately because he was obviously experienced in logistics planning, he was smart and a strong personality.

But he was open about the areas where he needed help. I have seen many gigs go south because the person in charge has an ego that doesn't allow anyone else to have expertise greater than his own. That outlook can be a disaster, and Terry wasn't like that. He had a background in project management and logistics and he could feel elements of the elephant project getting out of control.

He threatened to send me a whole lot of emails and documents and I sensed a man who was overwhelmed by a task, and so I told him he could send me the corporate hogwash if he wanted, but now we were talking he could just tell me what was going on. He took a deep breath and told me that they were trying to get eight elephants to a Thai Navy airport south of Bangkok, in the Pattaya area, where they were going to be flown by an Antonov cargo plane to Australia. They'd come via the Cocos and Keeling Islands, where they would stay for a thirty-day quarantine. There were some large logistics and project management tasks in this. There was red tape on the Thai side and red tape on the Australian side. You can't just take elephants out of Thailand and you can't just fly them to Australia. So a team was working on it, with a whole lot of juggling and official representations.

Then there was the vet job: the elephants had to be checked by vets in Thailand, prepared by vets for air travel, checked by vets and signed off by the Quarantine Service in the Cocos Islands, and then checked by vets in Australia when they landed. There was going to be an orchestra of international animal doctors, not only to make sure the animals were healthy but to check that the original doctoring was correct.

Okay, so now I could see where Terry was getting his headache.

Then there was the freight task. They had a precise window with the Antonov company, booked to leave Thailand in early June 2006. They had to fabricate special steel travelling cages and they had to feed and water the animals during the flight, and, you guessed it, a vet had to travel on the plane with the beasts. There had to be trucks, police escorts and road closures at the Thai and the Australian ends of the project, and if the slightest piece of paperwork was wrong, or there was a mere hint of disease in the animals, the whole thing would seize up like an engine with no oil.

Terry took a breath, and got to the part where they had called Mike: there were a number of organised animal welfare actions against the project. And I use the word 'welfare' to distinguish them from the 'rights' movement. The welfare types claimed the elephants should be in an open-range setting such as Dubbo, or the Victorian version in that state. A high-profile group-of-groups were challenging the Environment Minister's decision to allow the eight elephants into the country. Even though the zoos had been given the go-ahead by January 2006, the threat and the delay and the uncertainty of further legal action weighed heavily on the whole thing.

These animal welfare groups were the relatively sane organisations who had retired judges and former politicians on their boards. But there's another layer of animal activism which focuses on the 'rights' of animals, and these organisations conduct acts of sabotage, vandalism, trespass, threats and assault to transmit their messages.

So while the legitimate animal welfare bodies were making their legal challenges and trying to change the conditions for the elephants, outlaws were at work in Thailand. The elephants had already been cut loose at one holding facility in the Thai jungle, which had resulted in days spent getting the animals back. And in one attempt to bring an elephant in a logging camp to the main holding area, a tree had been cut down across the road, stopping the transport. The activists in Thailand had sent letters of threat to the zoos and were lobbying the Thai government to stop the project. And they sent a constant supply of questionable claims to the media – some of which were reported by activist journalists.

Terry was most worried about the outlaw activists. He said, 'It's like these activists are always one step ahead of us.' And that's when I felt I had an inkling about what was happening.

'Are the details of this operation open knowledge?' I asked.

'Only among zoo staff,' he said, quite innocently.

'Okay,' I said. 'From this point forward, we'll put some operational security around this job, right?'

'Okay,' he said. 'What does that mean?'

'It means we eliminate anyone who doesn't need to know.'

He agreed. And so began our weekly meetings at the Shakespeare Hotel in Surry Hills. We called it our Other Office.

I was now the Zoo Guy.

2

Long before psychographics was used by industry and political parties, it was of interest to intelligence organisations. That is: what are the values and opinions and outlooks of a certain group of people? How might we fore-arm ourselves by understanding their values and motivations?

There is a certain group that we'll call Zoo Employees, and their psychographics are interesting. All around the developed world, there are three distinct personality types who work in zoos. There is the person who just needs a job; there is the lifelong lover of animals, who really wants to work with them; and there are the activists.

These three groups comprise roughly equal thirds of the zoo workforce, and the phenomenon is as obvious in Australia and Germany as it is in the United States and Britain. The 'just a job' people are fairly obvious, and who can blame them? Everyone needs an income. But it can be harder sorting the animal lovers from the activists. Usually the clue is in the CV: the animal lovers might want to work with dolphins or bears or tigers – whatever their particular thing is – and they have usually done work experience or they've volunteered in zoos, marine parks or habitats such as Sumatra or Siberia. They are very different from the activists, who – generally – are not really focused on the animals. They're more interested in punishing humans. They're political people, not animal people.

Terry and I got this straight that first afternoon we met for a drink. He knew there were leaks coming from the consortium's zoos, and the information was being transmitted to activists in Thailand, giving them a head start on their sabotage efforts. But the reasons for it were less clear. The Thai elephants were being taken away from the exploitative and cruel world of logging camps, and they were going to be part of a breeding program in Australia. Asian elephant numbers were (and are) dwindling as their habitat shrank. Terry told me that the logging elephants were currently in a rehabilitation facility in Thailand, because when they worked they spent their lives with one leg chained to a spike in the ground, so they had never learned to walk properly. You can't just free these animals – they have to be retrained.

So the project to get elephants out of the logging camps, and out of Thailand, and into a breeding program where their numbers could be boosted, was good for elephants. The zoo consortium was even calling it a 'breeding program' now. So why the trouble?

Terry mentioned a particular group of animal activists. They had a long name, like a Marxist outfit, but during this gig they were always called the Group. They were big among young people in the United States and Europe, and their main idea was not animal *welfare*, but animal *rights*. The way they see it, animals have as many rights as humans and therefore you can't lock them up, or farm them, or put them in circuses, rodeos or zoos. But Terry told me that he suspected a few of the zoo employees had ties or sympathies with the Group, and that's where the leaks were coming from. When there was a new transportation planned, or a date on which something was going to happen, the Group activists in Thailand were notified and the sabotage was put in place.

It would be a complete disaster to the logistics task if the activists were given a heads-up while the elephants were en route to Australia. So we agreed that from this point on, we'd have a working relationship at the zoo, but that the main intelligence exchange would happen at our Shakespeare Hotel meetings. Unfortunately we couldn't just shut down all the information about the elephants. The zoos had a lot riding on the venture – they were investing millions in doing the Asian elephant breeding project and with all the corporate sponsors and the need for buy-in from the state and federal governments, there had to be publicity about the progress and that meant lots of internal details about what was happening in Thailand.

That night I called my wife Liz from my hotel room in Sydney. I told her the job had engulfed me and I was going to be out of town for maybe a week – or at least long enough to get on top of the early details and get some structure in place. My deal with Liz is that I get her full support as long as I don't lie to her. She'll always be there for me, and I can count on her adapting to my sometimes-crazy life. But I can't treat her like a fool – can't bullshit her.

'I'll ask Si to watch over the house job,' I said. 'He'll need fifteen hundred on Friday – to pay the lads – and it'll have to be cash.'

'I'll sort it,' said Liz. 'But, gee, wouldn't it be great if we could all be paid in cash?'

I didn't want to get into it with her. She was a senior nurse who worked in emergency departments and there was Buckley's chance she'd ever be paid in pre-tax money. We'd had some terse conversations about why the trades thought they were a tax law unto themselves and I always challenged her to find me a couple of labourers who would work as hard as I demanded, but have 40 per cent of their money taken out in tax.

We briefly spoke about covering the mortgage for the month, and I said McKenzie, one of my labourers, would drop by for the keys to the ute at some point – and then she said, 'Be careful, Mike,' and I told her I loved her.

Next, I called Si, my builder mate, and asked if he could take over my site. We act as one another's backup on our jobs. When I have to drop what I'm doing and attend to my other 'contracting', Si steps in and runs my employees. When Si has to take the kids away on holidays, I cover for him. We trust one another with cash and tools, and reputations, so this is usually a fairly seamless handover. Until someone hits a sewer line or a gate is left open and the client's dog escapes, and then the phone calls fly.

'I should be a week,' I said.

'Stay longer and start paying me what you're paying those fucking labourers of yours,' said Si, who thought I was too generous. 'Jesus, Mike!'

The next day, I went up to the zoo and had a more formal meeting with the consortium. They told me that 'tens of millions of dollars' were being spent on bringing the eight elephants to Sydney and Melbourne and it was important it remained a positive public event – not a controversial one – because big zoos are big tourism drawcards and they need lots of goodwill from governments and their bureaucrats. All you need is one question being raised that can make a government look bad, and certain types of politician will shut everything down. Just think about the live cattle trade and the New South Wales greyhound industry – both of which were shut down by sudden government decisions – and you realise how hard any animal-based industry has to work to keep governments onside.

I asked the top guy what the exact complaints were from the Group, and he had a dossier ready to go. It was thick with newspaper clippings and a few letters addressed to left-wing politicians. But I wanted to hear it direct from him.

'They have the usual animal rights arguments, that you can't lock up a wild animal because it's cruel and the animal should be released to the wild,' he said. 'And they have a rather novel one, where the Thai affiliate of the Group is claiming that the elephants were caught in the jungle – that they're not even logging elephants.'

'Are they logging elephants?' I asked.

'Of course,' he said. 'They've been in logging camps all their lives, which is why they can't walk. Wild elephants can walk.'

I nodded at the file on the desk in front of me. 'That's a file of what, clippings and letters?'

'Yes, with our original statement to the media last year.'

I flipped through the pages until I got to the media release. It talked about eight elephants, a breeding program and a $37 million Asian elephant enclosure in Sydney. In my mind I added another $10 million for a new set-up in Melbourne and another $10–15 million for the logistics, plus at least $10 million for the upgrades that Terry told me were being completed in the Cocos Islands to recommission the old quarantine station. It was a lot of dough.

'Have you done an intelligence assessment on the risks of this project?' I asked.

He looked to his managers and they all looked away. 'Looks like we haven't.'

'Have you done any work on who is leading the Group's efforts in Australia – the funders, the managers, the decision makers?'

He leaned back in his chair, and opened his hands to me. 'You're the Zoo Guy, Mike. We're in your hands.'

3

What I do with most of my gigs – when I have sufficient warning and time – is to grab a pad and pen and make some maps: one is a map of what I know, and what I don't. I can do all sorts of tricky things later, but having done initial interviews and a perusal of the material, I simply list my knowns and unknowns.

I also draw a simple little map where I identify the weak points – the choke points – in the chain of events.

After half an hour of writing I sat back and looked at where I was up to. I knew a lot about Asian elephants, logging camps, the costs of the new elephant infrastructure and the transport arrangements.

But when I looked at what I didn't know, it was dominated by a heading that might seem obvious to someone like me, but had been all but ignored by the zoos: we knew almost nothing about the enemy. As I mentioned earlier, in the end, intelligence is about people. You have to know who they are, what they want and who else they're influencing or taking orders from. If you understand people, you can get in front of them or at least be on the same page.

With the animal activists, there was one clue which seemed to have found its way into my file. It was a flyer, printed on yellow paper, which contained the words, in large black lettering: *Don't Support Animal Cruelty. Tell KFC to stop buying tortured chickens. Your Joy – Their Pain.*

On the back of this flyer, a person had written, in blue ballpoint: *Received at Bourke St KFC, Melbourne, 2 February 2006. The Group??*

I didn't need to look it up. The Bourke Street KFC store was right in the middle of Melbourne, walking distance from the Town Hall and Her Majesty's Theatre and all the good stuff in central Melbourne. I'd perhaps eaten a family pack there, myself, once or twice.

Then I turned my attention to the choke points. This wasn't happy reading. As far as I could see, there were significant risks getting the elephants out of the bush and onto a plane in Thailand; there were risks in transporting the elephants via the Cocos Islands; and there were significant risks when the elephants landed in Sydney and one group had to be transported to Mosman while the others were taken to Melbourne.

From this early point I saw the entire transport chain as a sabotage opportunity for the Group and a potential nightmare for the zoos.

I started with the Group because in many ways all the roads led back to them. I made some initial searches on the internet and found some interesting material on their US site. I hadn't been aware of this, but there seemed to be several layers to these animal activist sites. There might be a layer where you have the hippy girls talking about how animals are people too and we need people to care, and to march, to stop bears being in circuses. Sort of the university-'Kumbaya' stuff. But if you had a look around in these sites – which I did – you could find harder material, where members boasted of criminal activities and how to get away with them. It was 2006, so the internet still had an anarchic edge to it. During one of my searches, I ended up in what used to be called the 'chat rooms', the Internet Relay Chat (IRC) scene. This is really where the animal rights people dwelt, along with the outlaw rave crowd and Occupy Wall Street types. A lot of the animal activist people claimed to be from the Group, and I could tell they were from all over the world. The parts I was most interested in were the discussions about how to use your position to fight against animal oppression. This subject had a 'string', some of which went on for hundreds of posts, and they were from people in government, in NGOs, in law enforcement, city councils and of course, zoos. They bantered about leaking sensitive information either to the Group (or other organisations) and to the media. People made technical suggestions, such as how to properly light your guerilla video recording in a dimly lit piggery or poultry shed.

By the time I'd spent an hour looking through this stuff, I had established several things: the Group's Australian presence was based in Melbourne, making the KFC flyer more likely to be material from the Group; there was a name bandied around, the man who led the Australian Group – let's call him Toomai; and there was probably a cell of people from the Group at Sydney's zoo, who were leaking information, and those leaks were being used by a very aggressive Thai affiliate.

I needed Terry's help on this and asked him to be as low-key as possible when he went about the task, and that was to collect and make copies of all the correspondence and material he could find from animal activists. If it said 'the Group' on it, that was a bonus. But I didn't expect it to be signed by anyone. The Group wasn't that kind of organisation. I just wanted anything and everything written to the zoo from an animal rights person, with any kind of negative message.

I also put out the word through a government agency and I reached out to law enforcement. I asked for the same thing: low-key approach, no discussion about it with anyone. I wasn't trying to be difficult, but some of the Group people in the chat rooms were employees of sheriff's departments, quarantine services and police departments, boasting about what they leaked to the Group and how to cover up their actions. I wanted to tighten the op-sec, right down to obscuring searches for material on the Group.

Early the next week I attended a meeting that Terry was having with the police. This was an initial sit-down to discuss Terry's proposal for the elephant trucking operation from the airport to the Sydney zoo. Actually, the traffic operation would begin at the transport company's yards in Western Sydney, because we needed protection for the trucks even before they got to the airport. Terry went through it with the police and they were talking about motorcycle escorts, highway patrol cars, unmarked cars, road closures, lane closures on the Harbour Bridge and a PolAir helicopter in the sky.

I could tell Terry was happy with the police approach. Finally, someone else was giving a shit about the details.

The guy from the police ended the meeting by telling us: 'We have an operation name. We're now working on Operation Burma.'

4

I asked a junior employee of Terry's to research everything he could find on the Group, everything we had on Toomai – starting with his birth name – and I wanted a map of the Group's global affiliates, chapters and splinter groups. I also wanted him to create a list of the Group's known sabotage MOs. Trees across the road might work in the Thai bush, but what would they try in Australia? Also – most crucially – I wanted to know where the funding was coming from. What or who provided their money?

Me? I took a mid-morning flight down to Melbourne to do what I do.

I booked in to a building of serviced apartments in the city, close enough to walk to Fitzroy Gardens. When I do gigs in Melbourne, I generally don't operate from Liz and my house. It's just easier – from an operational security perspective – to not worry about leading an enemy's surveillance tail to your door. The apartments were three blocks away from the KFC on Bourke Street, and as soon as I'd checked in, I went for a stroll into the city to have a look for myself. There was no one outside the fried chicken joint, so I went in and had a quick bite of lunch and took my time, hoping someone might turn up to hand out leaflets. I picked up my phone, rang directory assistance, and was put through to the Melbourne City Council.

I asked for the street permits and vendor licences desk, and I listened to some ramped-up organ music for just over five minutes, before a woman picked up the call.

'Gee, it'd be nice to go into Bourke Street KFC without those animal rights people coming at me,' I said, trying to keep it light.

'Oh, *them*,' she said. 'They can be a pain.'

'Do they have a permit for that?'

'They don't need one,' she said. 'They're not selling anything, they don't use any temporary structures such as a desk or a chair, and they don't require people to stop.'

'Fair enough, so what happened today? They give up?' I asked. 'They solve animal cruelty?'

'No, they'll probably be back tomorrow,' said the woman. 'Thursdays, Fridays and Saturdays – that's their days.'

Thanking her, I signed off. It was Wednesday afternoon, so I was in luck.

I was back at KFC at 11.30 the next morning, and I saw the person from the Group as I walked up to the door. He was wearing what I considered to be university arts student clothing: faded jeans, a black U2 t-shirt under an open flannie shirt, and longish unkempt hair with an African kufi hat that neither fit nor suited him.

He was mouthing something about eating and morality, and you are what you eat, and I took a flyer from him, wide-eyed. It was the same flyer that was sitting in the zoo clippings file. I went in, ordered my family pack and a Coke, and sat near the front windows where I could watch him. He was nineteen or twenty, and I noticed he had a little hippie bag over his shoulder. He didn't seem exactly engaged in what he was doing and I wondered how I could use that.

I made a production of reading and nodding so that whenever he turned and saw me through the glass, he saw someone who was absorbing the message – really getting it.

When I emerged, I paused and thanked him for what he was doing. 'Is this just you?' I asked, clearly impressed. 'Or is this, like, an organisation or something?'

We got talking and he quickly identified the name of the Group, and then I found out his name: Matt.

So within thirty seconds of meeting Matt, I'd confirmed that the material in the file belonged to the Group, and I was talking to one of their operatives. I'd done a lot of research and chat rooms by now, so I cued him in on battery versus free range and genetically modified chickens and all the stuff about how it's not really chicken anymore – it's the same DNA as a potato. I had no idea what I was talking about, but it seemed to strike the right chord.

Matt told me he was an English literature major at the University of Melbourne. As we talked I got the feeling he was someone who had some brains but little ambition; he'd probably drifted a bit until he'd found a passion he could get into. I asked him if I could give out some of the leaflets and he gave me a handful from his hippie bag, and we got into it together.

I told him I was a builder by trade and he said his father was a businessman but he didn't want to follow that path. Fair enough, I said, and I sensed that Matt was beginning to warm to me. We made a bit of a team that day. I shouted him a cup of coffee that afternoon, and kept him talking. 'This is just so outside of my world,' I said. 'How do you get to do something like this?'

Matt smiled and told me he wasn't supposed to talk about it.

'Really?' I said. 'But you're standing in front of KFC on Bourke Street, in the middle of the day. How do you keep that a secret?'

'Well,' he said, sheepishly, 'I'm in the public eye, but we're not allowed to talk about the people who run it.'

We had a bit of a chuckle about that and I asked him if I could do it again the next day, and he said, 'Sure, see you at eleven.'

I got back to my apartment and called Terry's employee. 'How's the research going?'

'Got Toomai's birth name and I ran a check. He's been violent – before he joined animal lib, he had a couple of assault convictions.'

It made sense. 'Anything else?'

'Yeah,' he said. 'The Group gets most of its funding from grants from your favourite political party.'

'What, the Nationals?'

'No,' he laughed.

The next morning I brought an extra coffee, for Matt, and we got into the animal rights spiel. My job was to build affinity quickly, and I poked around a bit, like a gardener preparing the beds.

'So,' I asked. 'Do the bosses ever come down here and do this?'

Matt laughed. 'No, mate. He wouldn't come down here.'

'Well, I reckon he should,' I said. 'He could see the way we're doing this and you'd get a promotion.'

He shook his head. 'You're only here, with me, because he's overseas. I'm not allowed to deal with anyone he doesn't know.'

'Shit,' I said. 'Sorry to put you in that position, mate.'

'It's okay,' he said. 'I'm sort of in charge at the moment.'

'Sort of?'

He looked away for a few seconds, a man summing up the situation. 'You can't tell anyone this.'

'Sure,' I said, mumbling, *Reject the cruelty model – you are what you eat* to a passing woman and handing her the flyer.

'I have the key.'

When you do this sort of work, it's okay to be energetic in your rummaging, but once you unearth the gem, you don't want to turn a spotlight on it. That can alert the person to their indiscretion. So I let it go and instead went for a tangential answer that let him off the hook.

'Got the company car, huh? Nice job.'

He nodded, and I turned away and told a university girl – as I gave her the flyer – that KFC chickens were so genetically altered that when you ran a genome sequence on them you couldn't differentiate a drumstick from a turnip.

'I *know*,' she said, and walked in anyway.

The lunchtime crowd was starting when Matt came over and stood shoulder to shoulder with me and admitted that the key wasn't for a car – it was for the office.

'Cool,' I enthused. 'They must really trust you. I must say, you seem pretty responsible.'

'Ha!' he said, rolling his eyes. 'He doesn't trust me at all.'

'Who, *you*?!' I said, aghast. 'Matt, you stand out here all day, you know your stuff, you keep it together when people argue with you. That's management level, mate. It's no wonder he left the key with you.'

Matt kicked at the ground.

'We should go down there,' I said. 'I'd love to learn more about this organisation and its aims.'

'No way,' said Matt with a wry smile. 'He'd kill me for that. I shouldn't even be talking to you.'

I let it drift, and when we met on the Saturday we gave out some flyers and had a yak and at 1 pm I said, 'I'm calling a stop-work meeting at the pub,' and he laughed at that and we found a pub and had a couple of beers.

He was not enjoying university, although he was enjoying a bunch of poets with names like Sidney and Spenser and Donne, but he wasn't enormously engaged. No girlfriend, no car, no sport that he played. And no money. He'd worn the same clothes three days in row and he was having trouble staying in his flat. He wasn't appreciated and he was broke.

At some point, you have to decide how you're going to get access to the information you need. I reckoned I could persuade Matt to open up the office, but then I'd have to get him to open up the computer and show me the interesting files. And how would I trick him into that? The other way to do it is to come clean – something you can do if you've built the right affinity.

'You know, Matt,' I said, 'I need a small amount of information from the Group, just really to check up. It would be more like keeping all of you out of trouble, protecting you from one person's violent impulses. I'm sure you know what I mean.'

He didn't react badly. 'You a cop?'

'Nope,' I said.

'You a private investigator?'

'Something like that,' I said. 'You need $200 a week to stay in your flat – I'll pay you $300 a week, and you get a few bits and pieces for me. No one gets hurt.'

'Bits and pieces, like what?'

When he asked me that, I knew we had a deal.

'Like, what other groups is Toomai talking to? What's he asking you to do? Where are you being sent?'

He looked at me but I was sure he'd already made up his mind. If you want loyalty, don't treat the Matts of this world like shit.

I finished my glass and pointed to his, and Matt said, 'There's no point in wasting our dough here – there's beer in the fridge down at the office.'

Spoken like a true Aussie.

5

The Group's office was upstairs above a set of colonial high street shops, just south of Carlton. Matt jiggled at the deadlocks and we walked into a sort of Tardis of self-righteous rage. I was stunned when I first took in the posters and flags that covered the walls. When you see so much opposition to so many things, it looks like a joke. Aren't they *for* anything? Is there nothing about Australia they like? The democracy? The equal rights? The clean water?

Maybe not.

I said, 'Wow, Matt – this is pretty heavy.'

'I know,' he said, taking off his hippie bag and returning the flyers to their pile on a large desk. 'VB?'

He went to the fridge and I looked around. There was a desktop computer with a server under the desk. There were three banks – that I could see – of filing cabinets, and there was a door into another room. The kitchen area was open plan, containing a fridge, microwave and a coffee machine. And there were several large tables with chairs around them, piled high with printed flyers, letters, pamphlets and other literature. I pulled out my Nokia, which in 2006 had a 1.3-megapixel camera – not great, but okay for documents.

I snapped away as Matt twisted the tops off the VB stubbies and came over to me. 'Gee, it's not all about chickens, is it?' I said. 'Hell, tuna, elephants, kangaroos, bears, horses – and even rodeo bulls.'

'Yeah, we cover quite a bit of abuse.'

'What's the story with rodeo bulls?' I asked.

'Beats me, mate,' he said. 'I've never seen a rodeo.'

He gave me the tour, and when we walked into the next room, I was in the super-secret part of the Group's operation. I knew this because there was a large pinboard against one wall with a bunch of post-it notes and photographs pinned on it. There were large maps of Thailand, and a map of Australia and the Cocos Islands. I was mildly stunned at what I was seeing: the photos included an interior shot of the quarantine facility in Thailand, the quarantine facility on Cocos Islands and shots of Terry at both facilities.

I took photos on my phone of the pinboard and close-ups of some of the photographs. One of the post-its was stuck on the Thai Navy airport at U-Tapao. It said, *Outbound June 2006*.

Great – so they had a good idea of when we were moving.

This room was where they kept the bolt cutters and the crash helmets and the industrial breather-masks that stop the tear gas working. There were ladders and rappelling ropes and several sets of body armour of the type worn by riot police and rioters. Important to my investigations about MOs, there were two chainsaws on the racking that went to the roof. I filed that one away: it wasn't just a tactic in Thailand – they'd fell a tree here too, to stop a convoy. There were Sony Handycams and boxes packed with spray cans. But then my eyes lit up. In a cardboard box was a stash of folded black t-shirts. 'What's this?' I said, pulling one out. Across the front and back of the t-shirt, in large gold lettering, were the words *Animal Rescue*.

'We're not meant to touch those,' said Matt, a little worried. 'That's for the action teams – the boss has a select group who do jobs, and they're the only ones who can wear those.'

I nodded, pulled $300 in fifties from my pocket, and handed them to him. Before he touched the money I pulled back slightly. 'Are we okay about this?'

'Sure,' he said. 'You just need some information.'

'But it's our secret, right? You go blabbing about this and it's your arse, not mine. Okay?'

He nodded and I gave him the money.

'First act of faith,' I said, and I picked up three of the folded t-shirts.

'I'll get in trouble,' he said.

'And you're not already?' I laughed, giving him a slap on the shoulder.

I moved him into the main room and we drank our beers and I mentioned that this must be the nerve centre of it all. He told me he didn't have the keys to the filing cabinets, but he pointed at the computer and said, 'That's the real nerve centre, anyway.'

We were a little tipsy by now so I said, 'Let's have a look – imagine the pics they've got on there.'

'No one's allowed to touch it,' he said, rolling his eyes. 'That's a beating offence.'

'It's probably password-protected anyway.'

'Yeah, it is,' said Matt. 'But I know the password.'

He sat at the chair in front of the computer, booted it up, and the Windows XP logo came up. He input the password and then we were in. I was mildly drunk in Carlton, looking straight into the darkest secrets of the Group.

We went through the file lists and had a look. The majority were copies of letters sent to media, government, companies and NGOs. Mostly the wording was aggressive, high-handed and overloaded with adjectives. I clicked my phone camera where something was interesting. I grabbed two more VBs and pointed at a folder on the screen. 'What's that one there – the one that says *Proposals?*'

He scrolled down the file list and opened *Proposals*, and now we were in Aladdin's cave. The documents had innocuous names, but when he double-clicked on them, I was looking at conspiracy to commit many crimes. They were written like business plans but most were proposals to sabotage companies, by either wrecking parts of their operations or by lying to the media about traces of poisons found in food, etc. Some were extortionist: they'd threaten to do something antisocial unless something was done about chickens or tuna.

There was quite a bit on the Thai elephants but not in one coherent file. It consisted largely of ideas and intelligence passed on from the Group in Australia to the affiliate in Thailand. I read as quickly as I could but the documents gave no indication of who was the mole at the zoos. I didn't want to compromise my new confidential informant (CI) on the first day by emailing this material to myself and blowing his cover, so I clicked my phone camera. As we went further into this mess of threatened violence, I noticed that Toomai's favoured theme was fire. As in, *If they don't do as instructed, we set fire to their warehouse/office building/vehicle pool.*

Matt was embarrassed about those documents, so we looked elsewhere and found a file of mentions of the Group in the media. But Matt came to his senses because he was worried someone else from the Group might be dropping in. So he shut down the computer and we got out of there.

I took one last look around. You never get the time or the access you really want, but having had a nosy through the headquarters, I had seen the Group's proposals for activity and picked up on favoured MOs; I'd found the phone number, the email address, the street number and I'd grabbed the email address that Toomai sent ideas and intelligence to in Thailand. I'd also seen a name.

We went our separate ways and I never saw Matt again. However, now I had his phone number, and he was my CI. As a final act, I got Matt to take a picture of myself, in the Animal Rescue t-shirt, in front of the entrance to the building.

You can't stay in front of every adversary, but you can maybe goad them into a mistake.

6

Back in Sydney we worked pretty much full-time on Operation Burma, through March, April and into May. The legal problems seemed to be over by then and we had a 'load date' for the elephants, in early June – the same one, I noticed, already assumed by the Group

The work with the police and Terry's ever-expanding logistics team became very intense and my lists kept growing. At one point we were having three or four meetings a week between the zoo and the police and it was doing my head in, but it was also making me revise my 'unknowns' list. One night, when I couldn't sleep, I picked up my pad and added to my list: *If elephant(s) escape in an urban area.*

Don't laugh – what would you do if an adult elephant got out of its transport truck on William Street and started panicking? The big ones can weigh four tonnes, and they run wherever they want to. Now think about more than one on the loose.

At the next meeting I brought this up, and I was assuming that between the zoo logistics people and the police there would be a standard operating procedure for a rampant elephant loose in a built-up area. There wasn't. But the police and Terry felt they had enough on their plates, and so within a couple of minutes all eyes were on me and there were smiles and nods. It was agreed that Mike – the Zoo Guy – was now the weapons officer. I had the firearm licences and the government clearance to discharge a weapon in public. And I had proficiencies from a number of military agencies. So they pointed at me and that was it.

I had to consult widely, including with the senior weapons officer at a very large, very famous American zoo, and ensure I had the right firearm, the right rounds, and tactics that would work. I needed an H&H .375 rifle (aka, an elephant gun), and a Remington 870 pump-action shotgun loaded with 1 oz Brenneke solid slugs.

The real trick was how to actually stop a rampaging elephant. Effectively, you use the 870 to incapacitate the animal, and then you have to finish the job with the H&H, shooting down into the brain from behind the ear. None of this is discussed in a cavalier way. These are beautiful animals and we were bringing them around the world, to a new country, to care for them and give them a safe home. No one wanted that to end with a weapons officer. And as my adviser told me, I'd have to travel as the nearest person to the transport trucks, and be the first to act if an elephant got loose.

You can't wimp out if you're the weapons officer – your job is to save everyone else by stopping the beast before it harms anyone. And you can't have cops shooting their Glock pistols at an elephant because it will spook them but not stop them. The tricky part? There's actually no better way to stop the elephant than standing right in front of it. That's when you have the best access to both front legs. As strange as it sounds, if you can hold your nerve and make your shots, fronting the beast gives you the best chance.

And then my adviser said, 'If you act fast enough, and get it right, you could save many lives. But the public will hate you for it.'

Don't you love Americans?

So while I was trying to stay ahead of the Group and keep things on track in Thailand, I was also immersing myself in this role: the lifesaver who'd be loathed by every Australian if they saw me shooting an elephant on the six o'clock news. I simply had to be ready for any eventuality, so I started to plan my role in the transportation process. I'd have to travel in the operation commander's vehicle, with my elephant guns in a sling along my right leg. I liaised closely with my driver and we discussed how it was going to work. Elephants can move at forty kilometres per hour, so if one got loose, my driver would have to be right on it. You can't give them too much of a head start, my American adviser told me, because once panicked, they'll run over everything and anyone. Scared elephants have been known to run through brick walls. You have to stop the animal.

As it happens, I was no stranger to the weapons officer role. A few months earlier, at a large Australian zoo, the agency I was doing work for seconded me to the role of weapons officer because just as one of the permanent officers had left on maternity leave, the other one broke his leg. So because of my firearms proficiencies and licences – and my hunting background – I was offered up as a stop-gap.

I was only there for a few weeks but it coincided with the great Charlie Insurgency. (Both of the following chimps have had their names changed.) Charlie was an adolescent chimpanzee at this zoo. He wasn't particularly large but he was very aggressive and cunning. Bobo, the alpha male of the chimps, had kept him in check. I'd only been at this temporary posting for three or four days when the alarms went off one morning and I was called to attend the chimp enclosure. The place was a mess, with blood and chunks of hairy skin sticking to the concrete walls. Standing on a lawn beside the moat, was Charlie, arms raised and jumping up and down, making one hell of a racket in what looked like a victory dance. The other chimps lay in various states of unconsciousness and fear; young chimps huddled under their battered mothers and most of the animals were bleeding. The worst affected was Bobo, who was unconscious, had had his ears ripped off, several of his fingers bitten off and was bleeding from the anus. The place was a charnel house, and there were visitors in the zoo.

I was armed with a Remington 870 pumpie loaded with Brenneke solid slugs, and I had a Smith & Wesson .44 revolver on my hip for backup. With the aid of a chimp keeper, we herded Charlie into a solitary enclosure without me having to discharge a weapon. But don't think that because I had this firepower that I was relaxed. An adult male chimpanzee has the strength of three men and has 0.005 per cent body fat, compared to an average male human's 20 per cent. So weapons officers in zoos around the world have tried to stop rampaging chimpanzees, and a single solid slug from a Remington pump-action shotgun doesn't usually stop them. Their muscle mass is so hard and their body fat so low, that bullets and slugs don't always penetrate their chests. You add to that their speed, and if a male chimp wanted to attack me or another zoo worker, I'd have the chance to take one – maybe two – shots before the ape landed on me and used its incredible hand and arm strength to rip me apart.

But Charlie went into his own cell and the rest of the chimps were taken to the vet to be stitched up and put back together. Charlie had attacked and sexually assaulted all of the other chimps – around fifteen in total – and the animals were contracted out to vets around the city for stitching and rehab. The group was slowly put back together and they now had a new alpha: Charlie. The female chimps had to make nice with Charlie, the juveniles were scared, and Bobo spent a week looking into a corner, head bowed, refusing to have eye contact with the other animals.

The young beast had taken over and Bobo was beaten and now occupying a new position.

My understanding of apes up to this point was gleaned through David Attenborough and shows like *Lancelot Link* and *BJ and the Bear*. I thought chimps were mini-humans – but boy, I had no idea what sort of humans. It turned out most zoo workers like gorillas and don't particularly like or trust chimpanzees.

I spent about four weeks at that zoo. In my last few days the alarm went again and I was dispatched to the chimp enclosure. My heart was pumping as I arrived, assuming that Charlie had gone wild again. But when I got to the fence, and pushed my way through the public, Charlie was a bloody, groggy mess. And he was being held aloft by Bobo, who stood on the edge of the security moat, shaking his tormentor at the onlookers. Apparently the old boy had crept up behind Charlie while the younger ape was vamping for the audience, and really attacked him. Looking at the scene I was witnessing, you could almost believe that the old alpha was shaking the young upstart at me and saying, *'It ain't over til it's over.'*

The other zoo workers pushed the public back and away from me, and I raised the shotgun to stop Bobo. But before I could fire, Bobo threw Charlie into the moat, where that 0.005 per cent body fat took him to the bottom like a stone. Now it was Bobo's turn to jump up and down in a victory stomp and I threatened to fire a round by loading my weapon, but I didn't shoot. Eventually we pushed him back, allowing two zoo workers into the moat. They dragged the young chimp out of the water and tried CPR on him before racing him to the zoo hospital. There was too much water in Charlie's lungs and he never recovered.

So I was experienced in my duties as weapons officer – just not on elephants and not in a public place. My main concern with Operation Burma was getting enough early warning on where the Group – and other protesters – were hiding and preparing an ambush. The police had seen my report on the Group, so they knew the disruption these people could cause.

But when the shit started flying, it wasn't from Australia. It was from Thailand.

7

In the last week of May, when the rehab on the elephants' walking was complete, and the logistics and security operations were being finalised by a lot of frazzled and tired people, we got word of some animal rights activity around the Thai elephant facility. So regardless of my warnings and attempts to control the information, we still had a leaker at an Australian zoo, and the Melbourne-based Group were briefing the Thai splinter group. I contacted Terry and asked him to set up a meeting with the senior management. I argued that there was a multi-million-dollar transport operation that relied on having the elephant crates on the Antonov in Thailand within a certain window. And so I asked that we shut down all internal memos regarding the elephant program, since we couldn't work out who was talking to the Group.

They were very reluctant but they agreed. These internal emails had been circulating every day, so when they stopped and the word got around about why, the hate mail from people associated with the Group really started. It was intense and aimed at specific people with some ugly threats. Toomai now loomed as someone I'd have to become personal with.

Terry was up in Thailand, preparing for the transportation

of the eight elephants on the six-hour journey to the airfield at U-Tapao. It was a long journey because there was only one airport that the Antonov could land at – the Navy airport – which meant transporting the elephants from Kanchanaburi in the west, all the way across the top of Bangkok. The situation allowed for a lot of ambushes and disruptions. It wasn't ideal but Terry was on top of it.

As we went into June, we were readying ourselves for Operation Burma in Australia when I got a call from an old associate who told me there was increased activity around the Group's headquarters and a lot of chatter. And then on 6 June, Terry rang me, in a total state. He was at Kanchanaburi quarantine station and the trucks were ready to roll out the following morning. But an activist group had put a blockade on the facility: there were more than 200 of them, some of them bussed in from Bangkok, and others were locals who were probably being paid. They were sitting on the access road and wouldn't let our elephant trucks leave.

Terry was beside himself, and as the day dragged on the whole project had to be called off because we'd missed the Antonov window.

Terry flew back to Sydney and he called me into a big consortium meeting, where high-level people from the zoos, and representatives of the governments and government agencies, were present.

I sat back and tried not to get involved. But after a bunch of them had tried to quantify the loss – somewhere between $5–8 million – they turned to me anyway.

'Don't we have a risk person?' asked one of the senior consortium people.

'That would be me,' I said.

'What happened?' he asked.

'My area is Australia,' I said. 'I understood Thailand was sorted.'

They said they needed me across all of the mission, so I said yes and shut up. And then they worked out when they could reschedule.

'Late July,' said Terry, 'but it won't be cheap at such short notice.'

The big chiefs said, 'Book it.'

8

Okay, so this had started as a logistics-support gig but that meeting between the consortium people was really a signal to me and Terry to do whatever it took. It was costing too much money to dance around with these protesters. Terry rebooked the Russian airlift, but there was a lot of to-ing and fro-ing because we'd lost the first window and they were all booked up. So Terry had to settle for two flights out of U-Tapao on Ilyushin cargo aircraft, as opposed to a single flight on the larger Antonov. At my end, it meant going into one of my lines of work that I don't publicise.

Obviously, I had to control the situation in Thailand or these elephants were never getting anywhere near Australia. The first thing I did was reach out to a local asset who is very effective in Thailand, let's call him Hari. Hari is an intel-trained private operator who is always doing work for the 5EYEs (the intelligence services of UK, USA, Canada, Australia and New Zealand). I'd worked with him before and so I gave him a call and we settled on a price for his services. I told him I needed all I could get on the ringleaders of the Group in Thailand, and before I finished the sentence he told me who they were: the woman was the pretty TV face of the Group, who we'll call Sami. And the ugly, violent side of the activists was represented by Jimi – a thug and an organiser and a pretty ruthless person by all accounts.

I told Hari what I needed. I wanted him to infiltrate the Group operating in the rural villages around the Kanchanaburi quarantine station, and find out what he could, especially about the chain of command and how much information was coming from Australia; and I wanted him to set up a counter-surveillance operation, so we could get pictures of them surveilling us. I wanted to get a clear idea of how they were operating and who the watchers were, and I wanted pictures of them watching us so I could mess with their minds when the time was right.

After four days I got confirmation from Hari: the activists in Thailand were getting information and funding from the Group in Australia. In fact, the source of the best intelligence in Thailand was Australia.

I was distracted in Australia during this time because I was in regular contact with Matt – my CI in Melbourne – and he said the pinboard had an increasing number of pictures on it that were interior and exterior shots of the Cocos Islands quarantine station. Obviously Toomai was planning to hit the Cocos Islands.

There wasn't much I could do about this until I knew how they were going to do it. It would be by boat or plane – I'd wait to see that unfold.

I now had a blanket ban on consortium emails or internal memos regarding elephants that would alert anyone to the date or place associated with our second attempt. Then I took some sick leave from work and I flew to Bangkok, without telling anyone. While most of the information leaks were coming from the consortium, I didn't know or trust most of the consortium-linked people working on this in Thailand. Terry had a lot of contracted people working for him up there: vets, animal handlers, truck drivers, logistics people. I didn't know them or their motivations, and so I didn't want them to know I was there and allow the Group to put pieces of information together. If someone took a photo of me? That would be a disaster.

I had some very good contacts in the Thai government. This is a back-scratching business and I had done more than enough of the right things in South East Asia to get a meeting and be taken seriously. These days everyone is aware of cybercrime and its counter-measures, but back in 2006 it was a relatively new field and a lot of the best counter-measures people were as dark as the hackers. I had access to some very competent people and we'd done some work for two South East Asian governments whose central bank computer systems were being attacked. They were effective operations, one of which allowed the security services to apprehend the hackers. People don't forget you if you made them look good.

I explained what I needed to my contacts. I needed to remove the violent leader of the activists and I was willing to pay for a local crew to get this done. I didn't want violence or death – I wanted a troublemaker placed in another part of Thailand so that he was unable to lie down in front of the Kanchanaburi quarantine station.

They agreed that what I was proposing was for the best. I also mentioned that I had a budget to pay for some high-level IT and telecoms people to make internet or cell phone communication difficult in the Kanchanaburi region during the transportation.

We agreed on a price for these services, and they gave me a very effective intel–law enforcement officer to work with.

I now went undercover and caught the bus out to Kanchanaburi. I moved around, having meetings with various locals, because firstly I had to locate Jimi. He was being highly annoying and provocative to the local police, and he was keeping a low profile. So I kept one too. I wore a tropical shirt and cargo shorts, and no cap. No watch. I carried a camera, a phone and a pad and pen and told people I was a freelance reporter for a British newspaper.

I moved around clandestinely, not even introducing myself to the consortium team. Years later I bumped into one of the senior operators working with Terry, and I told him I'd been up there, and he said, 'Bullshit.' And so I described what he'd been wearing and what he'd been drinking, and who with, and he gawped. 'Are you a fucking ghost?' he asked.

Well, not really. But I do my best work when I go dark.

My job up there was to find out who was doing what and get in front of them, and that meant knowing where Jimi was at any given time. Where there was Jimi, there was trouble. We had a Go date at the Navy airport, and we had to make that. And this time I was going to anticipate the activists' move and stop it.

I had a coffee with Hari in a small village one morning, and he told me he'd attended a meeting the night before. 'Look who turned up,' he said, passing me his phone. It was a Nokia N90, which back then had the class-leading two-megapixel Carl Zeiss camera. I made sure we weren't being watched and scrolled through the photographs of a Thai man – around twenty-eight – standing in the corner of a simple village restaurant, addressing about fifty people.

I handed back the phone. 'Nice, mate. What did he have to say?'

'He said they won't let the elephants get to U-Tapao.'

'Any details?'

Hari named the date and the time of the transport, and – yes – Jimi was right on the money.

'He have much of a crew for this one?' I asked. 'Or just those people in the photograph?'

'Those people are the organisers,' said Hari. 'There's more coming in.'

'He make you?' I asked.

Hari lowered his voice. 'I think I'm clean, but I followed him and he's staying in that guesthouse.'

I knew the guesthouse and the village and I'd eaten many times in the restaurant where Jimi had held his talk. They did great things with chicken and ginger.

It was now 20 July. We were ten days out from taking the elephants to the airport. We had one chance at this.

I was absent from 'work' and incognito in Thailand. But I had to stay in touch with Terry. We'd built a relationship and he had to know he could count on me, especially after the first elephant move had failed. So I was using my in-country burner phone to call into my Australian voice mail, ensuring that nothing was erupting back in Oz. I'd been in Thailand a few days when I collected a voice mail: Terry, panting with stress, swearing about the Russians playing games with whether they'd be at U-Tapao airport on the agreed day.

I rang, told him I was sick and not in the office, and what was up?

'The Russians are getting vague on the arrangements,' he said. 'They're telling me they need more money or they might not make it.'

'What?' I said. 'You have a contract?'

'Yes, of course,' he said. 'But that doesn't matter if they don't show – that's still $5 million further down the drain.'

We went through it and it was one of those situations. I could offer to front the Russians myself, but they can be stubborn bastards and if faced with the likes of me they might just dig their heels in so they could have the pleasure of telling me to fuck myself. I had another idea that didn't involve grown men banging chests and then having to drink an entire bottle of vodka to sort it out.

'I might have an alternative,' I said. 'Leave it with me.'

'It can't be shipping, Mike,' he said. 'The activists would have a hernia and we might lose the support of the governments. Ships are not happening.'

'I know. It's something else.'

I was sitting in a coffee house in a village in Western Thailand, and I made a call to my buddy at the Pentagon. I already owed him so many favours and I felt bad putting this on him. But if he couldn't help, he would know who could, and that would be worth the price of asking.

Stan picked up, and I told him the problem.

'Fucking Russians,' he said, 'can't live with them, and you can't nuke 'em.'

We talked it around and he put his phone to his chest, talked to someone, and came back on the line. 'I can get you five Globemasters out of Guam. I'll call it a training exercise.'

I was humbled by that response. Really humbled. I thanked him and called Terry, told him what I could do.

'Is this a joke?' he said. 'Shit, Mike – I'm desperate.'

'It's not a joke, Terry,' I said. 'If you want those Globemasters, you can have them. Just let me know.'

So Terry got back to the Russians, said he didn't need their planes after all, and the Russians smoothed it over, admitted there'd been a small communication problem, and committed in writing to a time for the airlift from U-Tapao. At the original price.

You have to love the Americans – once again, superior air power resolves a misunderstanding.

9

So Terry had his planes, and I had my activist headache. I moved in to the village to keep an eye on Jimi, but I remained on the periphery, staying in a guesthouse at a neighbouring settlement. Hari was the infiltration operator and he was doing his job well. There was no need to jeopardise a successful surveillance. By establishing and sticking to my story of being a British journalist doing a story on rainforest logging, I moved around fairly easily and always had an excuse to ask questions of the locals. I based myself in and around the general store-depot, where I could stay on top of town gossip – they also brewed a nice coffee.

There was an area on the edge of this village where they stacked rubbish and junked cars and washing machines, and this is where I was meeting Hari every night. He was in the activist group and accepted – if not friendly – so he was bringing me direct intel about the protestors' intentions and direct confirmation that they had the entire zoo consortium schedule. He was also building a gallery of pictures on his phone of the people doing most of the one-on-one meetings with Jimi. One of them looked more Indonesian than Thai and Hari checked her out, and we were right: her name was Lana, a rich man's daughter from Jakarta, playing at saving the world one elephant at a time.

As we approached the date for shifting the elephants, I saw Jimi leave the café-restaurant one afternoon, and he was joined by Lana, the Indonesian woman. Jimi wore black Levi's and his black ponytail fell on a black Sea Shepherd t-shirt. He was athletically built and strong in the arms, like a boxer, and he had a charismatic swagger about him. The girl? About twenty-two, very pretty and curvy. I followed them as they walked the dusty streets, and when they got close to the guesthouse, I ducked into shadows as Jimi cased the street. Then he pushed her through the entry door by the waist, and she wasn't exactly struggling – if you get my meaning.

I had initially lined-up my Thai friends to remove Jimi, only as a safety-net option. There were other things I could do, like using some false information to turn the troops against Jimi, fudging the transport date and leaving in the middle of the night. That sort of thing. I could even have fronted the bloke and intimidated him. But now I'd seen him up close and realised that he had a bit of a spell over his followers, there was only one way to go and that was to physically lift him out of this area and into another area.

That night I met Hari at the village dump and he said the chatter was about scores of protestors coming in from Bangkok. After I'd met with Hari I grabbed a driver with a car and he headed to the neighbouring settlement, and once I was in my room I called my guys in the government and told them I needed the job to happen tout suite. The next morning – two days shy of the elephant transport – I was having an early morning coffee at the café-restaurant where Jimi held court. I watched the guesthouse at an angle through the front window. A silver Nissan Patrol pulled up outside the guesthouse at 7.09 am, and three heavily built Thai men wearing dark polo shirts and jeans – and with 9mm handguns on their hips – emerged from the car and walked into the guesthouse.

They came back to the car around ninety seconds later, dragging a person into the back seat. I could see who he was because there was a black hood over his head, but the guy was built like a boxer. Jimi was driven into a less urbanised part of Thailand where his drivers showed him the pictures of he and his gang surveilling the zoo consortium's quarantine operation – pictures we'd taken – and then they told him that the angry white man was on to him, and it was over, time to go home. Apparently Jimi was arrogant and full of fight. But they didn't hurt him. By the way, this was conducted by Thai authorities, for national security reasons – it was totally lawful.

Now I used my local connections to access the cell tower network so we could listen-in on the voice, text and email chatter to see what the Group were going to do. We set up our interception gear and laptop in the back of Hari's Tarago people-mover and using the cell phone numbers and email addresses that Hari had acquired from these people, we got a pretty good picture of what was going on. As I'd hoped, there was confusion about Jimi's whereabouts and concerns about his welfare. Actually, the entire Thai affiliate of the Group went into meltdown about the disappearance of their leader. The PR woman who headed the Group in Thailand for TV appearances couldn't get the locals to lie down on the road because Jimi wasn't there and the troops demanded to know where he was. There was mention of CIA and 'drones' and 'spies' in the ranks, and some of the louder animal activists were talking about the imposter and how he would have to die.

I decided Hari was probably blown, so I pulled him out and we retreated to the neighbouring settlement, parked the Tarago around the back of the building, and maintained an undercover position for the next day. It's true that many activist types are middle-class poseurs going through a phase, but all it takes is one of them to egg-on another, and if they have access to weapons, someone gets hurt. It's easier to pull back a bit.

On the night before the move, I made a phone call and the internet went down and so did the cell towers. And as the sun rose the next morning, Hari and I were in our overwatch position, back in the jungle, not only observing the quarantine facility but the observation post that Jimi and the activists had previously used. This time, we could see no surveillance. I watched through my binoculars as the facility gates opened and the trucks, loaded with our eight elephants, rolled on to the highway and turned towards the Navy airport at U-Tapao.

Some still-keen activists gave chase in their cars and scooters, but they didn't seem organised. It was much easier for police to head off a bunch of vehicles on a road than stop people from lying in front of a gate. The convoy was finally on their way, and Hari and I brought up the rear of the convoy. Hari was in his own Tarago and I rode with the Thai authorities. I stayed in constant contact with Hari and we played a vehicular overwatch role, finding the vehicles that were tailing the convoy. There were a couple of them, and it was just lucky that they had problems with their registration and certain safety defects, at which point the authorities had to pull them over. The upshot was that the elephant convoy – eight trucks long with Terry's 4x4 at the front and a security detail at the back – got to the military airport on time. I stayed back, in the Thai government car. I would have loved to slap Terry's back and congratulate him as they pulled into the freight section of U-Tapao but I still needed to stay dark.

I'm glad I did. As soon as the trucks rolled up to the area where the giant Russian cargo plane was parked, I could see a ruckus developing at the other end of the freight section. The freight section went into shutdown and I sent Terry a text, asking *Everything okay mate?* Down the trucking road that we were parked on we could see activity, maybe thirty people at another entrance and a police car racing to where the people were. My phone buzzed, a text from Terry: *Protestors at the airport. We're here but on hold.*

We kept watch for five minutes: the convoy was parked on the tarmac of the freight section, beside the huge Russian plane and the security gate our elephant trucks had gone through was secured by armed guards. So the protestors had hit another gate and I wondered why. It didn't take long to find out. The sirens started at about the same time as smoke started billowing from warehouses that abutted the tarmac. The protestors had set fire to a military building. The military personnel – who were going to load the first plane – now had to fight the fire, and so the elephants were still sitting on the tarmac at 3 pm, with no one loading them. I watched this unfold from the government car, unable to break my cover. It was frustrating and the texts I swapped with Terry were blizzards of swearing. He was at the end of his rope.

We watched the scene and suddenly Terry burst out of his Land Cruiser, stomping like a mad man, got on a loader and started loading the elephant crates himself (he later told me he didn't want the elephants sitting in the heat of the day). Then the Russian crew was climbing down from the plane and joining Terry, and they loaded most of the elephants in their steel containers, before the military people got back. Now the arguing started because Terry and the Russians weren't allowed to touch the loading gear. So we watched lots of arguing and shouting on the tarmac. But the convoy had made it and the loading had been done and regardless of the fire, the protesters were kept away from the plane and the elephants.

Finally, the first Russian cargo plane took off for the Cocos Islands at sunset, while the rest of the convoy waited for the second plane to be wheeled-up and loaded with elephants.

But the story didn't stop there.

Back in Australia, some judicious sharing of credible intel with state and federal law enforcement and intelligence operations had managed to forestall the Group's operation in the Cocos and Keeling Islands. I won't detail it except to say that because of that island group's infrastructure and location (and because of some assets that none of us are privy to), Australia's major security agencies just ensured that none of the saboteurs could physically access the area.

But the Russian Ilyushin aircraft could land there, and they did. With one small problem. The zoo consortium had spent around $10 million renovating the Cocos Islands quarantine station so it could accept eight Asian elephants for ninety days, and had rebuilt the runway and other infrastructure so an Antonov An-225 – which is over forty-three metres long – could land there.

But when the first Ilyushin Il-76 landed at Cocos – itself larger than a Boeing 747 – it got to the end of the runway, and stopped at the turnaround. The tarmac wasn't wide enough for the aircraft's turning circle. So the four elephants on board had to be offloaded from the end of the runway, and when Terry's team had finished with that, they had to find trucks, a gravel pit and some earth-moving machinery to build a wider turning area. Otherwise the aircraft was never getting out of there and the second plane wouldn't be able to land.

While the earthworks were being done, one pilot wanted to stay with the aircraft but others in the aircrew wanted to go drinking. This set up a rolling argument that climaxed as the sun came up with one group coming back from their night out and the sober pilot on the tarmac, with an AK-47 in his hands, telling them they couldn't access the plane with so much booze in their systems.

Eventually, however, they got the two planes on the ground and the eight elephants into quarantine. Now came the final piece: getting the animals from the Australian airports to the zoos.

10

Six o'clock in the morning, Mosman Police Station. There were twenty police motorbikes, six zoo vehicles, ten police cars and four low-loader trucks. As planned, I sat in the commander's car. We pulled out and headed for the airport, on the other side of the city. The commander was able to coordinate the motorcyclists so we could move smoothly, avoiding the traffic jams at major intersections. It was quite impressive, the way he handled it.

As we got to the Southern Cross Drive turnoff into Mascot, the motorcade headed into Qantas Drive which eventually leads around the airport to the international terminal. There, on the side of the road, was a parked van with protesters around it, obviously getting ready for action. The police by now were educated about these people, and as we passed the van an attachment of heavily armed officers pulled to the side of the road and apprehended them.

The pick-up of the elephants went smoothly, and now we had to get from Mascot to Mosman, with four trucks, five Asian elephants and a weapons officer who really dreaded the possibility of having to terminate a rogue elephant. I mean, I'd do it, if I had to. But after all the drama, and a cast of hundreds of people, and millions of dollars spent, I didn't relish being *that* person. I'd worked with the driver of the command vehicle and we both knew that if it came to it, he didn't want to be on *that* team. But we'd agreed that if it came to it, we could save some lives, some property, and some anguish for the animal by moving on it really quickly.

The move went very well, except for the TV network helicopter that buzzed the motorcade way too low, and had to be called off by the commander. When the helicopter didn't back off fast enough, the commander called the PolAir guys, who actually herded the TV helicopter away. It was quite a sight and saved us one less hassle: you don't want elephants to become riled when they're on the back of a truck. That's four tonnes of ballast, at a high centre of gravity, and if any animal wanted to start swinging and lurching, we'd have a hell of a time keeping the truck upright. When the convoy finally motored through Mosman and onto Bradley's Head Road, and then turned into the zoo's internal service roads, I felt as if I could breathe again for the first time in weeks. I was so drained I could barely get through one schooner of beer when the consortium crew met for a drink later that night.

The various police forces had become sick of the activists by the time the circus moved to Melbourne. I'm not sure how they handled moving their Asian elephants down there, but the police managed to keep all the activists in their burrows during the trip to the zoo.

It was one of those exhausting gigs that had a bit of everything in it. Terry became a renowned animal logistics manager after this escapade, and now sells his expert services to zoos and governments around the world. His knowledge of animal rights activists is second to none, and when we meet for a drink, he always jokes that his first chore on a new gig is to do the intelligence assessment . . . before he does much else.

Toomai, the Group's leader? He became more aggressive after the elephant transfer was a success, and made a couple of threats to the wrong people. So I sent him an early Christmas card. It was the photo of me outside the Group's headquarters, in the Animal Rescue t-shirt. Matt left Melbourne, completed his degree at another university and last I heard was living a peaceful and useful life.

And Jimi? He returned to Kanchanaburi five days after he left. He was dishevelled, but not hurt. Apparently he walked into his favourite café-restaurant and asked where everyone had gone. But the show had moved on. It always does.

On 16 January 2010, a girl Asian elephant named Mali was born at Melbourne Zoo: she was the first calf born at Melbourne Zoo, the first female elephant to be born in Australia, and the first conceived by artificial insemination. I have a picture of that baby elephant on the wall of my office. It reminds me of a time when my job was to hold a couple of weapons and stop the elephants rampaging.

I love my job, but I'm glad I didn't have to do it that day.

PALACE COUP

1

There was a voice, right behind me, and it was not quite right. I mean, the hairs on the back of my neck were sticking up.

I was with a bunch of data-storage executives, led by a guy called Chris and we were having morning tea at a coffee shop on Macquarie Street and discussing the security aspects of the organisation I was consulting to.

Chris, who'd brought me on board for this client, was trying to negotiate the integration of an electronic detection system with the human version. It was a case of the IT engineers over-claiming on the thermal signatures and face recognition and me sitting there, asking what happens when a bird sits on your camera or the computer tells you a terrorist is crawling through the undergrowth, but it's actually a wombat. I wasn't being totally argumentative because I think good security is a balance of assets, not one or the other. And also, I was a bit distracted because of the voice behind me. It had a nice base of Tamil English, with an overlay of perhaps Arab or Iranian. The person I was hearing wasn't being interrupted or spoken over, which meant he was the boss. The two Lebanese chaps in their mid-twenties who were with the talker were just *listening*, which is very strange for a couple of young Sydney Lebanese males. However, when they did speak

I could verify they had the Aussie-Leb accent. So I was thinking we had a foreign smooth dude and a couple of local patsies. Most important, the Tamil's tone was furtive – it reminded me of how I spoke to my crew when in public. By the sound of it this bloke was a foot from my left shoulder, and I didn't want to spook him by turning and having a butcher's. So I asked the waitress where the lav was, and I made for the loo.

I gave it fifteen seconds, had a look in the mirror and gave myself the order: *Don't get all Mike about this*, and pushed back through into the coffee shop.

I'd picked a nice set-up because now I had the chance to stop beside the shop counter and fish for my wallet: 'You boys need another coffee?' I asked, just loud enough so the smooth Tamil looked up at me briefly from his conversation. Which is what I wanted. I nodded at the boys, got their orders and turned to the girl behind the counter, and it was lucky she'd heard the palaver about soy lattes and espressos with two sugars, because my mind was now in hyperdrive. The Tamil who'd looked up at me was a face – the term we use for a person logged in an intel or law enforcement database, and who has a sheet attached. The guy was known. I couldn't place him – couldn't think of a name – but a good guess would be 'money man'. He was nicely dressed, well groomed, and had excellent English. A lot of the funding conduits for Islamic terror organisations were run by middle-class Tamils, and while cops and courts have to give persons of interest the benefit of the doubt about their guilt, I certainly don't.

I resumed my seat at the table and let the conversation about algorithms and 99.998 per cent uptime wash over me. I was totally, completely focused on the Tamil and his conversation with the two muppets beside him. I had the young blokes pegged as Lakemba panelbeaters, who probably prayed at the right mosque and had been baited and hooked by envelopes of $8000 in cash, given to them with enough regularity that they stayed interested.

Their involvement would escalate until the day the Federal Police pinged them for storing C-4 explosive and illegal detonators at their business, while the Tamil was sitting on his yacht off Pattaya Beach, sipping on a cold beer.

That's what it looked like, and perhaps the Tamil pegged me for a face too, because his conversation turned to small talk, and ninety seconds later he was saying his goodbyes and standing.

I gave him a one-minute head start, then stood and looked out the window of the café. He was walking north along Macquarie Street, towards the Harbour Bridge, with his two friends. I told my meeting that something had come up. I said everything they were saying made sense and I was looking forward to going over their beta security design, but that my two cents' worth was that we needed both human and electronic assets in place, for a mutual counter-balance. There were a lot of sage nods. I gave Chris the wink and he replied with a flick of the head, and I told him I'd ring him later.

I eased onto the street, scanning for cars and eyes. Did the Tamil have backup? Or were the muppets his muscle? Were those tradie vans legit, or did this bloke have a support crew standing off? I let my subjects have a head start, pulled my black baseball cap from my back pocket and put in on my head. Hitting a speed dial on my phone I called Andrew, a mate of mine who worked for a foreign government but who was based in an office just around the corner from where I was standing.

'Mate, I'm tailing someone who might interest you,' I said. 'I'm walking north on Macquarie Street, over the road from the eye hospital.'

Andrew told me he'd pop down and we signed off. The subjects walked slowly but they didn't seem overly alert about surveillance. I decided I hadn't been made in the coffee shop and stopped at a shop window as they paused for a chat at the top of Martin Place. This was a couple of years before Martin Place became famous for the Lindt Chocolate Café siege and a hostage-taker named Man Haron Monis – an Iranian immigrant who used to send vilification letters to the families of Aussie diggers who had died in Afghanistan. He was a piece of work, that Monis, and I wasn't surprised when his personality finally led him to strap on a suicide vest, chop down a shotgun and take the coffee drinkers at the Lindt Café hostage on that morning in December 2014. What had always angered me was the speed with which the courts and parole system had always put this person back on the street.

Anyway, that was all in front of us. For now, by the time the Tamil and his buddies had walked another thirty paces, I saw Andrew walking up Martin Place, past the Reserve Bank of Australia building. Andrew was in his early forties, a former college baseball player who had kept his physique and his sense of humour. He came up the hill towards me, that African-American athlete's build and those small agile steps the giveaway sign that this guy could rock 'n' roll when the circumstances required it. Don't let the nicely tailored suit fool you: Andrew was a veteran of two agencies and he was highly qualified in just about every intel-surveillance technique you could name. It was Andrew who had sponsored me into some of the world's best counter-terrorism programs. And it was Andrew who was responsible for my lifelong motto: *There is nothing better than a competent American.*

'Hey, Unit,' he said, not bothering with handshakes. 'What've we got?'

2

We walked north on Macquarie Street. In front of us the Tamil was talking, his hands making gestures as if giving a lesson.

'Got a name?' asked Andrew as we strolled. He was straight into surveillance mode as if he was born to it.

'Nope,' I said. 'He's a face – just can't place it.'

'Which one?' he asked, and I told him I was interested in the tall guy with the nice haircut wearing the Dunhill blazer.

'Indian?'

I reckoned Tamil.

'Who're those other dudes?'

'Sidekicks,' I said, lining up with a lamppost to take myself out of the picture should the Tamil turn and look. 'They did the listening, he was the talker.'

It was a beautiful day in March, a slight breeze coming up from Circular Quay, and we were in front of the lunch rush hour, so the footpaths were not densely populated. In surveillance terms, there was enough traffic to hide in and not so much that you got delayed and lost your subject.

We slowed and held back at Hunter Street, waiting for the crossing light to go green, before we entered the crossing as the Tamil entourage were stepping back on the footpath on the other side.

Now our crossing light was flashing red but we kept our slow pace, ignoring the taxi that was trying to edge into our kneecaps as it made a left turn.

We walked down the hill now, towards Circular Quay, and I was starting to relax. There was no counter-surveillance going on, and if there was any surveillance-detection – say, from a service van or another person behind us – I wasn't picking it up.

Andrew was quite chatty as we walked past the Royal Automobile Club – he wasn't concerned about these people and we caught up on his recent trip back home. The subjects walked all the way to the bottom of Macquarie Street, where the Opera House is in front of you and a large residential building nicknamed The Toaster is on the left. We pulled back a bit and I crossed the road alone, because the smooth Tamil had stopped outside the residential portico to the building and seemed to be having a last-minute briefing with the Lebanese blokes.

I sat on a park bench, in shadows, and watched, and Andrew joined me.

'Nice place he has here,' said my friend, and he fished a plastic device from his pocket – about the size of a box of matches – and slipped it over the top of his iPhone.

I looked over his shoulder: the device was a powerful telescopic lens, housed in a tiny package, and built so the camera pointed lengthwise, out of the top of the phone. It meant Andrew could place the phone on his thigh and look down to adjust the picture rather than having to hold it up and alert the person he was following. You could adjust the lens housing so it worked the other way, and the lens projected ninety degrees from the top of the phone, making it great for pointing over the top of a car dashboard.

The optics on the spy-camera were incredible, and I watched Andrew zero in on the Tamil's face by spreading his fingers on the screen. Once he had the screen filled with our subject's face,

Andrew waited ten, fifteen, twenty seconds, and when the Tamil turned slightly to look over one of the muppets' shoulders, Andrew tapped the shutter button several times.

And that was that: now there was a RAW picture file in his phone, taken with what would be a 300-millimetre lens if it was on a big DSLR camera. Then the Tamil turned and used a swipe card to get into the foyer, and the muppets dispersed. We weren't interested in them, although I'm sure they could have led us to something interesting.

'I'll let you know,' said Andrew, standing.

I shook his hand and he asked if I was walking back with him and I said, 'No mate, I'm going to see if this bloke leaves again.'

Andrew grinned and shook his head. Among his community I was known as the Aussie who was even more paranoid than they were.

'By the way,' he said as he was about to walk away. 'You around?'

'Not going anywhere,' I said.

'Might be something for you,' he said, turning and walking. 'I'll be in touch.'

I sat on that seat for the rest of the morning and into the afternoon. I should have been with Chris, helping him with the major corporate client we'd been meeting with in the café. They had physical security on their properties and they had cyber-security IT contractors for their systems. But Chris was a specialist, also from the intelligence community. You called Chris when you'd had breaches or threats, and you were moving away from day-to-day passive security and into what we call 'counter-measures' – you know, fighting fire with fire, visiting the bad guy where he lives and shitting in his nest.

I stayed watching that building for too long until finally, as I was about to give up and leave, the Tamil re-emerged. He looked around quickly and got into a waiting taxi. He was more casual now, in a pair of expensive jeans, a Ralph Lauren polo shirt and

Timberland yacht shoes. I'd have put him at forty-five, forty-six years old, and it was obvious he worked out or played a sport. He carried a cabin-luggage wheelie suitcase which I noticed he kept with him in the back seat of the cab.

I stood and started walking up the hill, not wanting the guy to see my face. I kept it cool, and as the taxi accelerated past me on the right, I looked sideways briefly and the Tamil wasn't looking at me. As I walked I saw the taxi slow for traffic that was stopped while a truck made a right-hand turn into one of the service roads. As that happened I saw that another taxi had snuck through from the other side and was driving downhill towards me. I thought, *What the hell*, and threw out my hand. The cab did a U-ie and stopped by the footpath and I got in and asked the cabbie to take me to Cronulla.

Once I'd given the driver a few sudden instructions, I decided he was kosher and I told him I needed him to stay behind the cab in front of us. He didn't ask me why, he just shrugged and got on with the job. By the time we were going down Southern Cross Drive I had a fair idea where the Tamil was headed. Now it was just a matter of whether it was domestic or international. Why was I in this cab, tailing this person who I'd initially only *heard* in a café, when I'd been meeting to discuss something entirely different? I really couldn't tell you. What I can tell you is that I have good instincts and a really good memory. I can't always access it as fast as I'd like, but I had a feeling about this bloke and I wanted to know more.

We came into the Kingsford Smith Airport precinct and rather than get off Southern Cross and into the departures lanes for the domestic terminals, we stayed on the freeway and drove around the Kogarah Golf Club, took an off-ramp and drove north. So he was flying international. As we drove up the elevated drop-off ramp of the international terminal, I took off my dark blue sports jacket and rolled it into a ball. Now to a casual onlooker I was predominantly wearing a white business shirt with green and blue pinstripes down it. I took off my baseball cap too, getting rid of any patterns the subject might pick up on.

The drop-off apron was pretty busy and there was now one car between my cab and the Tamil's. My subject's cab stopped halfway up the apron and I asked my cabbie to stop and flicked him two $50 notes. I moved straight to the sliding doors that led into the large departures area of Sydney International and walked across to the Travelex money bureau. From there I could see the Tamil entering the crowded departures hall. He walked in about twenty seconds later and didn't look around. He knew where he was going and headed straight for the Singapore Airlines desks. I moved around the end of the SIA set-up – at ninety degrees to the entrance doors – and melded into the crowds lining up for economy class check-in. The Tamil walked around this queue and entered a queue of three people in the business class line. He waited a minute and was served and I noticed he didn't even carry a ticket – just handed over his passport. A frequent traveller.

I stayed put and waited for the passport to come back to him. If it was a Sri Lankan passport, it would be red, and an Indian passport was usually black. When his was handed back I saw it was green, which could mean Indonesia. I filed that away and followed my subject to the security gate, where you have to have a ticket to enter. He walked right in, at a brisk enough pace to suggest he had a flight to make. I went back to the departure boards and looked at my watch: 16.18.

I scanned the boards for an SIA flight due to depart at 17.00 or thereabouts. Some travellers cut it fine – some don't. There were three Singapore Airlines flights inside the next hour: one to Frankfurt at 16.40 – probably too early – another to Singapore at 17.10, and the last one to Jakarta at 17.20.

I stared at that board for a couple of minutes, and decided it had to be Jakarta. I had no idea why, except for that green passport and a negative instinct about the bloke. And not for the first time in my life I wondered why I'd just done what I'd done. I'd flown to Sydney to consult to a large data processing and storage organisation with government and defence contracts, and Chris had wanted me to gee up those managers and engineers in the café, make them feel good about the money they'd have to spend to secure their business. The real work would begin tomorrow at the formal meetings, but I knew he'd be disappointed in me for doing the Harold today. A lot of security work is about relationships and trust, and you do that in the social environment, not in the big meeting.

I had to let the Tamil go. He wasn't paying my salary – Chris and the data company were. So I walked to the end of the departures hall and caught the escalator down to the train station.

On the second escalator, I sensed that one of the people I'd seen around the Singapore Airlines desk was now behind me. Let me rephrase: I was 90 per cent certain I was being tailed by a Pakistani bloke, in jeans and a windbreaker and almost my height.

There was a toilet on the landing before you reached the train platform, and I skewed off and walked into the gents. I went into one of the cubicles and crouched on the seat, and stayed there for six minutes. People came and went and finally – when the place was deserted – the Pakistani crept in. I could see him through the crack I kept open in the door. In the movies, I'd wait for him to push my door. But in real life, I pulled open the cubicle door as soon as he was in the room, and gave him a big smile.

'All right, mate?' I asked. 'Lost?'

His hand went to his waistband but he was too slow. My left toe connected hard under his right kneecap and I soft-slapped him under his left earlobe, connecting with the carotid artery and the main nerve, and collapsing him like a rag doll. Dragging him to my cubicle, I propped him up on the lav and pulled the door shut.

I guess the Tamil had backup after all. My bad.

3

I got through the next day which was all site visits and strat meetings, executive outreaches and long sessions where IT gurus used PowerPoint the way nannies once used brandy and milk. The main part of my work in these gigs lies in writing the report on weaknesses and threats and what has to be done about it. But this is just boilerplate stuff: my real expertise is in thinking through an incursion or interruption, based on the terrorist's or hacker's way of thinking, and seeing if the organisation has those moves covered. Usually what happens is that my report raises eyebrows and gets the paranoia going, and they ask Chris about me, and he suggests that they get me back for one of my all-dayers, where I brief the senior management on what these terror and political organisations can get up to and let them in on some of the cases that are routinely kept from the newspapers.

In this case there'd been an almost-incursion, so we were well beyond talking about passwords. They wanted some countering. I was thinking it might even turn into an infiltration gig: slip into the IT division and pretend to be someone I'm not, see where the slackness and the weakness was coming from. There might be a coding guru who also played *Halo* with his online 'buddies', not knowing they were Russian or Chinese.

When the meetings were over in downtown Sydney I had two beers with Chris and the guys from the data company, and when the rest of them had gone and we were down to the guy with 'chief' in front of his title, the big boss said, 'Mike, can you get these bastards?' and I nodded, and he told Chris, 'Do it.'

So Chris had another security contract and I had another retainer. With all the paperwork and contracts in this industry, I wasn't expecting to start overnight. Chris would let me know when we were on, so I left him to it and walked back to the Hotel Ibis across the old Pyrmont Bridge. It wasn't until I was almost at the far side of the old swing bridge that I realised I had a tail. I was expecting another emissary from the subcontinent, but when I stopped and put my foot on the sightseer bench to tie my shoe, I saw it was Max – an operator from the industry.

'Feel like a beer?' he asked, and kept walking.

There was a bar and grill called the Blue Fish on the western side of the Darling Harbour tourist precinct and we ducked in there, out of the early evening heat. It wasn't crowded and we didn't need a reservation. Max seemed to know where he was going, and when he got to one of the outdoor tables overlooking the glassy inlet of Darling Harbour, there was a man sitting there.

'Mike, meet Connor,' Max said, and gestured for the waitress.

I shook hands with the middle-aged man with a mid-Atlantic accent, who was obviously from my world. How did I know? Well, he didn't offer a name or a title or an organisation or a justification for having his colleague Max hauling me off Pyrmont Bridge. In my world an introduction from someone like Max means you don't ask for identification – it would just be rude. We just sat and made small talk, and when our beers were delivered, Max waited for the waitress to leave and got into it.

'Need something done, Mike. You around?'

I watched tourists walk along the quay at Darling Harbour and pondered what would happen in my life if for once I just told someone 'No'. I thought about what kind of movie that would be. Aussie tradie gets a gig to build a house. He builds the house, hires other tradies, goes home at night, drinks two beers and watches *The Chase*. Maybe a Friday night at the RSL with the missus, watching a Cold Chisel cover band.

But I didn't say 'No'.

'Depends what I'm around for, Max,' I said, 'you know that.'

'Surveillance,' said Max, like he was talking about where he had parked. 'We need to have a listen.'

I nodded. Either the gig was me planting a listening device, or it was me pretending to be someone I'm not and getting someone talking into the wire. 'Listen to who?'

'We'll get to that,' said the man named Connor. I noticed he had a toughness about him yet his skin was doughy. 'Max says you're very good.'

'And?' I said, smiling.

'And we can't use a face, not for this set-up.'

When a higher-up tells me he already has a set-up, I usually bristle: if I'm the one who might end up in a prison cell, I'm the one designing the gig. Max saw my face, and leapt in.

'Connor means, we have an *idea* of the best way to do this, right, Connor?'

Connor looked at Max a bit too long and then came back to meet my eyes. 'He's right, I have an *idea* of how to do this, and I don't want a face in it. Max tells me you're the best private contractor for this job – interested?'

I nodded slowly. 'And I don't get the details until I'm in, right?'

'You got it,' said Connor, a person who had clearly spent a lifetime hiding his emotions.

'We would thank you,' said Max, with a smirk.

'How much would you thank me?' I smiled back, knowing better than to ask who 'we' was as I drained the beer.

'Twenty thousand for the week,' he said, 'and another twenty if successful.'

I signalled for another round, and finally Connor cracked a smile. 'I'll take that as a yes.'

'It's a yes,' I said as the waitress came over.

'Good,' said Connor. 'I'll need you in Jakarta, day after tomorrow.'

4

I should probably have turned down this gig. I knew how all this worked because Wife Number One had borne the brunt of a hectic lifestyle in which I'd been married to my job as an employee of a government, and then as an attempt to save something from the ruins of that marriage I'd left the all-consuming government job and gone private. This had not developed into more time in the living room with my pipe and slippers, however; it turned out that employers wanted me to either lead security teams out of Kabul and Baghdad on minimum six-month engagements, or immerse myself in South East Asia, where I was expected to root out corrupt employees, mobbed-up truck drivers, pirates, thieving wharfies and saboteurs being paid to ruin mining and forestry machinery. In other words, I went from being a dude orbiting Sydney and working seventy hours a week, to being an operative who wasn't even in the same country as my wife half the time, let alone the same city. This was a big miscalculation, and one I paid for. As an aside, I now tell every young person who comes into this game: when you pull on a ballistic vest to go to work, you're about six months away from the missus giving up. So make a decision!

At this time I'd become serious with Liz and was trying desperately to have an even work–life balance. But even though I'd picked up some building work in Melbourne with decent income, my other career was still mainly in Sydney and overseas. Sydney and Melbourne are not enormously different, but Sydney has that same trouble-magnet as a Hong Kong or Jakarta. If you're an Australian working in my world, most briefings, meetings and shit-storms will be in Sydney.

So I took the gig, even as I regretted it in advance. I really just wanted to be with Liz, having a glass of wine and getting the barbecue on. As I accepted, Max and Connor told me that as soon as the contract was signed and emailed, they'd transfer the first half of my fee and have my expenses package sent over. On this one it was $5000 for the week. There's a whole other formula for subsequent weeks, but I didn't intend to be in Jakarta that long.

I raced back to the Ibis and flopped on the bed, my mind racing. I just never seemed to be able to break out of the foreign work. But I could at least get back to Melbourne for one day before I had to fly out. Liz might give me some brownie points for that.

So I took a cool shower, shook out the beers, and that night, in the hotel room, I wrote the security overview and recommendations for the data centre. My expertise would largely be accessed by Chris calling me on my mobile and me kicking my IT team into action. So I didn't have to be on deck in the way Chris did. The part of my report where I add my own bits of magic? They were listed as 'counter-measures', deep down in the dot points. I could keep that part vague because I knew Chris would go over it and add his own touches. As he used to say to me, 'Mike, you're the dancing bear – I'm the box office.'

As I was finishing off my version of SWOT – strengths, weaknesses, opportunities, threats – the PDFs from Southern Land Management Corp. came through on my email. They already had my BVI bank details, and the payment schedule was as they'd promised. So I zapped the PDF with my e-signature and sent the document back.

I did a final edit on the security document for Chris, giving them a bit of a scare about what is possible with sniffers – devices that can suck up data traffic from routers and switches – and also embedded some 'opportunity', to make them see there were things they could do. Just as I was about to email it to Chris, I heard a ping and the 'iMessage received' box popped up on my screen. It was my bank in the British Virgin Islands telling me that activity had just been recorded in my account. I opened my internet banking and there was a fresh deposit of US$10,000 – no GST for foreign payments.

*

The next morning I flew to Melbourne on the 6 am flight. I got to the house we were sharing – Liz's house, but I was contributing, doing renovations – at around 8.30. She was watching morning TV and having a hot chocolate. She'd worked the night shift and this was her wind-down before having a nap. I told her I had to go away for a week, and she knew not to ask where. When I'd first told her the bones of what I do, I'd explained that the best way to deal with the details was to not force me to lie. Many people in my business, who work for governments and the military, tell the missus that they work in logistics or management and that they have to go to Denpasar for that major VP meeting. But they're really in San Francisco running an operation. Misinformation is one way to do it, but then you're lying to your wife and you're really bringing your work home with you. And then you arrive back from your meeting in Bali, and the missus is saying, how come your flight got out through all that ash? That volcano erupted! And you look both dishonest and amateur. So I now do it the other way around: I give very basic information, and ask that she not press me on where and with whom. Liz understands that – doesn't like it, but she understands.

I gave her a cuddle and she gave me a kiss; and then both of us were getting short of breath and we took it to the bedroom. I'm a one-woman man and I count myself lucky that I don't tire of intimacy with my wife. We enjoyed one another and then we dozed the day away. When I got up in the early afternoon I had a shower and made a sandwich and booked a flight to Sydney for the following day, and then booked the afternoon flight from Sydney to Jakarta. I also booked six nights at the Pullman Hotel. It's comfortable, small enough to feel private and big enough to not be noticed. And it's not one of the major spy hangouts like the Shangri-La or Grand Hyatt.

I brought out my businessman uniform: dark blue suit, dark brown shoes, striped English business shirts and a secondary package of chinos, polo shirts and a light Asian sports jacket. Oh, and a pair of yacht shoes that are actually tactical boots. Packed it all in a wheelie that would be accepted as cabin luggage. As usual, I didn't plan to travel with my laptop or my phone.

Because Max had been with his superior when he'd met me in Sydney, I was assuming this was a Tier 1 intelligence operation in which all hand-offs and briefings would be deniable and all payments would be traced only to a company out of Singapore. Tier 1 operations are conducted as close as you can get to the executive government. They are undertaken by people and agencies that newspapers know little about. If I got caught or caused embarrassment, I'd be left to burn, or rot, or die of lead poisoning, whatever the Indonesians thought was best. And if I didn't get caught but I squealed to the media, there was a clause in that PDF that talked about certain pieces of national security legislation that would see me put away for a long time.

Nice to feel wanted, right?

One of my covers has always been a tourist-photographer, made possible by the fact that I've been published in online publications and I maintain a presence on Flickr – I do 'temples of South East

Asia', architecture and also vehicles. So in keeping with my 'stick to the truth' method of cover, I grabbed my Pelican camera case and put my Canon, two lenses, a flash and a mini-tripod in the case. I decided I'd make a song and dance about that case: get Garuda to put 'fragile' stickers on it, hold it out in front of me and tell the immigration and customs guys at Jakarta to be careful.

Nothing fancy – just a tourist-photographer.

I felt ready.

5

The flight into Sydney landed just after 9 am and I walked down to the taxi ranks of the domestic terminals and through the concrete and glass canyons for five minutes before I emerged into the morning sun, walked around the corner and into the Stamford Plaza Hotel. The Stamford is a hotel but it also contains corporate suites and bars and cafés, and I went into the corporate entrance and up one flight of stairs until I was face to face with a frosted glass door calling itself Spectral Holdings Ltd.

Pushing on the buzzer I was asked to identify myself, and having shown my face to the surveillance camera I was let in. The woman who met me looked like an Avis girl and showed me through to a meeting room where three men sat around a long table, talking and drinking coffee.

'Mike,' said Max, looking at his watch. 'Thought you'd got lost.'

'Just flew in,' I said, sitting. 'Connor,' I said, and he nodded and smiled.

'Mike, this is Adam, one of our technicians.'

I shook his hand – he was early thirties, a bit po-faced, but I assumed he knew what he was doing.

'Okay, Max, shall we?' said Connor, and Max put a briefcase on the table and distributed four blue folders, each containing not more than ten pages. I noticed Adam lifting his own black plastic security case onto the table.

Max got straight into it. 'Mike, no fancy operation names on this one. We're under a time constraint, and we need to get a listening device into a premises in Jakarta.'

I sat back and listened and followed as we spoke about the operator – me – and the device, which Adam held up. I'd used them before. This one was shaped like a small portable hard drive, with the stickers on it suggesting that that's exactly what it was. However, this one was going to live in the Toshiba laptop that Adam had also planted on the table, and when I got to Jakarta, I was going to take it out, connect it to a building's PABX system (private automatic branch exchange, if you're interested) with crocodile clips, and it was going to transmit every word uttered on the lines I connected it to. Then I was going to create what we call a diversion. How? They wanted me to carry two pink USB drives, which would be plugged into another part of the PABX room. The pink USBs contained legitimate files of family pictures and MS Word files but they were also 'killers' – anything I plugged them into was going to be melted from the inside, shutting down one system and forcing the people in this building to switch their chatter from the data lines to the voice lines, which we would hoover up with the listening device. I'd done this before and I understood the mechanics. But I was interested in the 'how'.

'There's a way you want to do this?' I asked.

'You'll be going to a Construction Indonesia dinner with Jenny Warren – page four,' he said, looking over. 'It'll be a chance meeting. She's not indoctrinated so you don't need to discuss what you're doing. She's just your ticket.'

The black and white picture showed an attractive, smart-looking dark blonde, mid-thirties, dressed in corporate clothes.

'You meet her at the Front Page Bar in South Jakarta, 1900, in three days, okay?'

I nodded.

'It's a blind meeting; I'll let you work it from there. I'm assuming she learns you're a building contractor and she needs a date anyway, so . . .'

'When's the dinner?' I asked.

'One night later, on Thursday,' said Max. 'And we'll need proof that the device is in place, okay?'

'How?'

'You'll have a burner phone in-country I take it?'

'I will,' I said.

'On your first meeting with Jenny, you give her the number. If the transmitter is working you'll get a text saying *Your pizza is ready*. If they can't get a signal, the text will read, *Your order has been delayed.*'

'And?'

'And you'll have to go back to the transmitter, check it and refit it.'

I nodded as I leaned forward and grabbed one of the water bottles on the table. I was intensely aware of Connor's silence, and by the time I'd removed the screw top on the bottle, Connor was speaking to Adam. 'Could you give us a minute, mate?'

Adam left, nodding my way – I winked.

'So, are we going to talk about where this all goes down?' I asked, sipping.

'Go to the last page,' said Max, and I flipped through the folder. The final page was a diagram of the PABX room I'd be working in. A close-up drawing of the phone lines was captioned: *Attach to lines 1046 and 1048. Could also be labelled 'Presiden'.*

I almost laughed. 'Where is this building?' I asked Max.

He cleared his throat. 'Merdeka Palace.'

Now I did laugh. The silly bastards were going to bug the president's phone line, in his own palace. So what did that make me?

6

I slept for most of the flight and the drive from the airport took around eighty minutes – not outrageous by Jakarta standards. I took my room card and made my way upstairs, happy they'd given me one of the rooms that looked over the swimming pool. I probably should have taken a hotel a bit further afield. But I liked the Pullman, I knew the Pullman, so I took a shower, lay on the bed in a big fluffy robe and watched CNBC *Mad Money* and *Closing Bell* until I fell into a deep sleep . . .

I woke just after 5 pm. Now I felt energised and alert and ready to go. I ordered up a cheese, tomato and mushroom omelette and a pot of coffee, and watched CNBC again. I like to eat when I can because you never know what's going to happen in the course of a day.

After my meal, I laid out my camera gear and did a check on my battery charge. The Canon I was travelling with would have looked like a behemoth even ten years earlier, and I would not have used something that big then. But now that everyone had a big camera, they looked much the same to the security people, and the fact that I was using a top-of-the-line professional camera would not have been obvious to most people unless they really knew their cameras. However, I do use a Canon rather than a

Nikon. Nikon is the standard fleet for the military and intelligence agencies of most nations, and the security folks at an airport are more likely to show interest in you if you have a big, serious Nikon.

To the camera I attached my favourite lens, a 70–300 millimetre zoom, which has perfect optics, incredible magnification, and anti-vibration technology. But the thing I like is that the lens doesn't look as hi-spec as it is.

I dressed in my chinos, polo shirt and baseball cap, threw the camera strap over my shoulder and slipped out of the hotel. I wanted to have a look around and see the ground for myself before I had to do the Jenny meeting. So I pulled down my black baseball cap and strolled south, towards the Front Page Bar, to do some perimeters of the area, do surveillance-detection and see who was around and what I might be walking into. Why would I do this almost twenty-four hours before the meeting? Firstly, I like to see the site in advance. And secondly, I could see a pattern that might be absent tomorrow.

If you go into a South East Asian city, you won't see a lot of the Indonesian or Thai versions of CIA or FBI operatives. There'll be a few, and I can often pick them. But in South East Asia, the intelligence services use the hotel system for their intel-gathering. The staff of these places help the security agencies and all across South East Asia, every hotel faxes or emails a list of their guest register to their Interior Minister at 3 pm every day. The hospitality industry in this part of the world works for intel.

I walked for five minutes, just a tourist enjoying the evening light of Jakarta. I strolled down the boulevard over the road from the Front Page, which was a bar-restaurant under a high-rise building. I made notes of where I would set up if I was the one surveilling me, and I took some shots from down low on my hip, shooting at ninety degrees from where my body was facing. On the drive in from the airport I'd used my camera to chuck off maybe thirty or forty 'tourist' pictures of Jakarta so that if anyone wanted to look at my shots, they'd scroll through twenty standard tourism pics and would probably never get to the images of the Front Page Bar.

I watched for staff movements, which wasn't too hard because there were windows that gave me a direct line of sight into the place. I didn't see anything amiss, and by the time I was halfway back to the Pullman I'd calmed down a bit. If Connor was holding something back, well, that was probably his job. I thought about it this way: without the jobs that no one else wants, private contractors wouldn't have work. And I'd chosen the private world so I could also have a family life, right? This was a gift to Liz and I.

I fired up the cappuccino machine in the hotel room and made myself a coffee. Then I got comfortable and thought about my next steps: having made contact with Jenny Warren, I would become her Plus One partner at a Construction Indonesia formal dinner at the Presidential Palace. There'd apparently be a lot of Western construction and banking types at the dinner. It would be a big affair with none of that teetotal garbage they pull at the same events in Dubai or Riyadh.

I was to excuse myself, find the telecoms room which contained the PABX entry point for the palace, and secure the device as per Adam's diagram. The transmitting device connected to the 1046 and 1048 'pair' via red and black crocodile clips and Adam suggested I mount the wireless transmitter behind the phone conduit, not in front.

On the other side of the telecoms room would be a rack of switches and routers, and I had to get the USB sticks into the right slots. The USB plugging had to be done after I'd attached the listening device, because as soon as the USBs were in place, they would activate and fuse all the hard drives. When that went down, I'd want to be back in the hall, innocently smiling at the guards.

Adam and Max had narrowed the telecoms room down to three locations in what was a large palace – which meant the planners didn't have a clue. That was okay. I always do my own proof of concept on these things, anyway, because I can tell you from bitter, painful experience that there is no consolation in being the guy who didn't make the mistake. If you're the guy who could end up in a basement interrogation room, then it's all your fault, all the time. You have to find the time to verify 'facts'. It isn't so different from taking a building contract: the architect says something will work and they have a piece of paper from a city council to prove it. But then they have to go through Mike's proof of concept: I'm the guy who walks the property and second-guesses the architect and shows other builders the plans and then tells the property owner to change them. Not because I'm a smart-arse, but because if the piers are wrong for a sloping property or the roof beams won't work, I don't want to be laying off my employees for four weeks while the whole project is redrafted. That hurts me financially, so I test and I prove. And knowing where the PABX and data lines entered the Presidential Palace was no different.

The part that annoyed me was proving my work. If the technicians couldn't get a signal, I'd have to go back and refit the transmitter. It could be a long night.

There were two features of the mission that anyone in this job would instantly notice; firstly, there was no extraction plan – either a Plan A or Plan B. That made it very deniable for my employers, but it actually didn't concern me too much. I know South East Asia well enough that I like planning my own exfils. If you're really worried about operational security, then you don't want any bastard knowing which door you're going to duck out through.

The other part that grabbed my attention? Bugging the Indonesian President in his own palace. You'd have to be mad or desperate to dream up that one.

7

I woke late, at around 9 am, and thought about my day. My only solid date before the construction dinner at the Presidential Palace was going to be meeting Jenny Warren at the Front Page Bar. I looked forward to it: it was a chance to assess her and see how it was going to go, what I had to watch for. But for now I had some work to do, which was finding that PABX entry point at the palace. The briefing blueprint that narrowed it down to three possible sites wasn't entirely useless. It gave me some starting points.

There was a bus loop over the road from the hotel that went north, up to the whole Merdeka precinct, which included a big park and lots of government buildings. I jumped on a bus, and found the palace tours people operating out of a kiosk on the edge of Merdeka. I paid my money and milled around, making sure my big Canon was fully charged and set up for what I wanted.

The tour started on time and I small-talked and gee-whizzed along with the Americans and Japanese. We walked through the Merdeka Park around the palace, listening to the story of how the area was owned by a rich Dutch dude at the start of the 1800s, but the colonial government bought it from him and converted the palace and grounds into the administrative centre. Since then, Dutch governors-general, Japanese generals and Indonesian presidents had either lived there or ruled from there. The last four or five presidents had lived elsewhere but used the palace for their offices. My impression of the place, when we broke from some trees and walked about 150 metres away from the building, was of a solid colonial structure built long before PABX boxes. I hoped to find it retro-fitted on the side of the building.

The front view of the palace was of a large white portico with about six thick white Doric pillars rising two storeys in front of a large Asian verandah, although the building itself was single-storey. It wasn't unlike the front-on view of the Bondi Pavilion.

We oohed and aahed and I took my shots as I yakked with a very chatty, very funny middle-aged woman from Minnesota. The Canon was wearing the 70–300 millimetre lens so as we walked I pulled in really close on some of the features at the front of the palace and I took the shots, but it was not what I was looking for.

We circled the building, moving in and out of stands of trees, and after some walking I spotted a grey steel box bolted to the side of the palace and almost touching the ground. From under the telecom box extended a conduit about two inches thick, covered in piping. I took my shots, convinced that this was what I was looking for. I must have stood in one place for too long, and perhaps I checked my shots for too long. But when I looked up, the tourist guide was standing beside my right shoulder, looking at the Canon's screen. I jumped a little – I'd been in my own world and just starting to relax with my shots in the can.

'Nice shots of a wall,' said the guide, and right at the point where I was thinking that Indonesian intel was about to swoop and end my vacation, he smiled, slapped me on the bicep and said, 'You builders find it sexy right?'

I thought my heart was going to jump out of my chest. Holy shit. Indonesians like to pull your leg – they're like Australians in that regard – and here was this guy thinking it was funny that an Aussie builder is taking pictures of the palace wall. I was freaked but I stayed on the tour, maintaining a social hubbub which I find helps me build my cover. If nothing else, making friends when you travel is a great prop for surveillance: there's always someone's shoulder to peer over.

I took public transport back to the Pullman and sat at the table in the hotel room and pulled an important piece of kit from my photography case: a screen magnifier that clips onto the back of the camera. You look into the big cupped eyepiece and it optically magnifies whatever is on the camera screen. For me, it means I don't have to travel with a laptop and download my pictures to look at them.

I grabbed a hotel pad and pen, and fitted the magnifier. I scrolled through the shots until I got to the telecom box on the side of the palace. I ran through all the photos: there was a series of about thirty-five. Then I went back, found the closest of the close-ups, and used the Canon system to zoom in to that photo. With the magnifier and the Canon's photo editor working on a shot that I'd already shot with a 300-millimetre zoom, the detail was quite amazing. I was counting bolt heads and I could see tiny scratches in the steel. Then I pulled back until I was looking at the entire eastern side of the palace. I opened the tour brochure, turned to the page with the palace dimensions and saw that it was sixty-five metres deep – which I took as my first measurement as I sketched the palace on the pad. I remembered some of the layout from my briefing notes, and sketched that in too, along with the state room that the dinner would be held in – essentially an interior space with doors leading off every wall. I sketched in the windows as I could see them on my camera, and I placed the PABX box as precisely as I could – about one-third of the way down the eastern wall.

I added in the basics of the internal layout, especially as they related to the state room. And when I sat back and looked at it, I could see two routes to get to that PABX box, and I was very clear about which windows they fell between and their relation to the roof features. Given my photographs, the construction of the building, and the placement of both my dinner venue and the PABX, I was confident I would at least not get lost.

On some of these gigs, you work with a technical crew who give you the tips and the insider view on how to do things. I didn't have a crew, I didn't have insiders, and the notes and diagrams I'd seen were clear but rudimentary. Still, I felt okay about it. Not great, but okay.

8

The bar was a lot like the media ones I've seen in the US: people talking very intensely, drinking quickly and only half-listening to the person speaking.

I looked around briefly and couldn't see Jenny, so I fronted the bar and waited to be served. While I was standing there I realised Jenny was down the other end of the bar, alone, and doing a good job of appearing single and slightly uncomfortable with it. Her sandy-blonde hair was pulled back with a tortoise-shell clip, and she wore a loose-fitting black dress with a little beige jacket thingy. Good looking and not going for skinny. About thirty-eight, I reckoned.

I ordered my drink and moved to the other end of the bar, where I could drag the barman in for a chat. When he wasn't serving I gestured him over and got him talking – man to man – about whether we thought this woman was alone, or was she waiting for someone?

He was a friendly Javanese bloke, about twenty-five, and he instantly followed my drift. He found it funny that there were two Anglo men at a table in the middle of the room who were checking her out. I asked him if he could maybe have a chat with her, find out for me. He moved down the bar, wiping it, and I could see him having a big smile with her. A few minutes later he was back and said, 'She's alone, brother,' and I ordered another beer and gave him a US$5 tip.

'And, oh yeah,' he said. 'She's Australian too.'

The point here is that it's good to make friends with the locals, but it's even better if they remember you in such a way that they can alibi you. If they have to have a chat with the security agents about the big Aussie, they can accurately remember that the Aussie didn't know the woman – 'He asked me to find out if she was alone.'

I sipped on the beer, had a look around and then moved down the bar, giving the barman a *Wish me luck* shrug as I passed his new customer. Jenny saw me coming closer and she gave a perfect act of looking away, not exactly a *Stay away*, but certainly an *I'm not available*.

'G'day,' I said, loud enough so the barman could hear. 'I hear you're an Aussie too?'

'Sure am,' she said, but she didn't turn her body towards me, and she kept her eyes on the drink.

'Business or pleasure?' I asked her, and she smirked, and took a look at me with pale blue eyes. 'Business, with a day of holiday at the end, if I'm lucky.'

'I'm all holiday – I win. Mike, from Melbourne,' I said, extending my hand.

'Jenny,' she said, and we started in on all the small talk that is supposed to bond two Australians when they're overseas. I took her in as she spoke: the defined cheekbones and strong jaw, even teeth and a curvy shape under the dress. She didn't seem uncomfortable about being appraised, in fact I think she was used to it.

I caught a look from the barman and he gave me the knowing smile, and when he turned his attention to a bunch of drinkers at the other end of the bar, I was about to talk and Jenny said, 'Shall we find a seat?'

I found us a table behind a pillar and I had the chance to get my chair up against the wall, where I could see who was coming and going from the place. But I didn't see other spooks coming and going – I saw a lot of male eyes checking her out as she sat in her chair. Besides her looks, she was a highly intelligent person who claimed to be in beef marketing.

'Didn't they shut that down?' I asked.

'Live cattle, yes,' she said. 'Chilled, no. They still like their beefcake up here.'

'Really?'

'You'd know that,' she said, nodding at me. 'Big bloke like you.'

She was trying to put me off balance, the typical approach of female intelligence operators.

So I asked her if she had any questions.

'Are you single?'

'I'm plus-one,' I said. 'We on for the conference soiree?'

'What do you want me to wear?' she asked, and leaned forward at me so I could look down the top of her dress.

'What does the invite say?'

'It doesn't,' she said. 'I can wear whatever I want.'

'What you're wearing is great.' I said. 'You might be a bit hot with the jacket thing.'

I shouldn't have said that because she took off the jacket and what I'd taken for loose-fitting was actually a very low neckline, and I could see her waiting for my eyes to drop. They didn't: disciplined Mike held her gaze.

'Have you done many pair-ups?' I asked, and she shrugged and said, 'I help out when I can. It's what you do, right?'

I relaxed right there. She was a bit flirty but she wasn't a muppet. Walking into the Presidential Palace was going to be casual with her – she wasn't going to pull any Lara Croft.

'The invites say Plus One. So if you can get me on the list tomorrow first thing, that would work well.'

She said, 'Done,' and I went over the cover story: keep it truthful. We met in a bar, we're both Aussies, she needed a date and I'm a construction person. Perfect.

I would normally arrange for a cab to take us to the dinner, but the backstory for me being at the event was that Jenny bumped into an Australian who she got along with and asked to the bash. So for this one I'd meet her on the steps of the palace and we'd go in together.

People in her position don't like to ask it – they don't want to appear scared. So I asked it for her. 'And if I get caught?'

She gave me an inquiring look, as if to say, *Please go on*.

'Let them grab you, don't run, plead innocence, okay? You just met me – you have no idea what's going on.'

Sometimes truth is the best option. Jenny actually didn't know what I was going to do and we had to use that to keep her clear if the crap started.

I gave her the number for my burner phone and she made to stand up. I thought we were finished for the night. I was about to stand too, but she asked if I wanted another Heineken. She was okay, this bird. I had a good feeling – but not too good a feeling. In this business there are many women I work with in many different ways. And many of them are confident, funny, good-looking women of the type that in another time and place I'd have a crack at. We had two more drinks, got to know each other slightly better, and we called it a night.

Then I went back to my room and re-checked my photographs, looking for what I'd missed the first time. I'm always looking, because there's always something.

9

I'd limited my intake to three Heinekens the previous night, so I wasn't technically hungover the next morning but at the hotel restaurant I piled the rockmelon on my plate to take the edge off. I saw a stack of *Asian Wall Street Journal*s and *Jakarta Post*s on a sloping table close to where I was sitting, and as I reached the papers and grabbed the *Journal*, I saw him. A tough, smooth African-American was standing at the maître d' station, pointing around the room, and I knew he was doing what I've done a thousand times: telling the maître d' that he's travelling alone and he'd like to be matched with someone who's also solo, and then heading for their target before the maître d' can answer. I headed back to my table and sure enough, a few seconds later Andrew walked up with the maître d', and before she could say anything, he told me he was travelling alone and did I mind if he joined me. And I did what all humans do and I said, 'Please, be my guest,' and Andrew sat. When the girl had gone, I shook my head and suppressed a chuckle. 'Not following me, are you, mate?'

'Coffee smells good here,' he said, turning over his cup on its saucer and pointing at my pot. 'You mind?'

And that, folks, is how you do it. You want to meet someone in a place like Jakarta or Kuala Lumpur or Saigon, and not alert the hotel workers that you know one another? You set up an 'I'm alone' discussion with the maître d', and before she can assign you to a random singleton, you start walking towards the person you want to meet.

'Pullman's a great hotel, eh?' I said, watching him pour coffee as I picked up a big curved slice of rockmelon and ate it two-handed, like a natural-born true blue Aussie.

He winced. 'Any of that actually going in your mouth?'

'But, I mean, why the Pullman when there's a perfectly good Embassy compound across town?'

Andrew stirred sugar into his coffee, put his hand on his big thigh. 'You were right, Big Unit.'

'About?'

'That Tamil – he's a face. And no good.'

That morning in Sydney seemed a long time ago, though it had only been a few days. He didn't mention the Tamil's security and what I'd done about it.

'So who is he?' I asked.

Andrew looked around and told me the Tamil was Nitish Fernandes, and as soon as I heard that name, I remembered. This was the person Australia's intelligence organisations had been looking for in the wake of a foiled attack on a domestic army base. A number of terrorists from an African Islamist terror organisation had been arrested over the plot to invade the army base with assault rifles and shoot as many army personnel as possible. Fernandes was an organiser and financier who stood between the source of money at al-Qaeda and the offshoot splinters in Somalia and its new Australian affiliate, based in Melbourne. While al-Qaeda was headquartered in places like Afghanistan and Pakistan, the money and middle management was often out of South East Asia.

'He was sitting beside you, Mike,' said Andrew. 'You got it right.'

All I could do was shake my head and let out a very slow *fuuuuc-cckkk*. I reached for my coffee and skolled the thing.

'He's got several aliases,' said Andrew. 'We believe he left Sydney the other day as Rafael Iyengar, on an Indonesian passport.'

I thought about the events: the way the guy had creeped me. I'd *known* he was all wrong and I hadn't acted – I'd let him walk.

'Sorry, mate,' I said. 'I should have jumped on the bloke.'

'No,' said Andrew, laughing. 'You played it just right. Now we have the name he's travelling under and the passport, and we know he's cooking something here. It's okay.'

I poured myself another coffee, furious with Andrew's organisation. They wanted to let Fernandes run, but I'd like him in a glass jar.

'Got something for you,' said Andrew, picking up one of my rockmelon slices.

'I'm in the middle of something right now.'

'After the something?'

I don't like distractions when I'm focused on a gig. And Andrew kind of knew that. So I said, 'I'll be free by Friday – perhaps we could have breakfast?'

'Sounds good to me. They do hash browns here?'

We stood and walked to the buffet, and scooped breakfast onto our plates.

10

The day flew by in a blur and when the late afternoon arrived I pulled out my suit, brushed it down, and put an extra shine on my dark brown shoes. My shirts were freshly ironed and pressed Jermyn Street cotton oxfords, and I unfolded a plain white number with a thin pinstripe and put it on a hanger. Then I unfurled a pale-red silk tie that I'd bought in Spain a number of years earlier. It was a long time ago and I'd only bought it as a cover, to stay close to a subject who was at the shop's counter. Rather than let him move away from me, I'd picked up the first item I could find – a $200 tie – and stood at the counter wondering, *Who the fuck would pay $200 for this?* A strange afternoon in which the object of my surveillance was suddenly snatched from in front of me when the Spanish version of the FBI braced him on the street and led him away. Talk about an anticlimax, and one that had cost me $200. But I ended up loving that piece of silk and it was still my A-game tie.

I've always been a tidy dresser, but during indoctrination into a government agency, they'd given me a grooming and deportment course. The lesson: be so well presented that there is nothing amiss for anyone to notice. I remembered that advice and have always put effort into creating a good first impression. Women get style points for standing out; men are rewarded for blending into the herd.

My burner phone was charging, and the Toshiba laptop was upside down in front of me. I used the tiny screwdriver from my key ring to open the underside panel, and found the device precisely where Adam had told me it would be. I pulled on my cotton photographers' gloves, eased the device from where it had been transported from Sydney and placed it on a new handkerchief I'd laid flat. Adam had told me to test the transmitter's battery by switching it on, and when I did so, the green light came on. The device looked like one of those portable chargers people carry to stop their phones running out of juice. So I left the charger cable from my burner phone in the device, to make it look legit. I switched it off again and, using the handkerchief, I carried it to my suit, and deposited it in the inside pocket of the jacket. Then I picked up the red and black wires with the crocodile clips on either end and twisted each one into a flat loop, and folded them under the turn-up on my trousers. The USBs went on my key ring, right where everyone else puts them.

I had a quick shower and shaved and dressed like a man going on a date with a good-looking woman. Which I was. A glimpse in the mirror told me that I looked like an American presidential candidate.

Then it was 6.30 pm – time to go.

*

The cab pulled up at an area to the side of the Presidential Palace, and my antennae were swinging on full alert. Among the women in cocktail dresses and the men in suits, I could make out Indonesian intel in dark sports jackets and open-necked shirts, prowling the periphery of the social whirl. I got out of the cab and there was Jenny, in a stunning peacock-blue off-the-shoulder silk dress. Her hair was up and I felt pretty special walking over to her and letting her peck me on the cheek.

'So you didn't wear that other dress?' I said, smiling.

'Do I look like a woman who takes fashion tips from a man?' she said. 'I only asked as a test.'

'Did I pass?' I said, looking over her shoulder and counting security.

'You told me I looked great the way I was,' she said, grabbing the crook of my left arm and getting into partner-mode. 'That's a pass.'

I noticed that off to my left, around the side of the big white building, were two black vehicles, one a late-model Land Cruiser with all the big aerials out the top and the run-flat tyres, and behind it a black van, with its side windows heavily tinted to hide the watchers and their cameras who were no doubt sitting in that vehicle. There was a dignitary and his wife shaking hands as everyone filed into the palace – the minister of finance or infrastructure, something like that – and when the factotum whispered in his ear, he smiled at me and said, 'Aaah, Mr Daly.'

And we exchanged pleasantries and I was in. As we reached the top of the front steps, to my right – tucked into the shadows of the massive Graeco-Roman portico – I saw the intel guy who in another time and place would have been me. Hands clasped across his belt buckle, sunglasses still on even though the dusk was almost with us. Aloof, yet very, very active in this whole thing.

I didn't look at him directly, but as we disappeared into this monument to European colonialism, I knew he was looking at me.

11

We were ushered into a very large, 200-year-old hall that could have been a banquet room or a ballroom. It was spacious and impressive, and a little quartet was playing in the corner and lots of grog was being served. I grabbed us a champagne flute each and we clinked glasses as I looked around and got my bearings. This was not the room that Max had estimated we'd be in. And I saw what the problem was; at the northern end of this ballroom I could see a large panel door ajar, and people in white aprons scurrying in and out. We were going to schmooze in this room and eat in the next one. But as I counted back the architectural features on the inside – trying to determine where the telecoms room would be – I realised it was straight through the side wall I was looking at as I spoke with Jenny. A plan started to form: the best way to conceal my movement would be during the schmoozing, and I wouldn't have to be too far from the crowd, which is what would happen if I waited for the sit-down dinner. In these gigs, the central problem is always going to be explaining to the security man why you're in their telecoms room. Closer is better when you're going to rely on, 'Sorry, I thought this was a toilet.'

And now I was closer. I knew my mind was in the gig because I felt excited, not scared.

My first job was to scope the scene, and to do this I asked Jenny to remain in one place as I orbited her slowly. I'd stand there with my champagne, talking, but every time I shifted weight I'd be moving slightly to my right. In three minutes I'd do a full 360 degrees, returning to where I started. The point of this was to familiarise myself with the inside of the place. The circling turned more into a dance, Jenny looking up at me and me able to look over her shoulder at the architecture, the security people and the male eyes staring at the rear-view of my date. We got through to 270 degrees of our surveillance circle and I realised she was touching me, and when I looked down I saw a beautiful woman smirking at me, probably excited by the confusion between sensual and totally uncomfortable.

I smirked in return, and then I stood back. I could bullshit you about how professional I am, but I'm also a one-woman man. Like any bloke, I'm flattered – just not tempted. I got back to my work: the room was twenty metres by twenty-five metres in floor area, with a raised walkway down the eastern side, edged by a small indoor version of the columns at the entry. The western side had a couple of big bi-fold doors that opened into another big state room, and the wall to the north had three wide doors in it, where I could see the waiters and chefs setting up the dinner. I reckoned there were 150 people in that space – they were expecting 200.

There were no obvious security cameras. I even made a big production of looking up into the central chandelier and talking about its grandeur, but I was looking for cameras. None there. The security personnel were a different story. I could see two obvious secret police in the room: one beside the chefs' doors, who had a habit of talking into his cuff. The other was the guy who'd been on the portico when I'd arrived and had come into the room maybe one minute after us. I could tell he was the boss, and he didn't consult his cuff. He kept his hands softly over his belt buckle, and while he was careful not to stare at me, his body language suggested he wanted to know more. This kind of surveillance is fairly standard and is no cause for panic. I'm a big guy who looks like trouble. The way the guy was standing off me, he was waiting to see if I was nervous or self-conscious. In these circumstances you show the watcher the thing that doesn't confirm their bias. He sees a big Aussie who could be a thug; I show him the gregarious bloke who's in Jakarta to have a laugh. But I needed a prop.

I kept up the banter with Jenny and she went with my flow very naturally. My job was to join us with another group, and get the attention off me. There was a gaggle of Americans about two paces from us, and they – having seen my interest in the chandelier – were talking about it too. So I caught the eye of one of the men and, betting the guy was an engineer, said to him, 'You'd need a nice piece of wire rope to hold that thing off the ground.'

'You would,' he said, peering at me, and proceeded to tell me what he thought the light fitting weighed and what he'd specify to hold it securely.

'Mike,' I said as he moved into our group. 'From Australia.'

'Carl, from San Diego,' he said, all smiles and confidence.

I liked this guy but I didn't just want Carl – I wanted the other three Yanks around me too, so I looked over at the remaining Americans and asked the middle-aged woman, 'You with Crazy Carl?'

And she hooted with laughter, 'Well, I'm his wife. Does that count?'

Soon we were all trading names and jokes and they were a good bunch of Americans, so there was a lot of loud calling of the waitress and grabbing of more booze. Ten minutes after I'd lured them over, I noticed that the security boss had moved on to the other side of the room, where he was standing off a couple of very slick-looking young men, waiting to see what kind of nerves they displayed.

With the boss guard gone, I had to make a decision. The Americans told me that the dinner was starting at 7.30, so we'd be sitting down at 7.15. It was just hitting 7 pm and so I had to make the call. Either go now and try to install the devices, and then return to Jenny for the dinner. Or wait to be seated in the dining area and then make my break later on. I leaned towards going now. The original floor layout I'd seen only listed the dining area – but now I was in here, I saw that where I was standing was much closer to the supposed site of the telecoms room. And proximity was an advantage, especially when your only plausible excuse was the lost lavatory.

12

I needed to move the crowd of Aussies and Americans towards the walkway down the side of the room, and more out of luck than good management I got the group adjacent to one of the pillars. Now I was on this side of the room, I leaned against the pillar and had a panoramic view. I told the group I needed to use the bathroom and moved sideways. I ducked into the colonnaded walkway and moved north, and as I approached a colonial wooden door at the end of the walkway, I saw a waitress near me and asked her, 'Is this the way to the toilet?'

She didn't understand properly and I thanked her anyway and pushed through the door. As I closed it behind me, I could feel my heart beating in my chest. It doesn't matter how many times you do this work, there is always a fear of the unknown, a fear of what happens if you're caught and can't fight your way out.

I breathed deeply, listening, and all I could hear was kitchen clanging and yelling from further down the hallway. People in white moved about but they paid me little attention. In the other direction, a dark corridor ran parallel to the wall against which the colonnade was situated in the state room. I walked down this dimly lit hall, noting four doors made of dark mahogany with brass colonial doorknobs.

I opened the first door and I stared into the gloom. It was now almost dark outside and from the small amount of light I could see it was a very small office with files stacked on a small desk. I backed out and moved to the next door. Locked, with a deadbolt. In the reverse side of my RM Williams belt buckle there were two flat steel spindles that I could use to jimmy that lock. But I didn't even know what was on the other side, so I went to the next door, and tried it. It opened easily, and as I pushed my head inside, I knew I was there. My briefers had assured me there was no security camera in this room, but I trusted my paranoia more than their touching display of certainty, so I didn't turn on the lights. If there was a camera in here, it would have to be infrared to get a good look at me.

The PABX system was in a cabinet against the outside wall. I began to move into the room, and as I did so I heard the sound of 200 delegates roaring into the quiet space of the hallway, and the light spilled in too. I ducked inside the telecoms room, and as I pulled back my head the security boss's face emerged from the door into the stateroom and slowly turned to look my way. I got my head in and shut the door, my heart pounding heavily. I had to control my breathing. I was trapped in a place that, realistically, I could not explain my way out of. If the security man caught me in here, I'd either have to cop it, or use my considerable experience – and size advantage – to hurt him and dispossess him of his gun. But then what? They'd put on a manhunt for me and once they'd finished kicking the shit out of me and torturing me, I'd do twenty years in an Indonesian prison. I know, I know: hadn't I thought about that before I took the gig? I always think about it, believe me. The same way I understand that there is a real chance that if I use a Skilsaw on a roof enough times, one day I'll slip and take off my finger. But just knowing the possibility wouldn't keep me off the roof.

So I'm standing in a dark room, in the Presidential Palace, about to be busted. At times like this you have to keep breathing, and thinking. You stop doing either of those things and the chances of disaster increase. I looked around. I could see in the darkness a stack of routers and switches in a rack against a side wall. I thought about hiding under the rack, but then I heard the creak of floorboards, and the rattling of a hand on a doorknob, one door away. Fuck – he was close. But then I thought, the lock! In the darkness I found the doorknob and it had a twist-turn locking mechanism on it. I gripped it and turned – *gently* – and breathed out slowly through my nose as the footsteps creaked to a stop outside the door and the knob rattled. I thought my heart was going to bang out of my ribcage. Standing there, less than a metre away from the security guy, I was convinced he was coming in and I'd have to kill him. As I prepped for what I was going to do, the security guy seemed to be satisfied that the room was locked, because he stopped rattling the knob and moved to the next door.

I breathed out long and hard, swearing to myself I wouldn't do a gig like this again. Let the wide-eyed twenty-six year olds do it – what the fuck was I doing trapped like a rat in a cage, praying for Indonesian intel to walk away? Those feet moved down the hallway again, and I think the guy started whistling. Me? I was panting for air, my forehead wet, and I felt myself drifting into existential questions. I pulled myself back, fast. You need a reset switch if you do this job. We all have emotions, and fear comes to all of us. The long-timers in my business know how to go through it, contain it and then pack it away when the threat is gone. You have to find a way, because if you let fear mess with you too much, you make bad decisions. When I heard the door at the end of the passage open and the roars flood in, and then the door shut again, I swallowed the adrenaline down a dry throat and wiped the sweat off my brow with my suit sleeve.

I went back to work. Opening my flip-top burner phone, I aimed the lit-up screen at the PABX cabinet – a three-foot-tall beige steel cabinet mounted about a foot off the floor. It was locked. Putting the phone on the floor and aiming the light at the lock, I fished the spindles from the back of my belt buckle and jimmied it. Then I reached inside my suit jacket and pulled out my handkerchief, using it to pull down the chrome handle that opened the cabinet. If someone pulls you up at the airport to ask a few searching questions, it pays to have no fingerprints on the scene that you know nothing about.

There were several blinking boxes in that PABX cabinet, and down the back of it – running vertically – were twenty-five or thirty telecom cables. I picked up the burner phone and shone its light on the cables: they were either blue or yellow, and each one had letters and numbers printed on a soft plastic tag that was wound around it like electrical tape. I pushed at them, trying to get a good view, and found the pair called 1046 and 1048. They were side by side and didn't include the word *Presiden*, although at the end of the numbers was a *P*.

I used the handkerchief to fish the red and black wires from my pants cuff, and put them on the floor of the cabinet. Then I brought out the transmitter device with my handkerchief, turned it on and verified the green light. Now I put the device on the floor of the cabinet and carefully attached the crocodile clips to the loops on the end of it. Then, picking it up with the handkerchief, I hid the device behind the bank of vertical lines so it was standing on its end, leaning against the back wall of the PABX cabinet. Now I pushed back the 1046 and 1048 lines slightly, to give a bit of cover to the crocodile clips, which I clipped onto the two lines.

I shut the cabinet door with my hanky and re-locked the door with my spindles. I stowed them in the slots behind my buckle and moved to the data system. In front of me were two nineteen-inch racks, each loaded with servers and switches and routers, and one of the racks was buzzing and blipping with mainly green lights. At the rear of both racks were thick braids of blue fibre-optic cabling which rose vertically up the wall and disappeared into the ceiling panels. About halfway down the blinking server rack was a slide-out shelf, which I pulled out. It looked like a laptop computer, but my main concern was giving myself access to the server above it and the USB plugs facing the wall. I was going to plant my USB plug in the rear of the servers so that at first glance, no one would see it. I reached up and around the back of the machine until I felt the vertical USB slots, and I pushed the first pink USB drive into one.

On the laptop screen, an icon came up. I double-clicked it open and hit the return button. Then I pushed the laptop component back flush with the rest of the rack and went to the neighbouring rack, pulling out its laptop. I paused, took a breath and had a look at my watch: I'd been in the 'toilet' for four and half minutes. I had to get back. So I reached up and around and plunged the second pink USB into the rear slot of the server above, hit return on the icon, and pushed the laptop back into its housing.

I closed my phone, moved to the door, and breathed out deeply. Then I opened the door: all quiet. I slipped out, snibbing the lock as I left, and wiped the inner and outer doorknobs with my handkerchief.

I put a big smile on my face as I slipped back into the party, easy now because some of the drinkers had moved onto the interior walkway and masked me as I came back into the room. The Americans had a drink waiting for me when I rejoined them, and Carl's wife raised her glass.

'To construction,' she toasted, and threw down half the glass in one shot.

'I'll drink to that,' I said, winking at Jenny. I was all smiles and I had a killer thirst. But I'd aged ten years.

13

Like Tom Petty says, the waiting is the hardest part. The organisers herded us to the dining area at the allotted time, and seated us in groups at round tables. It was lucky for me that Carl and his wife weren't seated with us because those two had a good old-fashioned American thirst and the missus was already talking about dragging Jenny and I along for a big night at a disco she knew of. I like a disco, and a lot of grog, but not when I'm working. The adrenaline let-down had already enticed me into two fast drinks, and now I was going with the sparkling water.

A speaker got on stage and the lights went down. He introduced himself as the MC and I felt the cold trickle of sweat down my back, sitting there in the dark and wanting to make a run for it. In the five minutes after I'd left that telecoms room, the pink USB would have burned out the first server rack, cutting the internet lines to the palace. The redundant second rack would have been brought online as soon as the first one failed, and as soon as it was booted up (probably remotely), the pink USB in that system would have disabled the internet in that system.

With the data lines down, the communicating parties would switch to the phone lines, and as they did so, the signals would be transmitted to the surveillance vans of another private contractor just like me.

And while all this was going on, I was supposed to keep the smile on my face. I dared not run for fear of drawing suspicion on me and Jenny, yet I also knew that a government IT person was going to come down to that telecom room at some point in the next half hour, and if they poked around enough they'd discover sabotage.

It's a fine line, by the way. Don't think that because I've done these gigs many times that the stress and nerves don't pile up on me. They do. The human in all of us wants to run, to avoid being trapped and hurt. But the professional knows that to race for the exits is like putting a target on your back. It's actually better to stay in character and bluff it out to the end, than to panic. If some parts of your cover are 'true' – a correct name, a real passport, a real profession – then being caught isn't always so bad. But to run is to give it all away.

For me, it was double-whammy nerves: if that device wasn't transmitting, I wasn't going anywhere. My job was to go back in and make it work. And my gut churned at that thought. I'd already blown my mainline of adrenaline with that security boss checking the doors. I was spent.

The speaker droned on and I found that when I leaned forward slightly, into the downward blast of the air-conditioning, the sweat down my back dried up. I was feeling better, but when the first guest speaker came on stage with his laptop and wanted to present something on the big screen, there was a problem. He turned and looked at the organiser, then shrugged and looked back at the screen of his computer. As an IT type was called onto the stage, I heard the speaker say, 'It's in the cloud – I can't connect.'

Okay, so when the internet goes down, there's no cloud. Now the sweat started down my back again. Around me, people chatted about the technology problem and I nodded at others at my table as if to say 'Fucking internet', but I was freaking out. The briefing in Australia had insisted that the first response to a data interruption at the Presidential Palace would be technical services, not intel. Indonesian intel would apparently become involved if they found evidence of phone intercepts or if the IT people found sabotage. And I hoped that they wouldn't find the two USBs until the day shift came through and inspected the whole thing.

The burner phone buzzed in my pocket, and looking down I saw the words, *Your pizza is ready*.

I felt my shoulders relax and I gave Jenny a smile. The thing had worked, so I'd get my bonus, and I felt $20,000 richer than I had ten seconds ago. But I still had to wait and worry. As I started squirming in my seat, wondering what would happen next, the guy with the laptop pulled a smartphone from his pocket and obviously set it up as a wi-fi hotspot, because just as quickly as they appeared, the support people were gone and the speaker started his presentation, something to do with economic multipliers from building transport infrastructure. I was happy for the reprieve, and I made myself breath out slowly through my mouth, staying in character with Jenny and the rest of the table. But mostly I didn't dare to turn around and look for that security boss. All eyes were on the speaker, but I sensed the security man's eyes on me.

14

The evening wound up at 9.30 pm and we were thanked as we left. By now I had a litre of fluid in my shoes from the bullets I was sweating. We moved out into the night, which was warm compared to the air-conditioned palace. Off to the right of the entrance portico was a bunch of cabs lined up for the guests and I helped Jenny into one and we drove south, into the area of expats and consular types.

'Hope it all went well,' she said, in character for the driver. 'Anything of use?'

'Infrastructure is good for everyone,' I said, my stomach tight and my throat a little dry. 'Especially the bankers. What about you?'

'I wanted to hear what that Canadian had to say about private tollways,' she said. 'You know, creating a benefit to the community and a return to the investors.'

We yakked and she was good at dropping enough information to the driver that if he was intel – and he probably was – he would report that by the sounds of the conversation the two Aussies had met in Jakarta and she had needed a date because Indonesians were suspicious about women venturing out alone. He'd be able to report that we spoke about infrastructure and construction and bored him senseless. I quietly thanked Jenny for that. Covers come undone because people miss the details, like talking in front of cabbies. Jenny didn't miss the details.

Jenny had a car she'd left in the car park of the Mandarin Oriental hotel, so I dropped her there, the driver having to line up on the under-car camera pad that sits in the drop-off apron out the front. I got out too and she gave me a quick hug and a peck on the cheek, and whispered, 'Be careful Mike,' and for a moment I felt her grip on my arms lingering longer than it should: she was giving me the opportunity to take the opportunity. But I didn't.

'Good night,' I said, like a brother, and she was gone, into the foyer of the Mandarin.

I got back in the cab, thinking through where or how I could be pinged. I'm cursed with paranoia because I have worked in government intel and *I* know what *I'd* be doing about me. If a data line goes down and people have to use phones and faxes, that's not considered a 'risk' in the IT manuals. But intelligence people are not IT people; intel people are nosy, suspicious, cunning bastards like me. And if that security boss had poked around in that telecom room, and pulled out the servers and looked at the USB slots, he'd have hit the alarm button. And, along with those yuppies he was checking out, he'd have come after me. As far as I knew, the security guy might be doing exactly that right at that moment. I hardly felt safe.

I had the cabbie drop me at the Front Page Bar, not only to avoid showing the driver where I was staying but also to continue my cover. If the security police wanted to have a chat about why I was at the Front Page Bar when I met Jenny, it would be easier to stick with the truth: the Front Page is a Western-style bar, close to my hotel, that serves Aussie beers and Bundy.

I paid the cabbie in local currency and tipped him. 'Well, that was a waste of four good hours,' I told him with a wink. 'But what can you do if a pretty woman asks you on a date?'

The cabbie was all smiles at that one. I gave him a wink and got out of the car. I scanned the area as the cab sped away and I was pretty sure the dark Nissan Maxima at the kerb, 100 metres away, had two people in the front seat. I didn't stare and I didn't dwell. I turned and walked into the bar. I wanted to run for the airport but I wasn't going to.

I pushed through to the bar and was served by the same barman who was there when I met Jenny. 'Crownie,' I said, pointing at the Aussie beers in the fridge behind him.

'How's your friend?' asked the barman, as he poured my beer from the bottle.

'She's a great girl,' I said, smiling and taking a much-needed mouthful of beer. 'But she's out of my league.'

'She looked so friendly,' he said, giving me the knowing grin.

I raised my glass at him. 'Here's to keeping it friendly,' I said, and drained the glass in two big gulps.

CODE ROUGE

1

I was halfway through my second Crown Lager and was considering a shot of Bundy when I sensed something out of pattern from the corner of my eye. Two non-Indonesian men had just walked into the bar and I had them as 'government' before they were even fully in the room.

I didn't look at them, but one came to the bar while the other peeled off. I allowed myself a quick glance to my left and almost spluttered on my drink. It was Andrew. He didn't look at me, which is the professional courtesy signal not to acknowledge. You bump into someone you know in our world, in a public place, and you hold back on your greetings – and especially on giving them a name – until you both signal it's okay. Andrew ignored me so I ignored him. I glanced over my shoulder and could see the other man – a tall white dude in his early forties – taking a table. He looked government-issue: beige chinos, white polo shirt and Timberland boat shoes. If he was wearing a U-Boat watch then I'd bet money he was intel of some kind.

Andrew ordered two Heinekens, paid and left, and when he was gone there was a beer coaster beside my left elbow. I slid it in front of me and waited until I was ordering another beer, then I flipped it while the barman's back was turned, and it said, *car 2300*.

The cheeky bugger – he knew I'd made their Maxima.

Looking at my watch I saw I had twenty minutes, so I finally took the weight off my feet, sat on one of the bar stools and resigned myself to a night of stress. When I drink at the bar, I often don't sit. I prefer to stand. It gives me more options. But with Andrew and his mate now riding shotgun, I let the pent-up air run out of me and gave my knotted muscles some time off. If shit started, I'd let Andrew deal with it. Fuck, I was tired, and I suspected my night had just started.

I left the bar at five to eleven and strolled away southbound, doing some basic surveillance-detection. Just because Andrew was tailing me didn't mean Indonesian intel weren't tailing him. It looked clean, though, and I turned and walked north on the wide footpath until I came adjacent with the Nissan, which was conveniently parked with some shadow cover from the overhead trees. I ducked onto the nature strip, in the darkness, and waited for Andrew and his friend to amble towards the car.

Andrew hit the key lock and the lights flashed, the locks disarmed, and he said, 'You wanna take a ride?'

I said, 'Who's your friend?'

Andrew opened the driver's door. 'He's with me – you coming?'

As I got to the rear passenger door, I saw the other guy up close. Slightly taller than me but not as heavily built. He had pale eyes and a wide face, with thinning blond hair brushed back on his head. He looked me in the eye and I looked back. If I was forced to take this guy, I'd have to kill him. And I guess he saw that in me too.

Oh, and he had a big, chunky stainless steel U-Boat. Definitely intelligence.

We drove through Jakarta, and after a couple of minutes I could see we were going north. Andrew kept it light, told me that he'd been busy with some things, and he introduced me to Sam, who didn't shake hands but waved.

We got to an area of North Jakarta known as Ancol, where the harbour opens into the Java Sea, giving maritime access to Sumatra and Singapore and the South China Sea. It's a place of theme parks and resorts and public beaches. There's also a famous cemetery where those executed by the Japanese in World War II were buried after they were reinterred from the mass graves. Andrew parked at a harbourside beach. A few drunk tourists floated around and some locals walked their dogs. Enough action for us to be unexceptional.

Andrew looked back at me. 'Sam has something to discuss with you.'

Then Andrew got out of the car, checked his phone, and went for a walk.

I sat back and watched the passing parade of tourists, keeping my annoyance to myself. If you want to be in this profession, you accept that you only have a licence to operate because you play by the rules. There are many rules, but the one you wouldn't know from watching spy movies is that the pecking order is real, and when a person with seniority starts talking, you shut up and listen. Yep, it's a bit old-fashioned, but the entire world runs on that rule.

Sam was obviously senior, by the way Andrew had to leave the car. He turned and looked at me. 'Andrew says you're a good operator.'

I shrugged.

'I like the way you played Fernandes,' he went on. 'We've been looking for him for a while. Now we have a tag on him.'

'You're welcome,' I said, not telling him that certain elements of the Australian special forces community would probably want a very different kind of tag on him, given that Fernandes's plot targeted an important military base.

Sam didn't take his eyes off me. 'I have a job for you, if you're interested.'

I looked out the window, where the famous harbour lapped and twinkled in all the city's lights.

'I need someone in Cambodia for a week, no more than ten days,' said Sam. 'It's a four-man team – I need an experienced guy.'

I didn't leap at it. I wanted to hear the brief but I also knew he wouldn't divulge much until I was committed.

'Pay is $50,000 US for the week, with $40,000 success payment. There's also $10,000 per day if you go over seven days. You'll be paid half up-front, the balance on completion.'

'Expenses?' I said.

'Anything reasonable,' he said. 'But I won't pay a bar bill or any of that crap.'

'What's the gig?' I asked.

'A snatch, but no one dies,' said Sam, now looking me in the eye. 'Your turn. You in?'

'When does it get done?' I asked.

'Before next weekend,' he said.

There was a big pregnant silence, because we were in Jakarta on a Thursday night. He was talking about an eight-day turnaround if I left for the airport right now.

'You got paperwork?' I asked, thinking, *What the hell?* and he said there was no contract. I could see Andrew having a cigarette over by a railing beside the promenade, and really I should have said no to the whole thing. Andrew was the Judas goat, the trusted one who had led me to Sam. As long as I could see Andrew in the picture – who knew nothing – then Sam thought I'd take the $25K up-front and work dark. And, in spite of my misgivings, he was right.

I accepted, and now Sam did shake my hand. And his eyes bore into me. You sign on to a gig with a man like Sam, and he shakes your hand, you're *his* guy. That's your loop, that's your indoctrination, and everyone else can get fucked. If Jesus himself called me into a room and asked about the Cambodia gig, the answer would be, *I'm not at liberty*. If you can't do that, you don't work again.

Sam gave me an address to be at the next day, and he tapped the car horn. Andrew flicked the cigarette and came back. I was back working for a foreign government, but I wasn't totally comfortable and I had a stipulation of my own. 'I need to get out of this country in one piece, can you do that?'

Finally Sam smiled. 'I'll see what I can do.'

*

The address was a low-rise grouping of professional office suites, in the precinct behind a major retail mall in north-western Jakarta. It was so unremarkable that it might have been designed by intelligence agency architects purely for the purpose of hosting front companies and anonymous meeting rooms. I was greeted by a receptionist in front of a bullshit sign and logo declaring something to do with customs clearing and freight forwarding. She ushered me into an internal room with white walls, decorated with Howard Johnson art and a flat-screen TV.

There was a teleconference box in the middle of the table, with a camera sticking out of it. The woman pointed at the camera and then leaned over and input a code. A male voice barked back, and she said, 'Guest is here,' and left the room.

Sam's face appeared on the screen and in a tiny box on the bottom right I could see my head and shoulders too.

'We all here?' said Sam, and I said yep, and there was a flurry of other affirmations. I noticed that the four of us listening in could only see Sam, not each other. He flicked the photographs of us on the screen, for just four or five seconds each, but didn't record our names. It was like, *This is the team, this is what you look like, don't ask any questions.* Not really team-building of the type they do in the corporate world: no white-water rafting, no 'Kumbaya'.

Sam went straight into the briefing. It was bare bones, of the type I actually prefer: a Thai gangster with nightclub, prostitution and gambling operations in Phnom Penh needed to be grabbed and dragged, and deposited – alive – at a freight depot on the outskirts of the Cambodian capital. Let's call him 'Chan'. Another team not known to any of us would be at the drop point: the leader would say, *Did you see the Red Wings on TV?* and one of us was to reply, *The Leafs need a new goalie.*

The job was to deliver Chan unhurt. Once he was in the freight depot, my team's job was done. We had open return tickets into and out of Phnom Penh. Sam had the address of a premises that Chan owned in Phnom Penh, and apparently frequented every day. And that was the only lead. Our job was to find the best way to do it. There was one other thing. We were all staying in the same hotel. That wasn't ideal, but by now it was clear I was not being asked for an opinion.

2

My flight out of Jakarta landed on time at Bangkok International and I spent a little under two hours wandering the massive light-filled concourses, looking for tails. I was dressed in my tourist gear – polo shirt, jeans, cap, backpack and wheelie cabin bag – and I carried my Canon D series on my shoulder. Just a tourist with a flash camera.

I ordered a coffee at a café and sat with my back against the wall. I wasn't entirely happy with the gig: for a start, I didn't know Sam and we hadn't nailed down his employer. Andrew wasn't saying. I also had a slight problem with the mission: kidnap a Thai national in Cambodia. Why Cambodia? What had he done? He was a bad person, I was assured.

There was also the issue of the duration: I was coming into a South East Asian city to kidnap a person, and I had essentially one week to do it and get clear. Two weeks is normal for this work because you need enough surveillance to establish pattern of life before you crash in and commit a crime. You have to know how a society works before you subvert it. There was a crew of four of us – none of whom had worked together – and to cap it off, the venue for this gig was trouble with a capital T: Phnom Penh, the place where overly confident Westerners go to be turned into pig food.

There were familiar aspects to it. Having a four-man team – rather than a six- or ten-man team – kept things low-key and made it easier to blend in. As long as everyone was in character as a tourist, we could get away with four.

Sitting there in Bangkok, waiting for my flight north, I was probably overthinking the negatives. On the plus side, I'd said yes because it was paying US$90,000. Hey, don't judge: that's a good earn. How long would I have to work to make that kind of income in the tradie world?

But if I was honest, it was also because the job was through Andrew and his government. I felt I owed his country a lot, certainly enough to feel it was time to top up. And I owed Andrew, who had mentored me and given me a great safety net when I needed it.

However, as a general rule I like to run the gig. So when I'd asked Sam in the car who was running the show, and he said, 'No one – you'll work off Slim,' I knew the leadership was being split. And I didn't like it, but by then I was basically in.

Lastly, and most crucial, was my name. I always endeavour to operate with my own passport. It's easier to be doing something dodgy behind the real you than it is to be doing something dodgy behind an invented identity. Fabricated identities just complicate matters, in my opinion. So I was more than annoyed that I was travelling into Cambodia on a fake passport under an assumed name. I didn't even have a say in the matter: when the teleconference in Jakarta wrapped up, the woman had handed me an envelope and asked me to open it. And inside was a New Zealand passport in the name of HARRIS: Martin, David. And my face peered out from the picture page.

That meant I'd have to fly back through Indonesia and fly out as Mike Daly. I was very unhappy with the arrangement not only because it goes against one of my op-sec rules but because it was making me nervy, the worst way to start a gig.

My flight was called and I gulped my coffee, stood and joined the river of humanity that flows around that airport. At least the air-con worked – this was the new Bangkok International; the old airport relied on ceiling fans, and a couple of hours in that place just before the monsoon was like walking around in a steam bath – a steam bath in which every bastard is chain-smoking.

I moved into one of the departure wings for Bangkok Airways, and as I walked past an airline service desk, I noticed a small movement behind the striped-mirror glass in the door that leads out the back. I didn't look for more than half a second, but peering through one of the non-mirror strips – from the other side – was a pair of dark eyes.

I kept walking, but when I hit the boarding queue and digested the last forty-eight hours, I didn't like how it stacked: if an agency needs something done, and they're rushing you, there's not much you can do. It's never personal. But when you're about to go into Cambodia to kidnap a major criminal, and you're being surveilled by the airline's staff, then you're wondering what the gig is really about and how much you're not being told.

As even the young players know, this would be the moment when you bail out. Of course you would, unless you do it for a living. Unless you're me.

3

I got to the Best Western River Palace on Friday afternoon, around 3.30 pm. It was a colonial building, converted by the American hotel chain, and it sat beside a secondary river that flows into the Mekong. I hadn't chosen the hotel but I was glad Sam had gone with Best Western because it was used by mid-level tourists and small business owners, so it has high throughput, and a bunch of Westerners staying for a week wouldn't arouse suspicion.

First points to Sam. I checked in, went up to my room and emptied the contents of my backpack onto the bed. There were three prepaid phone packages I'd bought at the airport and I plugged two of them into the power socket and charged them. I opened and activated the third, an LG flip phone. I was tempted to call Liz, but dismissed that urge. I'd already called her from a payphone in Jakarta, but I'd had to leave a voice mail. There was no way I was going to make an international call from Cambodia, even from a newly-bought burner phone. The assumption you have to make in South East Asia and the Middle East is that your international calls are monitored. You have to be especially alert to this assumption in the first hours you're in-country, when the watchers might just be checking to see who receives the first five or six international calls you make. If there's no action, they're unlikely to assign a team to you.

It was just before 3 pm when I'd checked in, so the security police would see a name on the hotel register, and if they ran it through a database I hoped to hell Sam's agency had done a thorough job on the passport and it was legit. I'd know by early evening.

I took a shower and hit the hay. I was tired and I still expected some blowback from the Jakarta job. The Indonesian intelligence services have no qualms about operating in other South East Asian countries. If they fingered me for the palace job, and they knew I was in Cambodia, they'd make some kind of approach.

I woke around 6 pm, washed my face and went downstairs to eat. I had a quick look in the restaurant – which featured a very useful set of internal mirrored pillars – and all I could see was an Indian family and two Western couples, having dinner early. No large male singletons, so I ducked into the bar, around the corner. It was an eccentric room with a coffee machine on the bar and a karaoke stage down the side. I was alone save for a strongly-built, dark-haired Anglo, maybe five years my junior, who was standing at the bar with a beer.

I recognised him from the teleconference. This was 'Slim'.

'Shit,' I said, fronting the bar and nodding at his beer. 'That looks good enough to drink.'

The bloke smiled and the barman asked what he could get me and I went for a Tiger from the tap. It was a perfect set-up because the meeting was random and would seem that way to the barman. Remember, barmen see patrons walk in a hundred times a day and they know the difference between people who know each other and people who don't.

I made small talk about the city and the weather and he got straight in character and asked me if I'd seen the river from the hotel. I said my room faced the other way, and he said, 'Check this out,' and I smiled at the barman, grabbed my beer and followed my new best American friend to the end of the rainbow-coloured bar, with its karaoke stage down the side.

At the end of the room, Slim pushed aside the sheer drapes and we were looking over the river.

'Tonle Sap,' he said, nodding at the river. 'It connects to that incredible lake, up in wild west country.'

'Khmer Rouge land,' I said, shrugging. 'All touristy now. Nice up there this time of year.'

'Get a houseboat, go touring around,' said Slim. 'Very nice. Not unlike Lake Michigan in summer.'

We were keeping it light for the audience but this was a tough and mean country with a really violent history. The Cambodian Communists – the Khmer Rouge – took over Cambodia in 1975, changed the country's name to Kampuchea, and turned the nation into a genocidal detention camp until 1979. They eliminated money, markets, private property and schools, and they shifted everyone they didn't execute into agricultural labour camps. Between the camps and the executions, the Khmer Rouge killed around two million people in four years. When the Khmer Rouge was defeated by the Vietnamese army in 1979, the country ended up with a power-sharing government but a lot of the genocidal KR leaders based themselves in north-western Cambodia and over the border in Thailand. These days, that same area was a big tourism money-spinner for Cambodia, but I'd worked in northern Cambodia in the late 1990s when it was still wild and crazy-violent. Back then my employers were establishing links between Indochinese drug lords and Western Sydney terrorist cells, and I'd spent some quality weeks infiltrating villages where slavery never went out of style. Times were different now, and I backed Cambodia as a country of the future. But even just making small talk about travelling upriver made my skin crawl.

The barman ducked down behind his bar and did something noisy, and I said, 'Martin.'

And the new American friend replied, 'Slim.'

We took a table by the window. 'I got in this morning, had a look around,' said Slim. He was wearing a Columbia outdoor shirt and a pair of loose cargo shorts. All nondescript and baggy but I could see he was muscly and strong – with the dark hair and tanned skin he looked like the American swimmer, Michael Phelps.

'You see the subject?'

Slim sipped. 'Yep, he's not exactly hiding.'

'At this bar that Sam briefed on?'

'It's a bar and strip joint and probably a whorehouse too,' said Slim, no trace of judgement. 'He stayed eighty, ninety minutes, and was gone.'

'Security?'

Slim shook his head slowly. 'There's one dude who accompanies him, a driver, but he's not muscle.'

I drank, keeping the body language friendly. 'I'll have a look tomorrow, see if we're being watched.'

'Sam said you're op-sec,' said Slim, and cut off as the barman approached. 'But the Land Cruiser rentals are fairly expensive for the insurance excess when you work it all out – the guided tours probably work out slightly more expensive, but they give you better deals on your hotels.'

'G'day, Wak,' I said, looking at the barman's name tag. 'What do you reckon? Would you recommend renting a Land Cruiser, driving myself around Tonle Sap Lake? Or go with a tour?'

Wak beamed. 'Tour guide very good, mister. But you drive yourself too, no problem. You need the boat? Ask me, I help.'

'I can see some of those river dolphins up there, can't I?'

'Yes, mister,' enthused Wak. 'So beautiful.'

We ordered another round and I asked Wak if we needed to book for dinner. He said we could book with him, and I said, 'Make it a table for two,' and as I did I held out my hand to Slim.

'Sure,' said Slim, staying with the story. 'I'm travelling alone but I prefer to eat with company.'

We stayed in the restaurant for around an hour, and went through the basics. My job was to do surveillance-detection on Chan. Slim wasn't so concerned that we'd be made – he was worried that a well-known gangster could easily have enemies casing him or have his own security crews standing off where we couldn't see them.

He named the two other operators: Rider, an Australian former SWAT cop responsible for the operational requirements: weapons, body bags, zip-ties, etc. He was already in-country and staying at the hotel.

The second, Altron, was expected that evening. He was an American analytics person from a military background who would assess all the photographs and maps, put together the patterns of life and any other ground intelligence, and make a plan. He'd start this with a pad and pen, from day one, and it would grow and develop so that by the time we were ready to do the gig, it would look like a business plan – or an investment proposal – and every person would know their parts in it.

That left Slim, whose role was to keep the higher-level view of the thing, allowing the rest of us to burrow down and be very specific about what we were doing. He would have the numbers for our burner phones and by keeping the higher view would be best placed to suggest when to say 'Go' – possibly the most crucial skill in these gigs and one that you only develop with experience. I'm usually the higher-view person in my gigs, not just because that's where I prefer to be, but because that's where employers see my effectiveness. I do the same thing on my building sites: I'm the eagle *and* the mouse. Not everyone can do that, but I can. On this job, though, I'd be the mouse, and I really wasn't sure how I felt about it.

4

There were three parts to the Chan routine, according to Slim and Rider, who ate breakfast with me in the hotel restaurant. Altron was having breakfast alone – an op-sec suggestion of mine. He seemed a bit older than the rest of us, which was perhaps an illusion because his thinning red hair had been shaved down to a chrome dome, giving him a very pale look that didn't really say 'tourist'. I wanted him to be included by us in a dramatic show of travellers suggesting a solo traveller join them for lunch or dinner. If we took the time to set up the illusion now, it would be worth the benefits if the security police came a'sniffing. But for now, only the three of us ate together.

The first part of Chan's routine was his hotel – the Raffles Hotel le Royal – closer to the central business district than we were. He left his hotel every morning at 10 am, and stayed at his bar and strip club for about ninety minutes. This was the second part of his routine. The third was that in the afternoon, around 3 pm, he was driven downtown, where he walked through the Central Market.

Our job was to find the best point at which to kidnap Chan without being made. Second, we had to ship him to the warehouse, without being made. And third, we had to extract ourselves from this country without being stopped or arrested.

A lot of the operation relied on whether we were being watched, and I suggested that we limit our public meetings to one a day, and, after our showy display of inviting Altron to eat with the rest of us to set up our 'travellers together' story, only ever three of us – not the full four – would socialise together. Secondly, I suggested that to keep our profile low, we have operational meetings in the biggest of the rooms. That was Altron's, as he was travelling as a business consultant and had a room twice the size of any of ours.

We arranged for the dinner that night to start with the three of us and then grow to four. I excused myself and, having loaded up with my camera and a bottle of water, I caught a cab across town to the Raffles Hotel le Royal. I wasn't expecting anything, really; I just wanted to see where he left from every morning, where he went to, and who was watching him when he did it. There was a small park over the road from the grand entrance of the Raffles, with some trees that gave shade. I slipped into those trees and had a wander, satisfying myself that there was no surveillance of the hotel entry. I waited for around twenty-five minutes on a park bench with a nice line of sight for my camera work. According to Slim and Rider, Chan was driven around in a black S-Class Mercedes with little evidence of muscle or security. I was interested in that, and at around 10.30, a black Mercedes rolled to the entrance, and a compact Thai man – about forty – danced down the front steps to where the driver was waiting with the back door opened. I had a good frame and good light so I took a few shots, and stood and walked to the kerb, where I hailed a cab, a yellow Toyota Camry.

We motored along, about ten car-lengths off the Mercedes's tail, and I decided not to tell the driver to follow the black car. We stayed far enough off his tail that I had a good view of the area and I made the driver get closer to the Merc, and to back off. I got him into different lanes and really worked all the angles for a tail. All the time, I'm talking about the beautiful temples and the colonial buildings and the profusion of street-trading, and the cabbie is talking back with great pride and no English, and this is giving me cover for firing off a few pictures on the Canon. Mostly, I went for shots of the number plate, and side shots of the Merc when the car turned into a cross street. You don't always get the full facial shots but you get profiles, which are useful in their own way. I was also picking up route shots – pictures that, when we put them together, can be analysed for choke points and handy cross streets.

By the time we were in the neighbourhood where Chan's nightspot was situated, my conclusion went along with my initial instincts: there were no signs of tails on Chan's movement from the hotel.

I paid the taxi driver and settled into Mike the Tourist mode – just an innocent Aussie in a polo shirt and cargo shorts, enjoying the sights of an old city in Indochina, with the cool camera he bought from Ted's. The Merc disappeared down a side street that had service lanes off it, running behind the businesses on the main street. I stood on the footpath and kept my eye on the alley that the Mercedes had turned left into, though I already knew where they would be stopping because Slim had told me the name of the nightspot – let's call it the Black Cat.

When the cab had gone, I took one of my gawker-tourist turns, through 180 degrees, just having a perv at the skyline of Phnom Penh. On my hip, the Canon was on auto-focus in multi-shot mode, which meant it was grabbing an image every second, and I was leaning on the shutter button. In a matter of five or six seconds I had a track shot of Position 2 of the subject – Position 1 being the hotel.

Then I walked to another corner and another observation point.

I was establishing three circles of surveillance. First circle is the subject himself and his routine; secondly, while you're doing that, you work out who or what might also be surveilling him, and the observation post *they* are using; and lastly, you ascertain who or what might be surveilling you, by figuring out where they'd be situated in order to watch you watch the subject. These last two are the job of surveillance-detection – my job – and they are the most difficult tasks and often the most important. If this were my gig I'd want two weeks – ten days at the very least – to establish these three circles of surveillance. If you're new to an area, and you're in a rush for intel, how are you to know whether that car is parked where it is parked because someone lives or works inside, or whether the car is used for third-party surveillance, taking pictures of *you* as you try to gain intel on the bad guy.

You think that's paranoid? Try this: I was once involved in an anti-terror operation conducted in a major Australian city. We were interested in the brother of someone who was organising an Islamist attack and the responsible agency needed to collect as much chatter about this plot as it could. So the agency had to rush in and conduct surveillance on the brother's house, and it involved entering the premises in order to intercept communications. The watchers waited patiently but there was nothing: no voice traffic, no conversations, no coded emails, no ambiguous texts. The guy being surveilled would come home from work, watch his TV and say or do nothing untoward.

After a week of this, and extreme frustration inside the agency team, the consensus emerged that this brother was a cleanskin and they'd wasted a week on him. I was an observer on behalf of another agency – not strictly 'operational'. So when the senior operator turned to me and asked, 'Mike, what do you think?' I was a little surprised, but also free to just have an opinion. And I told him that the brother might be clean, or maybe the agency itself was under surveillance. A lot of the al-Qaeda cells included people with good surveillance skills and I thought that before the agency upped sticks and moved on it should run some surveillance-detection.

There were a few rolled eyes. My style can be seen as deeply paranoid, and, besides, I was an observer representing another agency and this Aussie intel agency was quite parochial. Regardless, the senior bloke decided to do surveillance-detection for forty-eight hours and then at least the agency could tick that off in its report. Once the agency were looking for third-party surveillance, they found that when the brother went to work in his car – parked on the street – a neighbour's taxi cab would fill the gap. So a cabbie on the night shift would come home, park and sleep. When they reviewed their surveillance footage of the operation, they realised the car and the taxi did the switcheroo every day at more or less the same time. A closer inspection of the taxi showed that when it parked in front of the brother's house, its internal security camera – mounted by the rear-view mirror – was turned 180 degrees to face outwards into the street and at the house, rather than inwards to the passengers. So the terror cell was watching the agency's every move, using a parked taxi and its in-built security camera. With the taxi-camera discovery, the agency could track back to the operators of this cab and they were able to catch an outer circle of terror plotters.

So surveillance-detection is powerful but it has to be done right, and doing it right means taking the time. Phnom Penh was a busy city in South East Asia, with its own street rhythms, life patterns and criminal milieus. As I circled the Black Cat, taking my shots from all angles and waiting for Chan to move again, I had a strong feeling that the surveillance-detection couldn't be done in a week.

5

I found a café-bar with an outside table that gave me a forty-five-degree aspect on the Black Cat and its service alley. I ordered a beer and started a conversation with the young man who owned the place – let's call him Jack. (French-sounding names are common in Cambodia.)

I had already done my touristy walking tour of the area, along the front of the Black Cat and looking up to my right, to work out if there were any watchers in the rooms over the shops across the street who might be looking at Chan. I didn't see any. Even though this was the first day, I'd triangulated a few observation posts that a watcher might use, but I was sceptical. The size of the buildings and the nature of the streets and lanes that serviced the Black Cat made outer-circle surveillance fairly useless, in my opinion. Agencies have limited budgets for field operations (I've done many, and after two weeks the managers become antsy about the costs). So I didn't think there would be an observation post in the outer circle, 24/7, just to record Chan's comings and goings. As for closer-range surveillance? Well, you couldn't have someone sitting in that club between 11 am and 2 pm, because the club wasn't open then.

The best way to watch Chan's pattern was from where I was sitting, or from a shop in the vicinity, or from a room above the line of shops. Maybe one of the shop owners was being paid to make a call whenever Chan moved? Possible, but I didn't see anything to confirm that.

I put the Canon on my table; the action looked casual but the lens was now pointing at the strip club. From my left pocket I pulled out a small remote for the camera, giving me the opportunity to shoot pictures of people going in and out of the Black Cat without me picking up the camera and pointing it.

'So what *is* that place?' I asked Jack, after he'd brought me a cold Bintang.

'It a Chan business,' Jack said, wiping a table beside me. 'Chan have lots of business in Cambodia and Thailand.'

'So this is just a small place, right? He just forgets about it?'

Jack looked at me seriously, shaking his head. 'No, mister. He here every day!'

'What? In a strip club in Phnom Penh? I thought he was a big businessman?'

'I know,' said Jack, looking at the club. 'We not know – he in there right now.'

'In where?' I asked.

'The club,' said Jack. 'Every day.'

'Why?'

Jack shook his head again. 'He come every day, before lunch in the Mercedes-Benz. Then he leave in afternoon, go to the market.'

'The markets,' I said, feigning ignorance. 'The Central Market?'

Jack nodded. 'Yep.'

'Why would Chan go to the Central Market?'

Jack looked away, sighing. He either thought I was a stupid Aussie or he was about to censor himself. So I cued him. 'Don't tell me – Chan owns the Central Market too?'

Now Jack just gave me the universal look that says, *You tell me.*

I nodded. 'Good businessman, huh?'

Jack grimaced. 'Maybe more the criminal?'

'Really?' I said, wide-eyed. 'Thought the Cambodian government was cracking down on that?'

'Yes, they are,' said Jack, laughing. 'Take three months for me to have licence and I can't send money out of the country. But Chan . . . ?'

'So Chan, friend of the government?' I said, trying to get the conversation rolling.

'Maybe friend of the generals,' said Jack, ducking inside to deal with a customer.

And that – right there – is when I understood why this gig had a layer that I was not comfortable with.

6

The way these gigs are designed is so that each person does the task assigned them, and, to the greatest extent possible, unnecessary interactions between all the parties are cut out. The idea is to lessen the locals' perception that we are a big group of foreign whiteys operating as a unit. We stay in different rooms, we pretend to have met one another randomly and socially, and we ensure we don't know too much about one another – it reduces a teammate's ability to put others in the shit. We have our own jobs – our specialities – and we go out and do them, and return and share the spoils. We don't take cabs together. We group together in the hotel, but only as an ongoing piece of theatre for the employees, with a lot of 'Would you like to join us?'

So we come in at various times, and tell Slim what we have. But we are not necessarily together when these discussions take place. This is because another person is writing the operation manual from the pictures we provide, and no one has to know everything at once.

By the time I was at the Central Market in Phnom Penh, keeping a respectful distance behind Chan and his driver, I was focusing specifically on the extent to which we – the snatch crew – were under surveillance by the very person we were going to grab, or by another party. My first impression of the Central Market? It was so huge, with so many different elevations and angles – and so many thousands of people – that just about anyone could be under surveillance. It's a massive Art Deco building that is shaped like a cross. It is hundreds of feet high, with a huge windowed dome in the centre of the cross – a dome not unlike St Paul's in London. It sits in the middle of a very large roundabout which is really an entire block, with big concrete aprons on all its sides, and during the afternoon it's always busy. If I wanted to follow Chan, I'd start with the Central Market. I would put a tail on him, and because he only travelled with one person, he'd probably not notice the tail. I'd put someone on the inside of this massive structure, and I'd also cover the exterior from a building window, or just a van with two dudes and a camera.

Chan's black Merc pulled up at the north-western entrance of the market and I was a natural distance back in my cab, so I paid the fare, and started towards the entrance. Right off I noticed that Chan got out of the Mercedes alone and walked into the market by himself. He was either complacent or he felt protected – but by whom?

I walked past the hawkers, food stands and disabled beggars at the entrance until I was about thirty metres behind Chan, and had blended in with the tide of locals and sightseers. When we got inside the building proper I was astonished at how beautiful and functional it was. The height of the ceilings and the market's flow-through design cooled the air naturally, and the arrangement of the windows bathed it in light. This entrance housed clothing and shoe vendors, who stocked every knock-off you could imagine, from Lacoste and Nike to Chanel and Billabong.

I stayed loose, and didn't use the camera. I was more interested in who was looking at me and who was being paid to watch Chan. We kept going, and I gained the impression that Chan was strutting, perhaps quite slowly, and that the only looks he was getting were respectful – not surveillance. I looked up, checking for elevated observation posts in the domed, windowed interior, and could see none. I stayed back far enough that if Chan passed a trader and that trader suddenly leapt onto his phone, I'd see it. But I didn't see it. Security cameras? Not really.

Chan moved towards the centre of the building and I followed. Once we hit the centre – under the dome of a thousand windows – we were standing in a massive jewellery store, which would have given your average Rolex or Omega executive a total heart attack. I'm not an expert on watches, but I'm pretty sure Rolex Submariners can't be bought for US$20, and neither can those big Omegas that took a walk on the moon.

I was looking at the watches in their glass cases and discussing prices with the vendor because Chan had stopped right in the middle of the jewellery market, and what looked to be the senior trader in the building was talking to him. The other vendors stood off and tried not to look at him. Now I got it: Chan ran protection of vendors in Phnom Penh's biggest market. Chan would make sure that the thieves and pickpockets stayed out of the markets, and thereby didn't deter the tourists and their US dollars. Chan would stop other criminals trying to put the bite on. There were police around, sure, but Chan was the muscle.

He continued to talk with the senior trader, and at one point another vendor was called over and she did a lot of nodding and 'Yes, sir', and after fifteen minutes Chan pointed at the senior vendor, and then the other, and they both nodded, and Chan moved off again. I followed him on a leisurely stroll through the four 'arms' of the cross-shaped building – through the food stalls and the electronics sellers – and when he finally left, he did so through the north-eastern entrance, where his black Mercedes waited at the kerb. This entrance was less busy than the others: the one we'd come through was the official taxi rank and the south-western entrance led to the bus terminal.

I held back inside the entrance way. Outside, canvas shades covered people selling food and drinks. Chan didn't wait around: he walked up to the Merc and sped away. I held back in the shadows, behind a couple of cops, and scanned the windows and shopfronts across the road from the entrance. If the market was a daily ritual for Chan, and his watchers wanted to know when he was moving, they'd set up at this entrance. I was watching for movement: a body moving away from a window, a hand going up to an ear as a shopkeeper made a call, a craning neck of a watcher looking to make sure the guy had actually gone.

Nothing.

I brought the Canon up to my eye, zoomed in with the 70–300 millimetre lens, and glassed along the windows above the shops, over the road from the entrance. One of the things you look for is a cleaned window among all the dusty ones. Nothing.

I stowed the camera and turned on my heel, making straight back the way I'd come. I was looking for eyes, so I paused at the stacks of Blu-ray players and I asked the vendor for prices on compact cameras, and I allowed myself to be seen and known while all the time scanning the space. Even if the watchers weren't following Chan – which I was now sure they weren't – they could be following me.

Nothing.

I spent half an hour in the Central Market, trying to induce a tail to give himself away, wanting someone to look at me too hard. But I didn't detect a thing.

The streets were filled with tourists, so I went with the flow, walking around the massive roundabout, taking pictures of the market from every vantage point. A lot of my photographs covered the approaches to the entrances, especially the north-western and the north-eastern ones. I walked past the shops over the road from the north-eastern corner: there was a bar, a florist and a small grocer. I didn't notice anything. I strolled the back streets, behind and beside these shops, and I took some pictures of one laneway in particular. It was small and set back from the outlook of the Central Market.

And then I caught a taxi back to the Cara Hotel, a few blocks south of the Best Western, and I walked the remaining blocks, taking my time to lean on rails and look at the river, and stop and look at the great architecture around me. If I was being tailed I wanted the watchers to get out of their car and follow me on foot, but there were none that I could see.

By the time I got back to the hotel, I was actually frustrated that I wasn't being tailed.

7

Slim looked at the viewer panel on the back of my camera, scrolled through a few of the images, and made the suitable tourist noises about how great the Central Market was. We were in the bar at a table beside the window that overlooked the river, and we nursed a beer each while the karaoke girl set up her gear on stage. There were no more than fifteen people in the bar and lounge area, and none too close to us.

I'd told Slim that at first run-through I couldn't detect any surveillance on me or Chan, and that I was going further into it tomorrow. What he'd been looking at on the camera were my shots of the side street at the north-eastern entrance of the markets.

'This could be our grab point,' I said, making some enthusiastic gestures about my pictures. 'If we have a taxi ready to go, twenty metres from the main cross street, it won't be visible from the north-eastern entrance.'

'Where does the Mercedes park?' said Slim.

I asked him to scroll back to one of my shots looking out from the north-eastern entrance, and pointed to where the car had been parked.

'We could hide the taxi from the Mercedes, too. Is that what you're saying?'

'It's just a first go-over, but it's looking good.'

Slim stayed in character, made a big statement about how great these cameras are if you want to travel.

'What's your sense of it?' he asked.

I shrugged. 'He's a gangster who runs protection in the biggest market in town, maybe in Indochina. Everyone seems to know who he is.'

'We need two weeks of watching,' said Slim.

'I know,' I said. 'I'm going back, but I didn't see any tails on the streets, none in the market and none when he left.'

'Anyone tailing you – us?'

'I'm paranoid, but I don't think we're made,' I said. 'How much do you know about the gig?'

Slim smiled. 'I was contacted, asked to snatch a Thai gangster off the street and deliver him to a warehouse in Phnom Penh. Sound familiar?'

I nodded. 'How much background do you have on Chan?'

'Same as you,' said Slim. 'That briefing was about it.'

*

I walked three blocks east of the Best Western and hailed a cab from the kerb. We sped over to the Central Market, through the after-dinner strollers and clean-up crews, and I chatted with the driver about how I wanted to do some night photography. He was full of praise for the idea and when I paid him we parted the best of friends.

The Central Market was now deserted of crowds but bustling with all the cleaners and re-suppliers who worked under hundreds of yellowish lamps. As I walked around the northern aspects of the market, I came up to the north-eastern entrance and looked across the front of the entrance way – to where Chan's Mercedes had been parked. I zoomed in to the windows over the shops and I saw a family in front of a TV, a closed curtain and several windows with the lights switched off. It didn't look promising.

I ducked down the lane that I'd suggested we do the snatch from, took my first right and I was in an alley that ran along the back of the downstairs shops and provided car parks and stair access to the homes above. I was looking for a vehicle that was a little newer or more luxurious than other cars and scooters in the neighbourhood, but there was nothing that stood out. I got to the end of the stinking alley and walked further from the market.

I cabbed back to a bar one block north of the Best Western and had one beer before strolling back to the hotel. I texted Slim before I got there and he told me to drop in to his room. Altron was there too, producing his operations plan with pictures spread in front of him, printed at a backpackers' hostel. I grabbed a bottle of water from Slim's bar fridge and slumped in an armchair.

'Altron is working up your idea about parking the taxi in that side street,' said Slim, who was dunking a peppermint teabag in a mug. 'That's our Plan A.'

He could see the look on my face. 'Everything okay, Marty?'

I slurped on the water, breathed out and handed him the camera. 'Last twenty shots.'

Slim scrolled the wheel, looking at what I'd just shot. 'What am I looking for?'

'Your average racketeer is nervous, on the lookout for violence and incursions from his enemies,' I said, slipping further into the chair. 'But Mr Chan walks from his Mercedes across 100 metres of open ground, goes into one of the largest covered markets in South East Asia, a place which an experienced criminal would know is the perfect place to be assassinated, and he walks alone, he walks slowly, and he walks like a man who doesn't care who's following or who's watching.'

Altron nodded. 'You mean, it's like he almost wants us – or someone – to move on him?'

I looked away and shook my head. 'I don't know what the fuck's going on, boys, but you know what? I don't think he's carrying, either.'

'I agree,' said Slim. 'If the handguns are anywhere they're in the Merc.'

'So, Marty, what are you saying?' asked Altron. He was a bit older than me, perhaps mid-forties, with a build that had once been athletic but now lacked gym-time. I saw experience and a flicker of concern in his dark eyes.

I thought about it, yawned and rose to leave. 'I think we have to find the people who are watching this guy.'

'Can you do that?' asked Slim.

I gave him a wink and headed for the door. 'Yep, Slim – I can do that.'

8

After breakfast the next day I sat down with a pad and a pen and my camera, and I made an inventory of every security camera that Chan or his Mercedes would be exposed to on his daily route. The magnifying viewer on the back of a D series Canon is a powerful tool, and I reckoned I could get most of them from my photos.

I counted four around the Central Market – one on each entrance – but I hadn't seen any inside the building and I hadn't photographed any that I could see. I made a note to walk the Central Market again, and find the cameras.

The Black Cat nightspot, if I zoomed in to the picture as far as I could, showed a small blemish above the main door that might be a security camera, but because the place belonged to Chan I doubted this was part of any surveillance of the man. I made a note to visit the nightspot and look at it from inside – it was the one blank spot I had left.

The Raffles had the standard security camera set-up of all big tourist hotels in Asia: along the entry apron, in the foyer, over the reception desk and through the bars and restaurants. I wasn't going to waste my time at the hotel. Chan was in the hospitality game. The owners probably paid protection to him.

Next, I made a list of the positions at which those cameras

could capture me or the rest of the group and made a realistic assessment of what footage they would get and how useful it would be to them. We'd broken up our tails and our reconnaissance of the main points of his route. The security cameras I could see were broadly purposed and I dismissed the idea that someone was sitting there waiting to see my face or Rider's. Phnom Penh was crammed with Western businesspeople and tourists. It wasn't a suspicious thing to be.

I made my way downstairs, walked a block away and hailed a cab. As I got in the cab, I knew Rider was stationed outside Chan's hotel. The cab took me across town to where one of the French-built roundabouts collected vehicles from five different boulevards and distributed them again. There were a few canvas-awning stalls just off the big roundabout, and I found myself standing in shadow, buying coffee from one of the vendors. Sitting at a table near the road I got the Canon ready on my table: pointing at the roundabout and under a day-old *Bangkok Post*. I got the remote in my hand and sat where I could see the camera screen. I chatted with the coffee vendor, and for a couple of people who could not technically communicate, we got along fine. He thought it was going to get hotter and then rain; I liked his coffee and said he had a great place for his business. Blokes tend to be happy with that level of interaction.

The buzz came in my pocket just as I was draining my coffee. The text from Rider said, *package on its way*, and while still yakking with the coffee man, I looked at the camera screen hidden under the newspaper: it was aimed straight into the boulevard that met the roundabout. About ninety seconds after I received Rider's text, I saw the black Mercedes, its grille evident in my 70–300 milli-metre zoom lens, through the heat shimmers from the tarmac. When it was 200 metres away I started shooting on multi-shot mode. The Mercedes came up to the etoile, slowed and entered the circling traffic, passing by us not forty metres away, with me pulling back on the zoom, placing the middle of the etoile and the approach boulevard in the same shot. I kept the shutter button down, on multi-shot, and stayed in that position for at least a minute. Then I put down the remote, pulled off my black cap and wiped my brow. I was heating up and my frustration was growing. I knew I was no closer to finding any tails.

Buying a bottle of water from the coffee vendor, I caught a cab two blocks south of the Black Cat and walked the entire perimeter around the Chan business. No vans, no men on bus-stop benches reading tourist maps, no blokes staring into shops self-consciously and no people up high, on balconies or in first-floor windows having a perv in the direction of the Black Cat. It was clean.

Screw it, I thought. Putting on my goofiest look, and hanging my camera straight over my chest like a muppet, I walked to the Black Cat's main door and pushed. It was locked, but I could hear music playing inside. So I knocked, searching for a personality approach that married perv with nerd. A young local man opened the door a few centimetres and tried to wave me away and I hee-hawed and gee-whizzed and got my foot in the door opening and used what little English we had in common to suggest that it was time for the stupid white man to see some naked women.

The guy tried to see me off but I filled up the door and looked down on him and then he had a bunch of US dollars in front of his face, and I was allowed in the Black Cat. He let the door swing shut, locked it, and waved for me to follow him. The mop and the bucket stood in front of the bar suggesting he'd been cleaning. A glitter ball circled above one of three stages, the central one of which was a runway with drinkers' seats around it.

'So, when do the girls get here?' I asked, and the bloke shrugged slightly and as we looked for a way around the language barrier, an older man – the manager? – walked into the bar, saw me and yelled at the youth. The youth shrugged and gestured at me in an international sign of 'What can I do with this dickhead?'

The manager pointed to a curtained alcove, and the bloke shrugged again and bid me follow him. I followed, noticing that the manager had no interest in me whatsoever. We went through the red velvet curtain and we were in a red velvet lounge where four Cambodian and Thai women sat around, smoking and messing around with makeup. The music was 1970s disco and their uniform was G-strings and heels. I almost laughed – it was ridiculous, right down to the stink of baby oil. I could see the set-up and realised they'd want money from me for sex. I was about to talk it around to a private strip show instead, when a Cambodian middle-aged man appeared from a hallway, wearing an officer's uniform. He averted his eyes, and right behind him was a minder who eye-balled me like he wanted me to be scared. I played along, and quickly cut eye-contact.

When I turned back, two of the girls were on their feet and one had her hand on my bicep while arguing something with the youth who'd let me in. The youth was wide-eyed and saying 'no' to whatever was being suggested, but then the girl was leading me down the hallway and I had another behind me. I wasn't too concerned: my main priority was being able to get out of there.

They led me into a dimly-lit room and I saw the Jacuzzi in the corner, and then the girls were shutting the door and one of them was trying to get my shirt off, and I was pulling back. I was in here to have a look around – not to do a spa party with a couple of hookers. I gently but firmly pushed them away and we argued but they weren't backing down, so I showed them a stash of money and was starting to count it off when the door pushed inwards, and I was face-to-face with Mr Minder.

I took one look into his eyes and I didn't need a translator. This was shake-down time and I had to make a very good, split-second decision: really hurt this guy, or maintain my cover. I put up my hands and he kept coming, his hand reaching for me. I decided to not attack him, perhaps just divert his energy. Grabbing his right hand with my left, I got a grip on it and just twisted and pushed down, slightly but enough to make his knees buckle as he attempted to stop the pain in his wrist. I could predict the tough guy's next move, and it happened right to script: his left hand went into the back of his waistband, and as he dealt with my wrist-lock he tried to present a semi-automatic handgun. I was ready for the move and met him halfway with my right hand, before he could point the weapon. Using my strength and a couple of good holds I forced him to his knees and twisted the gun out of his hand.

As his face grimaced with the pain, I let go of his wrist and held the gun in front of him – but not pointing at him. I kept a smile on my face through most of this, the girls going into stunned silence while a Donna Summer classic played on the sound system.

'Sorry girls,' I said, staying polite. 'I think we were talking about a fee?'

I counted off two US$100 bills and handed them one each. While the minder rubbed his wrists and thought *What the fuck?* The girls freaked over their windfall, and I left the room with the minder's gun. I walked quickly down the hallway, strode across the main bar area – where the youth who had let me in was still mopping – and as he looked up I handed him the handgun.

'Someone dropped this,' I said, handing it to him. And I kept walking, through the entry doors and out into the sunlight of friendly Phnom Penh.

9

The next day – Tuesday – I did very little except go over what material I already had, and allowed some time for the minder to decide that there'd been little harm except some hurt pride. Sometimes it's a good idea to spend an entire day off the streets, breaking your own pattern of life. I started again on Wednesday, doing my rounds with Chan and watching for the watchers. Having surveilled Chan at the Central Market once again on Wednesday afternoon – and having seen no interior security except for the occasional Cambodian cops, in their pale-khaki uniforms and big dark peak caps – I turned my attention to a three-storey colonial building that looked over the place where Chan's Mercedes picked him up outside the Central Market. In terms of ticking boxes, this was the best place to do an 'over-watch' surveillance: watching the people who were watching my team watch Chan.

I walked straight up to the doorway where the residences and businesses were listed on brass letterboxes, and saw the main doors were open. I pushed inside, out of the heat, into the cool of a high-ceilinged foyer, with black and white marble on the floor and lots of dark timber. In front of me was an old cage elevator that had a large spiral staircase wrapped around it. When this place was built by the French in the 1880s, it would have been a fine piece of construction.

The staircase went all the way to the third storey, so I climbed to the first landing, and saw a small corridor leading to the front balcony. I gambled that the next floor had the same layout and I kept climbing, but as I did a middle-aged woman with greying hair in a bun came out of her door, dressed in her blue silk dress and shuffling in her plastic sandals, and she stared up at me.

I smiled and said, 'I'm looking for the fortune teller, she's just up here,' and she shook her head and made wide eyes at me and I reminded her that I knew the woman because I'd been here before and pretty soon I was nodding and smiling and telling her it was all okay, that I'd see myself up, and then I was walking up the next flight of stairs and she was shrugging to herself and returning to her office. I wasn't intimidating or anything. You see me and you think that I get where I have to go by monstering people, but I rarely do that because it gets you nowhere. I didn't even destroy the minder at the Black Cat – no one likes a bully.

I got to the next landing and headed straight for the small corridor leading to the balcony, but the door at the end was locked. I thought about using my RM Williams belt buckle, but then thought, *What the hell*, and just dropped my shoulder into the door. It flew open as the lock busted. Now I was standing on a colonial balcony, surrounded by filigree ironwork, and I looked down on the shops that overlooked Chan's car, from the side. Pulling up my camera I scoped the area on a decent zoom, looking for activity, looking for people, for binoculars, for telescopic lenses and people looking at that car while wearing a headset. There was no action around the shops in front of Chan's car and no action in the shops above.

Then I saw Chan, walking towards his car, and instead of watching him, I watched where the watchers should be, and there was nothing. When Chan reached the car, and the driver opened the door for him, I felt deflated.

I could now give the thumbs-up to Slim on surveillance-detection.

*

I slept through dinner and came down to the bar around 9 pm. Slim was by the window with a coffee, pretending to look at a tourist map, and I grabbed a Tiger and took a seat beside him.

'Just the man I wanted to see,' he said, as I leaned back. 'We've been pulled back to Thursday for the snatch.'

'Tomorrow?' I said, not liking it.

'Yep,' said Slim, and I could see him texting Rider. 'We need that camping equipment and Rider will need help.'

'Can't he take Altron?' I asked.

Slim made a face. 'Need someone like you, Marty.'

I nodded. Rider was picking up the body bags and handguns, and he expected trouble. 'Where do you need me?'

'He'll pick you up from that picnic place, just south of here on the river.'

Just to clarify this point, I generally don't use firearms in a foreign country unless it's absolutely necessary. If you know that a gig will only succeed because you can produce a gun at some point, then you must have the firearm and be prepared to use it. But if this Chan job had been my operation, I would not have procured firearms. We'd tailed him for long enough to know that he moved around unprotected, and we'd also seen that we would easily be able to subdue the driver without handguns. At least that was my take: do the snatch with brute strength, speed and surprise. That's the advantage of planning and using experienced operators, in my opinion. But Sam had stipulated a firearms component and so now we were heading into one of the main reasons that I avoid buying them in another country: you have to deal with gangsters to get it done, and that creates more risk than you avoid by having the gun.

Anyway, I was tapped for the job and when Rider picked me up in a cab we had a brief giggle about how if you need something done, you send the ANZACs. Rider was not very tall but had one of those builds that looks the same thickness from whatever angle you look at him. I'd worked with tradies and intel guys like this, and they were usually useful when it came time for the violence.

The pick-up point was a half-hour drive north along the river, in an old river-wharf area with crumbling warehouses, rotting wharf piles and little lighting. We were dropped on the outskirts of the docks area and Rider flicked the driver US$20 and asked him to wait right there for ten minutes. We walked down to the warehouse area in darkness, and I could see the place was overgrown with tall grasses and abandoned shipping containers. Ahead of us there was a white warehouse with a lamp over the main door.

'You want me to talk?' I asked.

'Stand back to begin with,' said Rider as a group of Cambodian men walked out of the shed. They were all carrying.

'Min,' said Rider, starting with the smiles. 'How's it goin'?'

Min, the tallest and oldest-looking of the group, nodded and sucked on a smoke. 'You got money?'

'Sure,' said Rider. 'You got our stuff?'

Min gave one of his guys a back-handed slap on the arm, and the bloke went back inside. Rider carefully lifted his shirt, showing Min a wad of US dollars folded in his waistband.

Min nodded, his long Asian face very solemn. He said, 'Okay,' and Rider carefully pulled out the notes.

'That's 500 US dollars,' said Rider, and the sidekick came out of the shed with a black Adidas sports bag, and placed it on the ground.

'Marty,' said Rider, and I knelt and unzipped the thing.

'Body bag,' I started, as I saw the folded black vinyl mat that would fold out to a body bag. I rummaged further and found the second one – needed if we had to lift the driver too. 'Four ballistic vests, four ceramic plates per vest.'

I dug under the vests and found a large zip-up vinyl bag, about the size of a bag that holds a doona. I looked in. 'Three nine-mil pistols – two Berettas and a Colt.'

'Okay,' said Rider.

'And a packet of zip-ties, three spare nine-mil clips, loaded.'

'Okay,' said Rider again, under his breath. 'There were supposed to be four pistols.'

We swapped a look and I made a small headshake – this was not worth being dropped for. Rider walked forward and offered the money. Min took it, put his smoke into his mouth and counted the notes like he was born with money in his hands.

'Okay?' said Rider.

'Okay,' said Min, and as he did so he reached back to his waistband and pulled out a Walther PPK 9mm, and showed it to Rider. I was still slightly forward of Rider, standing beside the Adidas bag, and I simply reacted. Before the PPK was level with Rider's face I slipped my front foot along the dirt, grabbed the pistol with my left hand and twisted it downwards, breaking Min's fingers. As Min's eyes rolled back in his head I slapped him in the side of the neck with my right hand, and he fell unconscious, his legs giving way beneath him. I tore the PPK from Min's fingers as the other gangsters reached into their waistbands but Rider was already moving through the air at the thug closest to him, coming down hard with a stamp-kick to the guy's right kneecap, and following through with an elbow strike to the nose. It sounded like a potato being thrown against a concrete wall, and by the time the victim was on the ground, Rider and I had a handgun each and the remaining two gangsters had their hands in the air, their eyes like saucers.

I panted as I stared at those two blokes, and waited for the telltale sound of backup moving inside the warehouse. Moths flitted around the warehouse exterior light and I suddenly felt hot. I lifted my finger to my lips, eyeballing the crim who was in front of me, dressed in a pair of knock-off Levi's and an Arsenal shirt – one of those gold-coloured ones with *Fly Emirates* on the front. He would have been no more than twenty and looked like he should have been playing on an Xbox, not selling guns to foreigners. He was in no state to give me any shit – I was going into a different mode now, leaving the aw-shucks Aussie tourist act behind – and I guess my face told him to play nice and make no sudden movements. At Rider's feet, the thug he'd dropped with the knee-kick and the elbow strike was moaning and writhing, blood pissing out of his face. Rider was formerly a SWAT police officer in a major Australian city and his methods focused on incapacitation rather than fancy kung fu.

I said to Rider, 'Can you cover these blokes while I check inside?'

'Got it,' he said, his weapon not deviating from the face of the thug in the bright blue shirt.

I gestured to the Arsenal bloke with my pistol – which I now held cup-and-saucer – and he turned and walked to the warehouse.

'Anyone in here, mate?' I asked as we got to the front door, which was a couple of pieces of corrugated iron nailed onto a wooden frame.

'No one here, mister,' he said, shaking his head. 'We wait for you. No one else.'

The bloke had some basic English and I heard fear in his voice. The lights were on in the warehouse, and as we pushed through the door, I stayed tucked in Arsenal's lee so I had a warm shield if someone wanted to open fire. But the bloke was right: there was no one in the office area of the warehouse. Just a table, chairs, stacked boxes and a shitty old 1960s GE refrigerator with the big chrome grille and handle.

I had a brief look around – I couldn't see anyone. And as the adrenaline slowly abated, my reasoning brain was returning and I realised we had a new problem: how to walk away from these people without them going to the cops, or even worse, without them going to a higher level of criminal operator who would come after us. If things really went pear-shaped, the organised crime figure who protected these people might even be Mr Chan.

We pushed out into the darkness again.

'We might have jumped the gun here, mate,' Rider said as I joined him.

'How so?'

'Tell him,' said Rider, waving his gun at the gangster in front of him.

'You buy four gun, right?' said Blue Shirt.

'Yeah, yeah, mate,' I said.

'There three in the bag,' he said, and I nodded. 'And Min giving you number four.'

'From here?' I asked, patting the back of my own waistband in imitation of what Min had done.

'Yep,' said Blue Shirt, nodding quickly. 'That one for you. You paid, you get four gun.'

Rider and I swapped a look. On the dirt in front of me, Min had regained consciousness and was dry-retching.

'Let's get inside,' I said to Rider, and the six of us moved through the door, the still-upright gangsters dragging their injured buddies.

My mind was spinning by the time we all sat down. Blue Shirt got waters and Cokes from the fridge and I realised that the next few minutes might have a pivotal effect on the whole gig.

'We either have to trust that they won't talk,' I said in Rider's ear, 'or, they don't walk out of here.'

Rider nodded, and the eye contact I had with Arsenal told me that he'd already worked out the crossroads we'd come to. I wasn't going to flush this gig down the toilet over a stupid misunderstanding. I wanted my bonus and I liked being on the right side of the IOU ledger when it came to the government I was working for.

Rider leaned in to me. 'Let me try this – it might work.'

Rider came from somewhere like Wagga Wagga or Gunnedah, and he spoke with a similar accent to me, and had similar values and sense of humour. I hadn't been in a situation like this with him before, but something in his voice told me to trust him.

'Okay,' I said, levelling my handgun on Arsenal.

By now Min was fully conscious and holding his broken fingers to his chest. He was in pain but he had assumed leadership again.

'Sorry about that, Min,' said Rider. 'We thought you were going for your gun.'

'I was *giving* it to you,' he said, his lips pale. 'It was the fourth gun – you don't count?'

'It was my fault, but I have a solution,' said Rider. He lifted the left side of his shirt, which was tucked into his pants, and pulled out another wad of US dollars. Min's eyes widened: there had to be a thousand dollars in that bundle.

'The way I see it, Min, we came here for guns and body bags – you came here for cash.'

Min sipped on a can of Coke. 'Sure – five hundred American.'

'Okay, well, what if we increased that fee?'

'Okay,' said Min, not quite getting it.

Rider smiled. 'Because of our mistake you now have medical expenses.'

Blue Shirt rinsed a piece of rag under a basin tap and gave it to the gangster who'd been floored by Rider – the gangster with the flattened nose.

'Okay,' said Min. 'We have medical expenses.'

'But given that we are both involved in a criminal enterprise, and neither of us want the police poking around, the way to do this is that we get the guns, and you get the cash for the guns and cash for your medical expenses, right?'

Min looked at his colleagues, who all nodded slowly at their leader, and Min looked back at Rider.

'Cambodia, expensive doctor,' he said, smirking. 'Not cheap.'

Lifting the wad, Rider said, 'Would that cover it?'

'Sure,' said Min, smiling.

It wasn't until we were halfway up the tree-lined bank, and almost back at the cab, that I think I finally exhaled. We placed the guns we'd confiscated in a pile under a tree – as agreed with the now cashed-up gangsters – and leapt into our waiting taxi with our Adidas bag.

A bystander would have seen two Aussie blokes hooting and cackling as we sped south for Phnom Penh. We were beside ourselves.

'I thought I was gone, mate!' yelled Rider. 'Fuck me dead!'

'Jesus wept,' I said, trying to stay positive. 'I'm having an angina attack, I swear to God.'

'Oh well, there goes the budget,' said Rider, giggling like a child, and I started giggling too. How do you account for $1000 that you gave to a gangster, having already paid him for the guns? The money you spent rather than kill four people? I thought it was worth it. The look on Min's face when we left was priceless, because he thought he had made out of the deal: his life had been spared and then he'd been paid to shut up and carry on.

We were through it, and we were alive, and I thanked the gods that Rider was with me that night. He had nothing to prove, not when he had $1000 cash on hand to make everybody happy.

But I was more adamant than ever. As I relaxed in the taxi's back seat, I vowed to never buy firearms in-country again.

10

I slept deep but short, waking at 4.45 am. The whole team had been assembled in Altron's room when we arrived back with the guns, and we'd done a forty-minute walk-through of the following day's job.

The team ate breakfast separately and we made our own ways out of the hotel. We wouldn't check out yet: that would be a staggered exit during the day. Our job was to each take our positions at the various points of the route, and phone in when Chan was at his known stops. In this way, we could track him and time our own movements. Also, if he chose this day to deviate from his routine, one of us could alert Slim and we could change the plan.

Plan A was this: we'd all descend on the Central Market and when it was time, the driver would get a clout, Chan would be lifted, we'd throw him in our waiting taxi and we'd go to the drop point. We had scoped a midway point on the warehouse route where we'd get out of the first taxi, grab another taxi and continue on to the warehouse with Chan. Rider had stopwatched the trip at twenty-four minutes in the mid-afternoon traffic we planned to do it in. The drive back to the hotel from the warehouse was thirty-nine to forty-one minutes, and from there we would scatter.

When we left we'd do so as individuals, with conversations about 'See you at Kratie', and 'Have fun at Angkor Wat'.

If security police are trying to find you, some disinformation from the hotel staff is a useful element. Not a lifesaver, but a half-day diversion that might buy you enough time to cross a border.

I'm always nervy on game day. But on this day I had a sense that we were all slightly off our game. Not only had I had two run-ins in less than a week, but I still felt we didn't have a full understanding of the life pattern. Now we had to do this a day early. Not ideal, but that was the call so that's what we were going to do.

My job covered the first leg of Chan's routine, so I caught a taxi to two blocks south of the Cara Hotel, walked up to the park bench over the road from the Raffles le Royal and took it easy with a bottle of water, a newspaper and my camera. I sent a text to Slim saying, *1 in place*, and waited. When the black Merc came up the entrance runway I stood and walked to the kerb, hailed a yellow Camry cab and we followed. I sent another text saying, *1 en route*, and we followed the Merc to the Black Cat, and when it turned off, I asked the cabbie to drive me to the cross street one block east of the market and I walked the rest of the way with the foot traffic. I strolled around the area, looking for all the types who I hadn't seen on the previous days, and I was none the calmer for not seeing anyone. It was getting warm and I was a ball of nerves. I walked the perimeter and took a seat in a café, observed the street and ate an omelette. It wasn't as hot as the day before, but I felt creeped out, sweaty and uncomfortable.

The phone buzzed in my pants at 2.37 pm and the text said, *2 approaching market*, and I deleted it immediately, stood up and started my walk to the north-eastern entrance. By now, Rider would be sitting in his taxi, parking in the side street, offering the guy money and telling him to stay put. Altron, Slim and I would not be together for the entire build-up, but while the other two appeared behind Chan, I would move to neutralise the driver who – if we timed it right – would be standing on the kerb beside Chan when we all came together, the five of us. I would take out the driver, and Slim and Altron would lift Chan across the road and into the taxi, parked out of sight and being held by Rider.

I took my agreed place at the coffee vendor outside the entrance and ordered a coffee. When I leaned forward and looked up to my right I could see the balcony I'd stood on the day before. No one up there.

I sat and waited . . . and waited, getting my calmness to where I wanted it. The higher your heart rate, the poorer your judgement and the clumsier your movements. I worked myself back into tourist mode, just chatty old Marty from New Zealand, gee-whizzing with the locals and gasbagging about life in Phnom Penh. It worked, and by the time I received my text from Slim – getting me into position – I was loose. I deleted the text, stood, said my goodbyes to the coffee man and wandered into the entrance of the market, all the way to the central dome, where I lurched sideways into a booth selling iPhones and Galaxies. I had a look at what the vendor had, and talked with the vendor.

Now I felt right. This is what I did, and I was ready for it. From the corner of my eye I saw a pale-blue Lacoste polo shirt, and as that image went past me I saw it was Chan. Right behind him were two Westerners, otherwise known as Slim and Altron, who were doing a great job of looking like foreign tourists. Altron wore a Vietnamese-style orange trop shirt over a pair of cargo shorts and hiking boots, and Slim wore a Billabong t-shirt and Aussie board shorts. We were all unarmed at this point: there were four handguns in the sports bag, hidden in a rubbish bin at our midway point. We'd decided not to carry them in public.

I peeled away from the smartphones and moved in the slip-stream of Slim and Altron. It was all very smooth. We walked out into the light and Chan pushed his sunnies down from where they'd been perched on his head while in the market, and the four of us walked across the apron towards the Mercedes. I have done this work quite a bit in my life and I know how to control my nerves. I was relaxed, and as we drew closer to the Mercedes, the driver stepped out to come around to the rear passenger door, and I could see Rider, waiting in front of the taxi, across the road. I accelerated around to the right of Slim and Altron so I could swiftly deal with the driver while the others grabbed Chan. And as I did so I felt a hard nudge from an object in my kidneys, and a hand grabbed the shoulder of my polo shirt.

I immediately raised my hands. I knew what that hard object was. The chatter started in my right ear, loud and fast, and from the left-hand side of my vision I could see Slim face-down on the ground and Altron being forced to his knees as the handcuffs came out. They were cops! Fucking *cops*!

My captor gave me a polite kick in the back of my knees and I knelt, allowing him to cuff me. The coup was done in fifteen seconds. They were professional and not particularly violent, and as the police truck pulled up, I saw Chan slip into his car, unruffled, and speed away.

Nicked in Cambodia.

Nine times out of ten, that means you're fucked. Really, really fucked.

11

The room was new and clean and the air-con worked. The plain-clothes guy held the black hood I'd been wearing since they'd thrown me in the police truck. It had stayed on my head during the drive and while I was being led from the truck into a room. Now I was in another room where the bloke had whipped the hood off my head and asked if I wanted water.

'Yep,' I said. I could also have said I wanted a new brain. I felt very stupid. You do these jobs and you stay out of trouble in some pretty bad places and circumstances, because you're careful. And then the day comes when the cops walk up from behind and bust the lot of you. Cold.

Completely embarrassing.

The plain-clothes guy left the room through a swinging door and from my angle I could see into the admin section of the building. I guessed by what I could see through the far windows that we were out near the airport somewhere. That would be Phnom Penh's airport – we hadn't driven far enough for this to be anywhere but Phnom Penh. Before the door swung shut I saw an office with a security cage around it so I assumed I was in a detention facility of some sort.

My wrists were still cuffed, but before they'd removed the hood they'd shifted the cuffs to be in front of me rather than behind, and I was now shackled by the wrists to a bolt on the table. The spring-loaded door flew back again and the Cambodian plain-clothes officer came back to the table. There was something about his dress and demeanour that was very confident, and when he started speaking in English with an Australian accent, I realised why: there wasn't going to be a language barrier with this bloke.

He tore the top off the water bottle he was carrying and put it where I could grab it. 'What's your name?'

'Martin Harris,' I said.

'Where are you staying?'

'Best Western,' I said. 'By the river.'

'What is your interest in Mr Chan?'

'Who?' I asked.

'Mr Chan – the man you were following.'

I shrugged. 'I wasn't following anyone.'

'Ever seen this man before?' he said, putting an eight-by-ten-inch photo of Chan on the table in front of me.

'No,' I said.

'Sure?'

'Yep.'

He paused, smiled slightly. 'We've been talking to your friends, Mr Harris.'

'Friends?'

'Yes, the three men who were with you.'

'I wasn't with three men, I was by myself.'

'Yet you travel in a group of four?'

I shrugged, my best innocent look. 'Four? I travel alone.'

'There's four of you,' he said, smiling. 'All Europeans, all at the same hotel.'

'I met some people who were staying at the hotel, sure,' I said. 'But they're not friends. I don't even know their names.'

We went around and around like this for a few minutes, and I told him he should talk to the hotel people. I was travelling alone. In the back of my mind I was thanking God for the decision to use a taxi – the driver had obviously scarpered.

'Why are you in Cambodia, travelling *alone*?' he asked, almost laughing at me.

'Tourist,' I said.

'Where are you headed?'

'Kratie, Tonle Sap Lake, Angkor Wat – all the good stuff.'

'Yet you spend a week in Phnom Penh?'

'It's nice, isn't it?' I said, maybe putting too much innocence into it.

Now he walked to the rear of the room where there was a table and a box on it. He reached into the box and out of it came a certain Canon D series SLR camera, with a big-ass 70–300 millimetre lens on it.

'This yours?' he said, holding the camera at me. Now I saw it in his hands, it looked way too big and expensive to be a tourist camera. The power-pack alone – on the bottom of the camera – made it a little beyond the enthusiast's rig.

'Looks like mine,' I said.

'Nice,' he said, weighing it in his hand. 'Professional?'

'No, just an enthusiast,' I said. 'Got the best camera I could afford.'

He switched it on and even as I wondered at how stupid we'd been to get caught, I thanked my residual op-sec expertise that I'd wiped all my surveillance photographs the night before. It's a basic hygiene habit; once I'm ready to do the actual gig, the operational pics can go. All he'd be looking at was tourist shots of the city and even the ones that I'd used for research still looked touristy. All the multi-shot pans of Chan and Chan's Mercedes were gone from the SD card.

'You like buildings?'

'Sure do,' I said. 'I'm a builder.'

'Where?'

'In Melbourne and Sydney,' I said.

'You're on a New Zealand passport?'

'Yep – live and work in Oz, but I'm a Kiwi.'

'That accounts for the Australian accent, I guess?'

Dammit. This guy was good. 'Yeah, picked it up pretty quick. Stopped me being called *Baa-Baa* on the building sites.'

'I'm sorry?' he asked.

'You know: Aussies have a thing about New Zealanders and sheep.'

He looked back at his notes, shaking his head like he was dealing with a drunk. 'You travelling up north with your friends?'

'I don't have friends here,' I said. 'I'm travelling alone.'

The intel man rubbed his chin, said nothing more and left the room. I waited, trying to stay comfortable. Someone, somewhere in the building, yelled. I convinced myself it was an emotional outburst, not a response to torture, and I controlled my breathing, keeping my heart rate down. The Cambodian cops – or intel, I hadn't been formally introduced – hadn't hit me or threatened me yet which I took as a good sign. There are certainly good cop/bad cop scenarios when you get caught, but they usually occur when something has actually gone down. I was in the unusual position of being apprehended before something happened, which meant there wasn't much for the bad cop to shout about. Still, Cambodia is a volatile place and I was really worried about where this could lead. I was sure those gangsters we'd bought the guns off would keep their mouths shut – there was nothing to be gained by them going to the police – and if these other people I was working with were professionals, there'd be no snitching. There was no need for it. That left three outstanding issues: a taxi driver paid to wait for us around a corner, a whorehouse minder with a sore wrist, and the cache of handguns hidden in a public park at the midway point where we'd planned to change cabs on our way to the warehouse. I couldn't control those situations: all I could do was stay calm and work on the situation right in front of me.

When the cop returned, he sat back in his chair and flipped through a notebook. 'Your friends certainly know you,' he said. 'I mean, you were going to Kratie with one of them, weren't you?'

I could have laughed. He was recycling tittle-tattle from the hotel workers, trying to make it look as though someone in the team had squealed. When I heard that I relaxed a bit because if that's all he had, the other guys were holding firm.

'No, I'm not going to Kratie with anyone, except me,' I said. 'An American I met at the hotel told me that tours might seem expensive but the insurance excess on a Toyota Land Cruiser is brutal. He wasn't inviting himself; least I don't think he was.'

'You usually travel with three cell phones?' he asked.

I shrugged. 'No offence, but in Asia you have pickpockets. I always buy two or three prepaid phones at the airport. They're not expensive.'

'Always?'

'Vietnam, Thailand, Indonesia – I don't like to be without a phone, so I have a couple back at the hotel in case the thieves get me.'

He tried some more triangulations, but now I was throwing a dead bat at him. One of the joys of travelling without a laptop or any written material is that the security people have nothing to talk about. And my habit of wiping my texts as soon as I've read them might seem paranoid, but I do it precisely because of these conversations.

An older Cambodian man, wearing a grey suit but no tie, came in and whispered in my interrogator's ear. They talked in the local language for a bit and then the old bloke sat in a chair opposite me and opened what I was supposed to believe was a file on me. I'd done this on many interrogations: slap a file on the table and occasionally look at it, but not delve into it. Guilty people can be pushed into all sorts of strange behaviour by simply putting a file on the table. Sometimes I've been known to leave the file in front of the interviewee, and vacate the room for half an hour. By the time I arrive back the perp is so chatty he can barely get all the words out.

'Is Martin Harris your real name?' he asked, not looking up.

'Yes,' I said, giving this guy a tick for not looking at me. He was listening for voice stress.

'You have another name?'

'No.'

Now he looked at me. 'You ever travelled under the name Daly?'

'No,' I said, not taking my eyes off him.

He made a gesture of turning his file slightly and looking confused. 'Is this you, perhaps you can help me?'

He turned the file and showed me a black and white off-take from a CCTV feed. By the look of it I was passing through immigration and customs at Tan Son Nhat Airport in Ho Chi Minh City, maybe six months earlier. You'd have to have a visual impairment and be high on drugs to think it was anyone other than me.

'Looks a little *like* me, I guess,' I said, trying to sound perplexed. 'But he's wearing the wrong clothes. I don't own a Quiksilver t-shirt.'

We looked at each other for five long seconds of mutual deadpan, and then he gave up. After whispering to the younger bloke again, the older man walked out of the interview room, and I got a good look at the admin area before the spring on the door could pull it back. Standing at the main desk was a senior policeman, with a big peak cap and tonnes of fruit salad. He was talking to a person I'd grown close to in the past week: Chan.

'Fuck,' I said to myself, my mind going haywire. 'Seriously?'

12

The walk from the terminal building to the plane was long and humiliating. The authorities waited until all the paying passengers were seated and then they walked us across the tarmac, our hands cuffed in front, and we were escorted up the rear stairway of the AirAsia A320.

Two uniformed cops pushed us down into the back row seats as the passengers all turned to look at us. The senior interrogation bloke in the grey suit chattered to the chief hostie as he gestured for a young uniformed cop to unlock our shackles.

'You get off Kuala Lumpur,' said the older bloke. 'No trouble from you, okay?'

I shrugged. 'So, no Kratie, huh?'

'No Kratie,' said the bloke, pushing our passports into our shirts so they dropped down to our bellybuttons. 'No more Cambodia for you.'

He walked away as if he'd just put out the trash, and headed for the rear cabin door.

Once we were in the air, Slim asked for drinks and we cracked a can each of Tiger and sipped in silence, all of us fuming. I was vibrating with anger – Rider's knuckles were white.

Finally, Slim ordered another Tiger and started talking. 'You were right, Marty,' he said, cracking open the beer.

'I don't want to be right,' I said.

'But you were,' said Slim. 'You said he must have protection.'

'But who knew they'd be the fucking cops?' said Rider.

There was a pause and then we all started laughing. Even as Cambodia was emerging into the modern world, the joint was still so corrupt that the police were the bodyguard for the city's biggest gangster. And we'd been looking for his goons the whole time.

I asked for another beer, and the hostie down the back with us started laughing too.

'What's up with you, love?' I asked.

'I'm glad to see you're laughing,' she said, handing out the beers. 'I thought for a minute there I'd have to stop you leaping out the cabin door.'

A nice attempt at humour, but none of us were up for it for a couple of hours. We were a hopeless bunch of sad drunks by the time we landed in Malaysia with more bruises to the egos than our bodies – thank God – but with a tonne of questions for those who had assigned us. Who was Sam? What was the set-up? Were we the patsies? But for what – for whom? None of us had a clue. Sam had obviously pulled together a crew of people who'd never worked with him before, and fed them to the wolves for a 'bigger game' reason. Slim, our American, was ropeable, and some of the commitments he made on that flight were quite seditious. He was convinced that we'd been sent in as a threat to Chan – that we were never supposed to succeed. Slim surmised that Chan had never cottoned on to our surveillance or our plan; the cops had been tipped.

'You,' he said, pointing at me as we got drunk. 'You're a paranoid bastard – did you detect any surveillance from the cops at the market?'

I shook my head. I'm good at what I do – the cops in that place weren't on to us and they didn't follow or surveil Chan.

'The cops were tipped to a Thursday,' I said, essentially working it out as I spoke. 'So let's track it back: who, at the last minute, changed it to a Thursday?'

'Fuuuccckkk!' yelled Slim, his face purple with rage.

And that, folks, is how the occasional gig ends. More than a century of experience is sent in to do a simple bag-and-drag, and a puppeteer with another agenda makes us all look like monkeys. The moral of the story? Don't look too hard for what you can't see, when what you can actually see is telling you all you need to know. Here's another lesson: don't settle for one week of surveillance when you need two; and don't ever let some spook in an office shift your timeline at the last minute. He doesn't want you to succeed.

And finally, remember to give your best energy to those who really matter.

As I flew south for KL, I was one week late and a couple of hundred miles north of where I ought to be. But I hadn't lied about it to my wife, and I was coming home in one piece. Ego bruised, integrity intact and ready for a couple of wines with my favourite lady.

I'll call that Mission Accomplished.